MODERN BASQUE HISTORY

Cameron Watson received a B.A. Honours Degree in History from the University of Ulster, Coleraine, Northern Ireland, in 1988; an M.A. in History from the University of Nevada, Reno, in 1992; and a Ph.D. in Basque Studies (History) from the University of Nevada, Reno, in 1996. He was Assistant Professor of History at the University of Nevada, Reno, from 1996 to 1999 and currently teaches at Mondragon Unibertsitatea in Euskal Herria and for the University Studies Abroad Consortium (USAC) Program at the University of the Basque Country. He is an Adjunct Professor of the Center for Basque Studies at the University of Nevada, Reno.

He has published "Ethnic Conflict and the League of Nations: The Case of Transylvania, 1918–1940," *Hungarian Studies* 9, nos. 1–2 (1994), pp. 173–80; "Folklore and Basque Nationalism: Language, Myth, Reality," *Nations and Nationalism* 2, no. 1 (1996), pp. 17–34; "Imagining ETA," in William A. Douglass, Carmelo Urza, Linda White, and Joseba Zulaika, eds., *Basque Politics and Nationalism on the Eve of the Millennium* (Reno: Basque Studies Program, 1999), pp. 94–114; and (with Pauliina Raento) "Gernika, Guernica, *Guernica*? Contested Meanings of a Basque Place," *Political Geography* 19 (2000), pp. 707–36.

His research interests include Basque and Iberian culture and history, Celtic identity and nationalism, modern European history and the impact of modernity on European society, nationalism and the construction of cultural identity, and ethnic conflict and political violence.

Cameron Watson

Modern Basque History
Eighteenth Century to the Present

Basque Textbooks Series

Center for Basque Studies
University of Nevada, Reno

This book was published with generous financial support from the Basque Government.

ISBN 1-877802-16-6 Paperback
ISBN 1-877802-17-4 Hardcover
ISBN 1-877802-18-2 Compact disk

Published by the Center for Basque Studies
University of Nevada, Reno / 322
Reno, Nevada 89557-0012

Printed in the United States of America

CONTENTS

Introduction

MODERNITY—THAT indefinable ideology associated
with the rational organizing principle of nation-
states and the rise of the democratic, technological
West—bequeathed European history a legacy of
thinking that the historical "meaning of civilization"
was intimately connected to the fortunes of the great
powers, from ancient Greece to the British Empire. Yet
beneath the surface of this idea lies another story—at
the same time just as interesting and often even more
dramatic than its traditionally more esteemed parallel.
This is what has come to be known as a "local" story,
part of a burgeoning trend of other histories that seek to
strengthen that most human of desires—the desire to
belong to a collective past predating the cultural homog-
enization implied by globalization. Today, amid this
blurring of international cultural, economic, and political boundaries, people are increasingly turning to local
culture as a means of defining their group identity.

I would advocate that the fortunes of the Basque
Country (or Euskal Herria as it is termed in Basque), an
ancient, small country tucked away in a corner of
western Europe, offer historians just as much insight
into the meaning of modern European history as the
more widely known events of the large European states.
Modern Basque history is replete with all the drama of
the modern period, beginning with the French Revolution and its effects on Basque society and traversing the
industrial and urban changes of the nineteenth century
through to the twentieth-century phenomena of war and
totalitarianism. I would similarly argue that the Basque
historical experience—especially the seemingly illogical
survival of the Basque language and its associated cultural forms—offers those of us from historically more

Late nineteenth-century couple from Gipuzkoa. The rural Basque figure was appropriated by Basque nationalists as a timeless symbol of the Basque essence.
By permission of Editorial Iparaguirre, S.A. archives.

powerful cultural backgrounds an important lesson in comprehending the tenacity of smaller cultures within our globalizing world.

In the following chapters, I will attempt to tell the story of the modern Basque Country while at the same time raising more general questions about the nature of history itself and the meaning of Europe, as well as issues such as how and why historical change takes place and the myriad ways in which culture drives history.

WHAT, THEN, of history? A sense of the past is central to what it means to be human. We define ourselves, in many ways, through our relationship with the past. History, memory, and individual or group awareness of the past thus shape and sometimes even determine the present. The central problem for historians, however, as the noted historian Eric Hobsbawm observes, is to analyze this *sense of the past* in society and to trace its changes and transformations.[1] But do history and memory alone guarantee that what we think happened in the past did in fact take place? The past is, in real terms, gone, and at best history can only re-create what it thinks took place. We cannot verify it through experiment, nor can we physically visit it.[2] Thus we are left with the difficult task of attempting to re-create something that we can never truly be sure took place.

Lest we think that a historical exploration of the sort we are about to embark on is doomed to a sense of uncertainty, let us affirm the benefits of an investigation of this type: In an account of critical historical investigation remarkable for its clarity and contemporary relevance, the fourteenth-century Arab scholar Ibn Khaldûn observed that history ultimately involves an attempt to get at the *truth*, the subtle explanation of the causes and origins of things, and a profound understanding of the *how* and *why* of things.[3]

The following assumptions underlie the theoretical structure of the study of Basque history undertaken here:

1. We should think and talk about the particular events, objects, and texts we examine within the *temporal* context of change. That is, we should always be aware of the time frame of our subject matter and what (if indeed anything) changes within this time frame.

2. We should analyze our subject matter within a broad *context*. Whereas a literary analyst might let a text stand alone in terms of their investigation, for example, the historian must relate the text to other objects around it at that same point in time. Ultimately the *subject* of the text should fit into the overall *object* of understanding linear time through the rubric of change.[4]

It is also vital to clarify at least working definitions (however subject to change they might be) of the key terms and concepts of this historical account. If any two words stand out immediately in an exploration of modern Basque history, they are *nation* and *state*. Throughout the time period studied here, Euskal Herria has been, according to many perspectives, a nation without a state (with state authority residing in France and Spain).

ANTHONY SMITH defines a nation, or at least the *ideal* aspired to by many nationalists, as a "named community of history and culture, possessing a unified territory, economy, mass education system and common legal rights."[5] As this definition applies to an ideal, he continues, many nations may lack one or more of these characteristics, but as the nation can never be a once-and-for-all, all-or-nothing concept, this should not obstruct what effectively constitutes a national basis. Smith then makes a statement of particular relevance to the present work: "historical nations are ongoing processes."[6] This idea tells us much about the nature of history, measured in many ways as the process of change through time.

The second major point to Smith's conception of the nation is that it cannot exist ex nihilo—it cannot appear as if by magic without at least some favorable elements in its social environment that encourage the ongoing process. Most significant among these is the existence of an ethnic community—a social group that historically has shared certain cultural attributes. Smith calls such communities *ethnies*. As a starting point, we might understand our examination of modern Basque history as the investigation of the Basque ethnie (although, as we will see, there are contrasting interpretations of this idea).

WALKER CONNOR makes an important distinction between two types of group loyalty, defining nationalism as loyalty to a nation and patriotism as loyalty to a state and its institutions.[7] Connor sees the nation as "a psychological bond that joins a people and differentiates it, in the subconscious conviction of its members, from all nonmembers in a most vital way."[8] He invokes the dictum that it is not *what is* but *what people perceive as is* that invariably determines social attitudes and behaviors. From this, we might infer that often it is not factual but sentient or felt history that is the key to understanding the nation—that in many respects (and potentially in conflict with the precepts of social science) what we might understand through study of the nation is *nonrational* (though not *irrational*) human behavior.

A key question I would ask you, the reader, to keep in mind before embarking on this book is how people *represent* the Basque Country. We immediately face a semantic problem when dealing with Basque history due to the fact that the Basque Country has not been a unified nation-state in modern times. As such, it does not possess the traditional guardians of history: unitary government, a single educational system, and the like— the assorted police officers of supposed historical truth. Consequently, Basque history is open to discussion, debate, and argument. Is there such a thing as a unified Basque history? Or must we subsume it within French and Spanish history as a regional element of these grander and more powerful tales?

CERTAIN WORKS of popular history, written principally for a general reading public rather than for teachers or students, provide more direct access to some of the issues encountered in any study of modern Basque history than do stricter academic investigations. "The Basques are a mystery race and their language an enigma," states Ian Gibson, whose description of the Basque Country forms one chapter of a book about Spain aimed at potential visitors to the 1992 Barcelona Olympic Games.[9] His account echoes some of the most enduring stereotypes of Euskal Herria. Culturally, he writes, Basques are, "fundamentally an agricultural and fishing people," "fiercely independent," "sexually more timid than other Spaniards," and "a non-swearing people."

He also maintains that "brother-sister incest occurs with some frequency" in the Basque Country and that "the men are famous for their long, straight noses, and the women have a characteristically 'Red Indian' look, with a pointed nose (which tends to get hooked in old age), square shoulders and small buttocks and breasts.

The Basque Country is divided by an international frontier. Three of the seven provinces are in France, four in Spain.

When a Basque woman wears her hair plaited and dons moccasin sandals she looks as if she has come straight off the set of a Western. Sometimes, through the industrial pall of a winter evening in Bilbao, you can see, standing at a bus-stop or crossing a street, a breathtaking female apparition from *Hiawatha*."[10]

After this cultural introduction, Gibson goes on to discuss the historical apparition of national feeling or nationalism in Euskal Herria: "Madrid's meddling with and final suppression of the Basques' traditional privileges had the effect of definitively alienating these independent-minded people, and made the rise of militant political nationalism inevitable."[11] In his opinion, historically the Basques were "a proud people, but far from being radical nationalists,"[12] and their language (Euskara or Euskera) "can never be a medium of international communication."[13]

Mark Kurlansky offers a highly personal account of his encounter with Basque culture and history in a work dedicated to Euskal Herria alone. "The most important word in Euskera is *gure*. It means 'our'—our people, our home, our village. ... [T]hat four-letter word, *gure*, is at the center of Basqueness, the feeling of belonging inalienably to a group. It is what the Basques mean by a nation, why they have remained a nation without a country, even stripped of their laws."[14]

For Kurlansky, old-fashioned kinds of Basques, although rooted in their "little country," are internationalists at heart. He sums up contemporary Basque culture thus: "Whatever the feelings of the rest of Spain, a united Europe is an idea that resonates with the Basques. They are not always happy with the way the new giant Europe is run. To the left, it seems too friendly to corporations and not open to individuals and small business ... but the idea of not having a border through the middle, of Europeans being borderless and tariffless partners, seems to many Basques what they call 'a natural idea.' ... The borders around Basqueland endure because they are cultural, not political."[15]

Kurlansky's view of Basque history is that "Basques are not isolationists. They never wanted to leave Europe. They only wanted to be Basque. Perhaps it is the French and the Spanish, relative newcomers, who will disappear in another 1,000 years. But the Basques will still be there, playing strange sports, speaking a language of *ks* and *xs* that no one else understands, naming their houses and facing them toward the eastern sunrise in a land of legends, on steep green mountains by a cobalt sea—still surviving, enduring by the grace of what Juan San Martin called *Euskaldun bizi nahia*, the will to live like a Basque."[16]

HERE IS AN example of the problems encountered in attempting to arrive at historical certainty or truth. Even a cursory reading of Gibson's and Kurlansky's texts reveals very different opinions about Basque history and culture. As is demonstrated by these two texts, we all have specific opinions about what *is*, resulting in distinct perspectives, truths, and certainties. At the outset of this investigation into Basque history, then, we need to be aware of the power of perception and how historical *representation*—the way we conceive of and write about history—is perhaps the critical factor in understanding history itself. Comprehending the power of historical representation is crucial to understanding modern Basque history.

Above all, the following account is a meditation on what it has meant to be Basque in the modern period. As such, a constant theme will be the impact of modernity—understood in general terms as the process by which unitary political states emerged during the

Basque peasant women doing laundry, Donibane-Garazi, Nafarroa Beherea, late nineteenth century. The daily wash required communal work between the families of the town.
By permission of the "Les Amis de la Vieille Navarre" Association archives.

nineteenth century based on the suppression of premodern social and cultural diversity. Here, the legacy of the Enlightenment and the French Revolution is crucial, not just for France, but for Europe as a whole (and consequently for the world). Postrevolutionary modern

France, with its centrist political organization and mono-cultural identity, served as the model for the new pow-erful nation-states of the "long nineteenth century" (the phrase used by Eric Hobsbawm to encompass the social, political, and economic changes associated with the period from 1789 to 1914).[17] A successful country, in nineteenth-century terms, was one that streamlined its social, cultural, and political identity to the needs of the nation-state alone. Competing identities—local, occupa-tional, or religious, for example—were to be disposed of as antiquated or fanatical.

THIS PROCESS of political modernity would have obvious implications for the Basque Country. In the following chapters, we will see how the emergence of France and Spain (understood in terms of modern nation-states) in the nineteenth century, together with concomitant social and economic changes in Basque society, in effect awakened a dormant Basque political identity. We will observe how, in an intense period dating from the late nineteenth through to the late twen-tieth century, cultural identity became a battleground in a struggle between the Basque nation and the more pow-erful nation-states of France and Spain. Modernity only allowed for one victor, and this imbued the struggle with an existential or ontological finite quality.

Toward the end of the twentieth century, however—a century that proved more destructive than any other in history—cracks in modernity began to appear. New pat-terns of identity, more redolent in many ways of the pre-modern era, began to emerge from the ruins of moder-nity, and suddenly the nation-states of Europe began to accept both subnational or local allegiances and a supra-national European identity.

As we will see, the case of the Basque Country is as pertinent to these recent developments as that of anywhere else in the European continent. For this reason, we might plausibly consider modern Basque history as a unique perspective—different from that with which we are likely to be familiar—of European history as a whole.

Sample lesson

REQUIRED READING

Anthony Smith, "The Origins of Nations," in Geoff Eley and Ronald Grigor Suny, eds., *Becoming National: A Reader* (New York and Oxford: Oxford University Press, 1996), pp. 106–30.

Mark Kurlansky, *The Basque History of the World* (New York: Walker & Company, 1999), pp. 326–51.

SUGGESTED READING

Walker Connor, *Ethnonationalism: The Quest For Understanding* (Princeton: Princeton University Press, 1994), pp. 196–209.

Ian Gibson, *Fire in the Blood: The New Spain* (London and Boston: Faber and Faber, 1992), pp. 131–46.

LEARNING OBJECTIVES

1. To understand the power of history, or how the way history is written influences the way we perceive facts, knowledge, and truth.
2. An introduction to key terms associated with the study of a particular national identity: nation and state.
3. An introduction to historical representation and the Basque Country.

WRITTEN LESSON FOR SUBMISSION

1. In a radio interview on January 10, 2000, the Spanish Minister of Defense, Eduardo Serra, defending previous comments he had made invoking Article 8 of the 1978 Spanish constitution (that the armed forces of the Spanish state were an integral guarantor of "territorial unity"), stated that he had been criticized by (among others) Basque nationalists because he "was a patriot, not a nationalist." "Patriotism," he went on to argue, "is love of one's own land [whereas] nationalism is hatred of one's neighbor's land." Why might he have made this distinction? What differences do you see between nationalism and patriotism?

2. Examine the approaches taken by Ian Gibson and Mark Kurlansky in their descriptions of Euskal Herria and Basque culture. What, in your opinion, are their principal differences? (Consider especially the themes of language, nationalism, and Bilbao.) Why might they differ, and what problems might this highlight about an exploration of Basque history? Which (if any) of the two texts do you find most stimulating or persuasive, and why?

1 · Old Regime Basque culture
Society and economy

The modern Basque Country, a land of around 20,000 square kilometers, lies at the western extent of the Pyrenees mountain range, facing the Bay of Biscay. For a territory of this size, there is a surprising complexity of ecological zones: At its northern extent, a temperate coastal area of natural harbors gives way to a hilly interior pierced by narrow river valleys. Further inland lie the commanding mountains of the western Pyrenees, whose higher reaches experience Alpine conditions. To the south is a broad zone of interior Continental and even Mediterranean-like climates.[18]

HISTORICALLY, Euskal Herria has been divided into seven provinces: Araba, Bizkaia, Gipuzkoa, and Nafarroa (called Álava, Vizcaya, Guipúzcoa, and Navarra in Spanish), which form Hegoalde, the southern side of the international border between the French and Spanish states, and Lapurdi, Nafarroa Beherea, and Zuberoa (Labourd, Basse Navarre, and Soule in French), which form Iparralde, the northern side. Between the tenth and twelfth centuries, much of the present-day Basque Country enjoyed a loose form of unity (which was normal in medieval political culture) within the kingdom of Nafarroa, but with the steady decline of this kingdom and parallel rise of the kingdom of Castile (the forerunner of contemporary Spain) and its capital in Madrid, the disparate Basque provinces began to follow different political trajectories.

The initial creation of an international dividing line between the kingdoms of France and Spain in 1512 marks a seminal date in Basque history. Among its repurcussions was a recurrent divisive political tendency (perhaps more than a cultural or social one) between Hegoalde and Iparralde.

R ACHEL BARD writes: "[F]or some seven centuries the political histories of Basse Navarre and Navarre were interlaced. Both were predominantly Basque and predominantly mountainous. ... [F]rom the tenth to the sixteenth century they were virtually one kingdom ... [yet after 1512] the two Basque nations, hitherto separated only by the rather artificial barrier of the Pyrenees, were forced to diverge by their involuntary absorption into two inimical states: France and Spain."[19]

As we can see, then, there were noteworthy political differences among the Basque provinces, but should this deter us from our search for an integrated Basque history? I think not. As Benedict Anderson notes, "nationality, or ... nation-ness, as well as nationalism, are cultural artifacts of a particular kind [and] to understand them properly we need to consider carefully how they have come into historical being, in what ways their meanings have changed over time, and why, today, they command such profound emotional legitimacy."[20]

We will discuss the political realities of Euskal Herria in the eighteenth century later, but we should first take account of the social, economic, and cultural aspects of Basque history to the eve of the French Revolution.

THE PEOPLE AND THE LAND

We live today in a world increasingly dominated by *large* concerns—mass markets, international media, the so-called global village, to name a few—that shape our general outlook. However, Old Regime (pre–French Revolution) Europe was markedly different. Around the eleventh century, the tribal social structure of the continent gave way to a peasant society (which would in turn be succeeded in the nineteenth century by the modern

industrial variant). Within this peasant society, the pattern of human activity revolved mostly around the
modest and intimate concerns of family and local community, the demands of Church and State in the form of
tithes and taxes, and the whims and rhythms of nature.
More than anything else, day-to-day living conditions
were dependent on the environment (soil type, altitude,
climate) and proximity to lines of communication
(ports, borders, rivers or other strategic routes). The
rural world of the eighteenth century was small: Many
people traveled no more than thirty or forty kilometers
from their farmstead during their entire lifetime;
indeed, as Eric Hobsbawm notes, most peasants, unless
snatched away for military service, lived and died in the
parish of their birth.[21] An individual's identity was
shaped by several key factors, usually prescribed at
birth: their *gender*, their *social rank*, their *religion*, the
political authority they served, the *local community* in
which they lived, and the *occupation* practiced by their
parents and grandparents.

IN THE EIGHTEENTH century, the overwhelming
majority of the Basque Country's people were
engaged in a peasant agricultural system based on the
baserri (*caserío* in Spanish). These *baserriak* (plural
spelling) were extended-family farmsteads that functioned largely as self-sufficient socioeconomic units.
Each *baserri* consisted of a number of small plots of
land that together formed a mixed farming economy
based on sheep, pigs, poultry, grains, apples, chestnuts,
honey, and fodder. Agriculture was labor-intensive and
the technology simple. The need for a cash income was
minimal, as the *baserriak* emphasized subsistence
farming and most trade was conducted through a barter
system.[22] For example, the pigs of Nafarroa Beherea and
the cheeses of Zuberoa were typically exchanged for the

Home. Typical Basque farmhouse, Larrabetzu, Bizkaia. Basque farmhouses operated as self-contained and self-sufficient units where people and animals lived together. Note the stable and barn area built into the main house.
By permission of Editorial Iparaguirre, S.A. archives.

wheat, wine, and olive oil of Nafarroa, encouraging a thriving trade between Iparralde and Hegoalde. The seasonal migration of pastoral herders and their animals in the Pyrenean reaches of Euskal Herria, where soil and climate could not sustain a strict agriculturally based economy, likewise encouraged an economic (and concomitantly social and cultural) exchange between

----

Basques on both sides of the Pyrenees. Through the nineteenth century, seasonal migration flowed mostly from north to south, with Basques from Iparralde traveling as far as the Ebro valley to work the large farms of southern Nafarroa.

THE MAJORITY OF Basques in the eighteenth century (except in the southern province of Nafarroa) were *Euskaldunak* (Basque speakers). Euskara, the Basque language, is the sole survivor of those languages spoken on the European continent before the arrival of Indo-European–speaking peoples around 4,000 years ago. This legacy bequeathed the Basques what James E. Jacob terms a kind of "linguistic particularism"[23]—so much so, in fact, that this distinction increasingly found itself at odds with the centralizing policies of the emergent French and Spanish states.

The Basque Country's predominantly oral culture (the spoken word carrying more weight than written text) served to highlight the differences between Basque identity and that of France or Spain. Modern Western society has, throughout history, emphasized the civilized nature of the literate world compared to its oral ancestor. Yet it is worth remembering that this forebear is at the root of Western civilization: Many of the great heroic figures of the Western intellectual tradition—Achilles and Odysseus, for example—are products of oral culture. Memory plays a more powerful role in oral culture than in its literary partner, for in the oral world the past is recalled in a very personal way. With no texts to refer to, the individual must remember in a more profound manner—often, it must be said, by overloading memory with heavy characters or heroes and memorable or spectacular deeds. As Walter Ong observes, social organization is defined by the interplay between the orality that humans are born with and the technology of writing, which no one is born into.[24]

Basque orality was expressed in a variety of cultural forms, from romantic ballads and war songs to the singing of marriage and funeral ceremonies. Where social conflict arose—between individual *baserritarrak* or even whole towns, for example—the situation was often resolved through singing duals, or *charivari*. The *foruak*—the series of rights and privileges guaranteeing Basque liberties (which will be discussed further in the next chapter)—were originally devised through the spoken word and only later written down or codified. In Iparralde, a distinctive form of popular outdoor theater emerged in the fifteenth century, known as the *pastoral*, where whole communities took part in typical tales of good versus evil. Perhaps the most visible expression of Basque oral culture was the *bertsolaritza*, a troubadourial contest between improvisational versifiers (*bertsolariak*), an art form that continues to this day. These various expressions of Basque oral culture should be considered the historical equivalents of the dominant literate cultures of Europe. Historically, they were the guardians of Basque-speaking culture, especially when this culture was faced with the assault of French and Castilian literate society.

IN 1539, THE EDICT of Villers-Cotterets, issued by the French sovereign François I, made the use of French compulsory for all official documents. Yet French, like Castilian (later known as Spanish) and even English, was far from being a standardized language. Indeed, beginning around this time, what would come to be the great imperial languages of the modern age were consciously *invented*, usually at the behest of royal leaders in an attempt to unite the disparate dialectical variants spoken by many of their subjects (this quite apart from

Donkey Academician. In 1635 the French Academy was
established to purify the language and codify its usage.
However, critics of the new institution quickly picked up
on its rigid, uncompromising nature. The allusion to a
donkey highlights these charcateristics.
From Grandville's Scènes de la vie privée et publique
des animaux, *1866.*

---

the separate languages spoken within their realms). In
1635, the Académie Française (French Academy) was
established to purify the language and codify its usage,
and by 1714, with the signing of the Treaty of Rastatt
between the kingdoms of France and Castile, French had

become the language of international diplomacy and the closest approximation of a universal language of communication.

On the other side of the border, it was not until the seventeenth century that Castile began to take more of an interest in domestic affairs rather than imperial designs. As a consequence, the Church was centralized, leading to its official use of Castilian for religious instruction and the naming of specifically Castilian-speaking bishops throughout the crown's lands. Furthermore, the Real Academia de la Lengua Española (Royal Academy of the Spanish Language), with its motto "cleanse, fix, and give splendor," was established in 1713 as a means of attaining linguistic standardization.[25]

ELEMENTS OF CHANGE

1. Early Modern Industry. If the Basque Country's history could be explained in terms of the simple bucolic rhythm of natural peasant cycles, it would perhaps prove less of a problematic endeavor. However, this would not give the whole story, for from the earliest times, alongside the traditional social and economic organization described above, there has also existed a modernizing, industrial thrust that has at times propelled the Basque Country to the forefront of European and world affairs. BY THE TURN of the fifteenth century, the Basque Country's long history of iron production had endowed it with a renown throughout Europe for the manufacture of arms, agricultural implements, and shipbuilding materials such as anchors and chains. Maritime exploration and commerce were likewise principal elements of early Basque modernization. Still today, the coat of arms of Miarritze (Biarritz) in the province of Lapurdi, dating from the fourteenth century,

depicts a whale hunt, suggesting the significance of this
endeavor. From the demands of the medieval whaling
industry (most likely the earliest of its kind in Europe)
emerged important developments in the design and production of ships, and this in turn encouraged Basque-
sponsored explorations of an ever-unfolding new world.
By the dawn of the modern era, Basque maritime knowledge, whether in the realm of exploration, fishing, or
trade, was in demand throughout Europe.

As commercial trade eclipsed the whaling industry in
the fifteenth and sixteenth centuries, one port in particular emerged as especially suited to protoindustrial and
commercial development, due principally to its proximity to both major iron-ore deposits and a navigable
river outlet to ocean-going routes: Bilbo (Bilbao).[26]
Bilbo (along with, to a lesser extent, Gipuzkoa, famed for
its maritime leaders) served as a channel for the wheat-
producing regions of Castile to the outside world, concentrating the early industrial development of Hegoalde
in the province of Bizkaia. This protoindustrial expansion was also facilitated by the Basque Country's de facto
status, established by the *foruak*, as a free-trade area:
Castile's customs frontier was established at the
southern extent of Euskal Herria, thus making trade in
and out of the Basque provinces tax-free.

FURTHER, AS Robert P. Clark notes, "Spanish interests in the Western Hemisphere demanded high
levels of commercial intercourse and a skilled and ener-
getic mercantile class. Such a class arose readily in the
coastal Basque provinces of Vizcaya and Guipúzcoa. For
the first time, there was a Basque elite whose economic
interests were identified with a strong and vigorous
Spanish state."[27]

Parallel developments in and around Baiona (Bayonne) in Lapurdi took place at the same time. As in

Bizkaia (although not of the same quality), there were iron-ore deposits in both Lapurdi and Nafarroa Beherea. These were exploited by forges in and around Baiona in the production of arms and tools. Baiona also made good use of the ready supply of wood from the dense forests of Nafarroa Beherea to develop a thriving ship-building industry in the eighteenth century. Much like Bilbo, Baiona benefited from a tax-free status within the French kingdom, encouraging the development of the city as a major manufacturing and commercial center.

OTHER SEAFARING Basques of Lapurdi enjoyed a different kind of success and fame, as corsairs or pirates authorized by successive French monarchs to plunder non-French ships. If Bilbo and, to a lesser extent, Baiona were increasingly becoming known as important trading and commercial centers in Europe, Donibane-Lohizune (St. Jean-de-Luz) and Miarritze enjoyed a more sinister reputation, as home of pirates and corsairs such as Duconté, Cepé, Harismendy, and Dolabaratz.

2. *Culture and Society.* Although the vast majority of the Basque population remained intrinsically tied to an orally based rural society, important cultural changes did take place in the early modern period. The first entire text in Euskara, a collection of religious and bawdy poems by a priest from Iparralde by the name of Bernard Dechepare, was published in 1545. Throughout most of the modern era up to the eighteenth century, Euskara as a literate form was confined to the publication of religious texts, principally in Iparralde; where a literate Basque culture did emerge, it was elitist and its language was French or Castilian.

In the eighteenth century, however, there was an increase in the integration of Euskara into literate cul-

ture with the work of writers such as Joannes
D'Etcheberry from Lapurdi; Manuel de Larramendi,
Augustín Cardaberaz, Sebastián Mendiburu, and Fray
Juan Antonio de Ubillos from Gipuzkoa; and Joaquín
Lizarraga from Nafarroa. This may well have been a reaction, of sorts, to the beginning of a retreat in the use of
the Basque language around the mid-eighteenth century. Coinciding with a moderate growth in trade sponsored by the French and Spanish kingdoms, the official
languages of these kingdoms were increasingly used.
The decline was most noteworthy in Araba and somewhat less pronounced in Nafarroa; the remaining
provinces remained overwhelmingly Basque speaking,
but a custom had already developed whereby a commercial bilingualism operated in the principal trading cities
of Bilbo, Donostia (San Sebastián), and Baiona. By the
end of the century, then, Basque was becoming a
socially and culturally marginalized language, increasingly stigmatized as the preserve of peasants.[28]

BY THE EIGHTEENTH century, there had emerged in
the coastal Basque provinces a growing social and
economic division between rural and urban areas, a tension that was increasingly exacerbated by internal pressures such as a stagnation in the iron industry due to
increasing foreign competition and a series of poor harvests as a result of especially harsh weather conditions.
Political opinions concerning how to resolve the crisis
were divided. According to Renato Barahona, "by the
start of the nineteenth century some of Vizcaya's most
enlightened minds were well aware that the liberties and
tariffs (and related government prohibitions) constituted fundamental barriers to local industrial development, and that change was critical."[29] These differences
of opinion would, together with other outside political
factors, ultimately lead to a series of conflicts affecting

Enduring dream. Passports issued by the Autonomous Basque Government during the Spanish Civil War (1936-39). For the first and only time in history some citizens of Euskal Herria obtained specifically Basque official national identity documents.
Photo by permission of Abertzaletasunaren Agiritegia. Sabino Arana Kultur Elkargoa archives.

Hegoalde throughout the nineteenth century and beyond. By contrast, the eighteenth century was, for Iparralde (most visibly in Baiona), a period of stability and economic growth after two hundred years of relative decline, but this growth would be destroyed by the effects of revolution and war that engulfed the region at century's end.

What of identity? Did the people of this territory consider themselves Basque? According to Peter Sahlins,
the standard notion of identity in historical accounts of
European rural society assumes a concentric-circle
model whereby "a sense of identity decreases in relation
to geographical and spatial distance from a social
'ego'—a village or parish." He notes, however, that this
model "fails to take account of the oppositional character of identities and loyalties."[30] The question of identity, then, is not one of spatial consideration but of what
anthropologists have come to term *segmentary organization*, where identities and loyalties shift in relation to
circumstance and change, especially where this implies
conflict between collectivities.

IN ONE SENSE, we might conclude that the very term
euskaldun—which means, literally, "a speaker of
Basque," but which has also come to mean simply
"Basque"—must have generated a sense of imagined
community. At least in linguistic terms, we can speak of
a sense of Basqueness, however remotely this was articulated. In another sense, though, the nature of conflict or
competition in this society also generated difference,
and this was increasingly the case after the seventeenth
century, with different societies emerging within Euskal
Herria as a result of economic change. Between the end
of the eighteenth and the beginning of the nineteenth
century, these tensions would generate a series of conflicts that would ultimately change the social fabric of
the Basque Country. Before we contemplate these
changes, however, it is first necessary to examine the
political, administrative, and judicial structure of the
Basque Country in relation to the Castilian and French
kingdoms.

Lesson one

Note: Chapters 1 and 2 should be considered jointly as an examination of social, political, and cultural developments in Euskal Herria. The reading lists that appear below and the written assignment in Lesson 2 all refer to the material covered in both Chapters 1 and 2.

REQUIRED READING (FOR CHAPTERS 1 AND 2)
Robert P. Clark, *The Basques: The Franco Years and Beyond* (Reno: University of Nevada Press, 1979), pp. 10–25.
Renato Barahona, *Vizcaya on the Eve of Carlism: Politics and Society, 1800–1833* (Reno and Las Vegas: University of Nevada Press, 1989), pp. 1–21.
James E. Jacob, *Hills of Conflict: Basque Nationalism in France* (Reno, Las Vegas, and London: University of Nevada Press, 1994), pp. xiii–xvi, 3–16.
Rachel Bard, "The Decline of a Basque State in France: Basse Navarre, 1512–1789," in William A. Douglass, Richard W. Etulain, and William H. Jacobs, eds., *Anglo-American Contributions to Basque Studies: Essays in Honor of Jon Bilbao* (Reno: Desert Research Institute, 1977), pp. 83–92.

SUGGESTED READING (FOR CHAPTERS 1 AND 2)
Román Basurto, "Bilbao in the Economy of the Basque Country and Northwestern Europe during the Modern Era," in William A. Douglass, ed., *Essays in Basque Social Anthropology and History* (Reno: Basque Studies Program, 1989), pp. 215–34.
William A. Douglass and Jon Bilbao, *Amerikanuak: Basques in the New World* (Reno: University of Nevada Press, 1975), pp. 9–59.

Jerome Blum, "The Internal Structure and Polity of the
European Village Community from the Fifteenth to
the Nineteenth Century," *Journal of Modern History*
43, no. 4 (1971), pp. 541–76.

Benedict Anderson, *Imagined Communities: Reflections
on the Origin and Spread of Nationalism*, rev. ed.
(London and New York: Verso, 1991), pp. 1–7, 9–36.

LEARNING OBJECTIVES

1. To establish the basis of social and economic organization in the Basque Country during the eighteenth
   century.
2. To critically evaluate what one might understand by
   the term "Basque culture," as opposed to "French
   culture" or "Spanish culture," in the eighteenth century.

2 · Old Regime Basque society
Political culture

In our attempts to discern whether Basque history constitutes a sufficiently "separate" quality to merit distinct
academic investigation, it is important to understand
the basis of political culture existent in both Iparralde
and Hegoalde. Surprisingly perhaps, for a nation divided
and ruled by two powerful kingdoms, there were many
parallels in the general political framework of Euskal
Herria. In particular, we will examine two of these
common political, administrative, and judicial elements:
the *foruak* (*fueros* in Spanish, *fors* in French), a series of
laws guaranteeing a measure of historical self-rule to the
Basque Country; and the concept of *collective nobility*, a
legal precedent peculiar to Euskal Herria.

FORUAK
As Robert P. Clark observes, the *foruak* were instituted
in Hegoalde in the twelfth century, when a foral system
was established throughout the dominions of the
kingdom of Castile as a necessary compromise between
the central authority in Madrid and the disparate peoples, with their own traditions and political cultures,
that were gathered under the hegemony of the crown.
OF CRUCIAL IMPORTANCE within this system were
the local councils or general assemblies (known
variously as *juntas*, *cortes*, or *hermandades*), which
elected, on a biennial basis, the executive branch of local
government known as the *diputación*. The councils
retained the right to veto crown laws; the *pase foral*, as
this was called, was a critical check on potentially overwhelming central authority and a guarantee of local
political control.

Juan de Yciar is best known for his 1550 instruction manual, *Arte Subtilissima*. He is the only Iberian writing master of world renown.
Engraving by Juan de Vingles.

Sancho asked "Which of you is my secretary?" and one of those standing by answered, "I, sir, for I can read and write, and I am a Basque."

"With that last qualification," said Sancho, "you could well be secretary to the Emperor himself."

(Miguel de Cervantes Saavedra: *The Ingenious Hidalgo Don Quixote de la Mancha*, chapter 47.)

By the eighteenth century, the local councils held the reins of political authority within the individual provinces of Hegoalde. Renato Barahona argues that "until the 1730s–1740s the juntas had been truly open, often generating a great deal of participation. But fear of disorder and unruliness—real or imaginary—had apparently induced the dominant provincial oligarchies to restrict attendance and hold the sessions in private."[31] Perhaps the most potent symbol of this local authority was the obligation on the part of the Castilian monarch to travel to the Bizkaian town of Gernika (Guernica) in order to swear an oath of obedience to the Basque *foruak* before Spanish political authority was extended to Bizkaia. Clearly, Barahona notes, "Vizcayans regarded their bond to the monarch as contractual" in more ways than one.[32]

THE OTHER key component of the foral system for Euskal Herria was its economic dimension. As noted in the previous chapter, Hegoalde and, to a certain extent, coastal Lapurdi operated as tax-free zones, with the official customs borders drawn at the lines between Euskal Herria and its royal patrons. The situation benefited the majority of the Basque population—peasants and the clergy, for example—while alienating the merchant classes of Bilbo, Donostia (San Sebastián), and, to some extent, Iruñea (Pamplona), who could not compete with goods flowing into the Basque Country from northern Europe and whose own exports to Castile were subject to import duties. As a consequence, the (minority) merchant classes progressively favored economic incorporation with Castile and the dismantling of this particular dimension of foral privilege.[33]

Clark writes of the *foruak*: "as the rights developed through the Middle Ages, they anticipated by several hundred years those liberties for which American colonists would struggle in the American Revolution. ... [A]t an institutional level, the *fueros* served primarily to isolate the provinces from central rule [but] above all, foral democracy was a state of mind. ... So long as Basques, Navarrese, Catalans, and so forth, were not required to think of themselves as Spanish, they were willing enough to pay homage to the Spanish Crown."[34]

Indeed, according to Barahona, "while part and parcel of the Spanish monarchy, Vizcaya showed a remarkable bent and capacity to act as a separate and quasi sovereign political entity."[35] But there was tension too. In particular, the *juntas* and *diputaciones* relied for their power base on the rural populace, and as such saw their own power as being intimately bound to the persistence of a rural socioeconomic organization, whereas more "progressive" urban environments, at the head of which quite clearly lay Bilbo, felt hemmed in by the more conservative policies of the foral institutions.

AS IN HEGOALDE, the *foruak* of Iparralde operated as a set of laws governing social and economic life, regulating the day-to-day existence of the overwhelmingly rural community. At the center of this foral power lay the *biltzar* (*bilçar*), a local decision-making body composed traditionally of village or town elders. As with the Castilian monarchy to the south, successive French rulers were obliged, on accession to the throne, to swear allegiance to these rights. However, as James E. Jacob points out, from the early seventeenth century these rights were gradually eroded as the French monarchy attempted to impose a more centralized and authoritative control over what it viewed as the peripheries of its domain.[36] Accordingly, royal commissaries (representatives of the French crown or central authority in the regions, roughly equivalent to the Castilian *corregidores*) were charged with overseeing these changes.

The most successful of the French monarchs to attempt such change during this era was Louis XIV, an aggressive centralist who gradually succeeded in establishing absolutist royal authority within the kingdom.

A S RACHEL BARD observes, "though Louis XIV gave some recognition to Basse Navarre's *fors*, during his reign [1643–1715] the old privileges continued to deteriorate. One that disappeared was the coining of money. When both Navarres were one, there had been mints at Pamplona and St. Palais, subject to the *Cortes'* direction. After 1512 the mint at St. Palais (founded in 1351) continued to function ... but as Basse Navarre lost autonomy and as French money was more widely used, the mint had less to do and by 1642 was inactive. Louis XIV officially closed it in 1663."[37]

Similarly, "between 1742 and 1762 alone," observes Jacob, "taxes levied in Soule increased from 8,000 to 30,000 livres. They symbolized the intrusion of the absolutist state into local liberty and the steady onslaught against foral privilege." Indeed, he continues, "the onerous impact of central authority continued to affect the three Basque Provinces until the Revolution."[38]

We might highlight the period between 1451 and 1589—with the progressive imposition of French authority over Lapurdi and Zuberoa—as the critical moment when much of Iparralde lost its separate political identity. Iparralde remained less socially divided than was Hegoalde, at least in those enclaves of modernization such as Bilbo; Baiona (Bayonne) never developed as separate an identity from its rural hinterland as had Bilbo or even Donostia. As such, in the face of increasing centralization imposed from Versailles (the seat of the French crown), Lapurdi and Zuberoa sought

measures to defend their traditional rights. Yet, as is a
central theme of Basque history, they lacked a unified
political base from which to launch protests. In fact, the
picture that emerges from a cursory glance at its political organization reveals a complex system of different
institutions, often operating solely at the most local of
levels, a system mirrored to some degree in Hegoalde as
well.

COLLECTIVE NOBILITY

Sustaining this diffuse and distinct system was a feature
of political culture specific to the Basque provinces on
both sides of the international border: the concept of
collective nobility. The actual extent to which this concept functioned in practice has been open to historical
debate, but what is certain is that there emerged, in the
aftermath of the Moorish retreat from the Iberian peninsula in the late fifteenth century, a legal framework (recognized in both Hegoalde and Iparralde) by which all
Basques were considered noble. This was possibly due
to the Basques' perceived racial purity (they had never
been assimilated by the Moors), together with the
unique application of the *foruak* within their borders.
As Stanley Payne observes, "that the Basque territories
developed *fueros* partially on a provincial level was due
not merely to geography but to some extent to their
ethno-cultural, or at least linguistic, distinctiveness,
which set them apart from the Castilian population as a
whole."[39]

THE CONFERRING of "noble" status meant, in reality,
a guarantee of property and land rights, and it took
distinct forms in the different Basque provinces. It was
most clearly apparent in Bizkaia and Gipuzkoa when
royal recognition of the noble status of all inhabitants
was conferred in 1526 and 1610, respectively. One-sixth

When both Nafarroas were one, there had been mints at Iruñea (Pamplona) and Donapaleu (St.Palais), in Lapurdi, Iparralde. However, use of the specifically Nafarroan coinage waned on the northern side of the Pyrenees during the late sixteenth century as its French counterpart became more important.
Photo by PhotoSpin.

of the population in Nafarroa Beherea and one-eighth in Araba were considered noble while Lapurdi remained the province of Iparralde least affected by the imposition of a feudal nobility. In Zuberoa, the body of customary law, codified as early as the sixteenth century, included the provision that, "all Souletins [inhabitants of the province] are free, of free condition, and with no trace of servitude," while in Nafarroa, although a more strictly feudal system remained in place, social mobility, namely the ability to gain freedom from feudal servitude, was generally easier than in Castile, and considerable numbers of peasants earned their freedom through the seventeenth and eighteenth centuries.

Throughout Euskal Herria, then, through the eighteenth century and from two different directions, there was an increasing and concerted effort on the part of the French and Spanish crowns to impose their central authority. This process began in 1512 with the first agreement between the two crowns aimed at establishing a common frontier, and initially culminated in 1659 with the signing of the Treaty of the Pyrenees. With this treaty, not only was the international border established once and for all, but the two crowns would be unified through marriage (Louis XIV of France would marry the Spanish *infanta* María Teresa, daughter of the Castilian monarch Felipe IV, the following year), and the king of France, while retaining the title of king of Nafarroa, relinquished any claim to the Nafarroan within the Castilian political orbit. The treaty thus marked a definitive political partition of the ancient kingdom.

WHERE THESE centralizing efforts did not collide with local interests—as was the case with the affluent classes of Bilbo—Basques gained much from the process, but this was the exception more than the rule, at least during the eighteenth century. More typical of the age were clashes between Basques and the two crowns. For example, after the accession of the French Bourbons (who had already established an absolutist policy) to the Castilian throne, a royal decree of 1717 declared that Basque imports should fall under the common tariff system of the country as a whole, thereby violating the foral privilege of tax exemption on all imports coming into Hegoalde. The response of the Bizkaian and Gipuzkoan peasantry was swift: declaring a *matxinada*, or peasant revolt, they rose up against the central forces of the state. Although the revolt was initially brutally suppressed, the previous tariff system was restored in 1722. Similar revolts against impositions by central authority took place in Iparralde (where women were especially prominent in defying royal authority), including revolts in Ainhoa (1724), in Lapurdi as a whole (1726), and in Baiona (1748).

IF ONE KEY theme dominates the history of the Basque Country on the eve of the modern age, it is the rise of political absolutism within the kingdoms of France and Castile—the attempt to centralize political and economic authority as well as to standardize the social and cultural environment—in other words, the beginning of the creation of the modern French and Spanish states. In the opinion of Joxe Azurmendi, the crowns of France and Castile were consolidating their political and legal authority through the sixteenth and seventeenth centuries, creating the basis of a social organization that would ultimately facilitate the implementation of the modern state. In contrast, during the same time Euskal Herria was effectively *unmaking* itself as a single political entity, for example through the decline of the kingdom of Nafarroa and the progressive loss of Basque ecclesiastical unity.[40] We should add that, during this period at least, Versailles was more successful than Madrid in these endeavors.

From a Basque perspective, for the majority of the people at least, the central political question (with concomitant social, economic, and cultural ramifications) was the preservation of specifically regional and local rights and privileges, and many of these distinct laws remained more or less in force during the late eighteenth century. It was this basic difference of opinion, the struggle between central and regional administrative power, that would subsequently come to define the modern political, economic, and cultural trajectory of Basque history. However, where the centralizing tendencies of the Old Regime emerged out of monarchical absolutism, the modern impulse toward uniformity would come from a relatively new political doctrine, Enlightenment liberalism.

Lesson two

LEARNING OBJECTIVES
1. To understand and critically examine the foral system and the concept of collective nobility.
2. To examine in rudimentary form the process of political change affecting this system and the consequences of this change.
3. To understand the political culture in Euskal Herria on the eve of the French Revolution.

WRITTEN LESSON FOR SUBMISSION (FOR CHAPTERS 1 AND 2)
1. What might Robert P. Clark mean by the statement that "above all, foral democracy was a state of mind" (*The Basques: The Franco Years and Beyond*, p. 21)? Carefully consider the foral systems of the different Basque provinces. In your opinion, and taking into account some of the theories of nationality you have already come across, did this system really, as James E. Jacob claims (*Hills of Conflict*, p. 8), constitute the basis for a kind of *protonationalistic ethnic pride*?

2. Critically examine the opening arguments of Benedict Anderson's *Imagined Communities* as they relate to the nationality question in the Basque Country (including the potential emergence of French and Spanish identities). In your answer, you should include some discussion of, though you need not limit it to, the idea that, "the very possibility of imagining the nation only arose historically when, and where, three fundamental cultural conceptions, all of great antiquity, lost their axiomatic grip on men's minds" (p. 36).

3 · The French Revolution (I)

IN THIS AND the following chapter, we will examine
the effects of political *modernity* (understood here as
a combination of Enlightenment idealism and French
Revolutionary upheaval) on Euskal Herria. According to
eighteenth-century French dictionaries, the word *revolution* carried with it no political connotation, instead
implying something more akin to "return" (of a planet
or a star, for example). This is worth noting, for the
French Revolution was in many ways an *invention*
without precedent in Europe and, quite possibly, the
world (even counting events on the other side of the
Atlantic). Among the myriad reasons for the tumultuous
events in France after 1789, we might distinguish the
involvement of the French army in the American Revolution, which brought the crown to the brink of financial
collapse; a succession of poor harvests throughout the
1780s, which drastically reduced the supply of essential
foodstuffs and consequently raised prices of these goods
beyond the reach of most people; and, more generally, a
new kind of tension produced by the emergence of a
social order—urban, educated, and wealthy but without
the political influence historically accorded to those with
their economic status—that was voraciously devouring a
set of ideas associated with a new philosophical movement, the Enlightenment.

THE ENLIGHTENMENT
In many ways, modern political history begins with
ideas associated with the eighteenth-century Enlightenment, in particular one doctrine: liberalism. From the
late 1700s on, Enlightenment liberalism would inexorably alter the fortunes of Euskal Herria.

But what exactly was liberalism? For the most part, liberalism referred to a belief in responsible constitutional government based on popular consent, understood as the will of the citizenry. We should not regard this as democratic in the modern sense, as the concept of the citizen extended only to urban-based propertied male individuals. Essentially, liberalism was a doctrine for Europe's emerging middle class, whose wealth and education could not gain them access to the Old Regime political structure. Indeed, liberals often felt as much contempt for the landless peasants below them in the social hierarchy as for the aristocrats above; a good deal of this antipathy also stemmed from rising rural-urban tensions.

IN VERY broad terms, the Enlightenment, a movement that began in the early 1700s but found its full force and expression toward the middle and end of the century, was initially an intellectual quest for *truth* through the use of reason. Enlightened thinkers operated under the principle that this truth was unfolding before their very eyes—in other words, that they were being progressively "enlightened." "Order" and "reason" became the watchwords of the movement as these progressive and liberal thinkers saw the acquisition of knowledge as a means to attaining human perfection. Society, it was thought, would gradually and rationally release itself from the irrational, dogmatic, and superstitious thought of the Old Regime, and as a consequence just political and legal systems would emerge from the people themselves—in other words, democratically.

At the heart of Enlightenment thought was the need, as Robert Darnton observes, to sort and classify or, maybe even more accurately stated, the need to *resort* and *reclassify*.[41] What would become important, then, with the French Revolution—understood in some

—

Encyclopedia, a multi-volume work encompassing
Enlightenment ideals about exactly what constituted
human knowledge. Eighteenth-century philosophers
believed that all understanding could be encompassed
within the pages of a book. Anything that could not be
logically written down was therefore deemed superstitious nonsense.

Photo: Photodisk Object Series..

respects as the political expression of Enlightenment
thought—was the sorting, classifying, and categorizing
of the new French state on terms radically different from
those that had gone before. "Pigeon-holing [catego-
rizing]," argues Darnton, "is ... an exercise in power."[42]

Moreover, according to the Enlightenment worldview, "all borders are dangerous. If left unguarded, they could break down, our categories could collapse, and our world dissolve in chaos. ... Setting up categories and policing them is therefore a serious business."[43]

Darnton critically examines the *Encyclopédie*, a multi-volume work compiled by Denis Diderot and Jean le Rond d'Alembert between 1751 and 1772, in terms of what it might tell us about Enlightenment ideas concerning what constitutes human knowledge. Above all, the *Encyclopédie* emphasized the classical humanistic tradition of learning: the application of reason to human affairs by a literate culture. While the authors of the *Encyclopédie* advocated the free dissemination of knowledge, they remained intensely hostile toward nonliterate forms (such as those of oral cultures—as in Euskal Herria), representing them as superstitious and nonrational.

The exclusion of such forms demonstrates the downside of the cult of reason—namely, a propensity toward seeing things in one way alone. By allowing only *one* correct answer, this mentality tended to deny other forms of expression, viewing them as counterproductive to the triumph of reason.

ANOTHER WATCHWORD of the Revolution related to the notion of recategorization was "uniformity," considered the basis of an egalitarian and strong state apparatus. The concept of political uniformity was not entirely new to France. As we have seen, the Old Regime French monarchy followed a similar objective in pursuing a policy of administrative centralization.

As a result of these guiding Enlightenment principles, Iparralde would experience a drastic change during the French Revolution.

THE ORIGINS OF THE MODERN FRENCH STATE

In January 1789, Louis XVI, faced with a financial crisis that threatened to bankrupt his kingdom, convoked the Estates General—a national council through which public grievances, known as *cahiers*, could be presented—for the first time since 1614. This convocation marked a very public admission that the kingdom was in trouble, presenting to those who wished to reform the political and social environment (most obviously the more politically active Enlightenment thinkers) an opportunity to achieve significant change. For those whose politico-cultural heritage depended on Old Regime society, however, the moment marked a potential threat to their own security, and the grievances they presented to the Estates General were more likely to call for reforms to the system that looked toward the past. The three Basque provinces fell into this latter category.

THE CENTRAL elements of the Basque *cahiers* related to the defense of foral privileges and traditions, such as local decision-making institutions, economic privileges, clericalism, and linguistic rights. It was, as James E. Jacob demonstrates, a conservative reaction to the unfolding events: Their revolution called for the full restoration of the privileges that had been steadily eroded during the previous two centuries. "The Basque expression for revolution, *iraultza*," observes Jacob, "suggests a timeless agricultural rhythm of the tilling of the soil or the orbiting of the planets in the sky."[44]

In May 1789, the Estates General convened to hear grievances from the competing perspectives of the various disenchanted groups. It soon became apparent that these complaints were deep and widespread, but had one uniting theme: a questioning of the political consensus of the French kingdom. By the summer, it was increasingly evident that, amid such profound social

---

and political protest, Louis XVI would have to respond in some way if he were to maintain the stability of his kingdom. He thus grudgingly accepted the transformation of the Estates General into the National Assembly, something more approximate to a parliamentary forum, in June 1789.

THIS PASSAGE from Estates General to National Assembly marked a significant change, for the Estates General symbolized Old Regime political culture and the new institution was, by contrast, more redolent of the new politics of representation that had been developing through the seventeenth and eighteenth centuries in countries such as Great Britain, the Netherlands, and the United States. Through the summer of 1789, the National Assembly called for more reform, and with a concomitant rise in popular protest as a result of the poor harvest, events culminated in August with the pronouncement of "The Declaration of the Rights of Man and the Citizen," the political manifesto that more than any other signified the definitive step out of the Old Regime and into the search for a new kind of society.

THE BASQUE REACTION

The reaction of the Basques of Iparralde was divided: Whereas the representatives of Nafarroa Beherea refused even to attend meetings of the new body, those of both Lapurdi and Zuberoa acquiesced to the will of the National Assembly. Yet while Zuberoa seems to have accepted the changes associated with the tumultuous events of 1789, however unwillingly, the *Biltzar* of Lapurdi attempted to convince its representatives in Paris to argue more favorably in defense of its foral privileges. Ultimately, though, this was doomed to failure, and the *Biltzar* met for the last time in November 1789. Nafarroa Beherea, from the first moments of the

convening of the Estates General through the creation of
the National Assembly, had attempted to preserve its
distinct status as an independent realm outside the
French polity in all communication with these bodies. It
became clear that these attempts too would fail as events
in Paris through the fall and early winter of 1789 led
increasingly to the reorganization of the political and
administrative basis of the country. In November, the
separate office of the kingdom of Nafarroa Beherea was
abolished, and in late December the province capitulated to the rule of the National Assembly.

THE SOCIAL AND CULTURAL BEGINNINGS OF THE FRENCH STATE

If the events of 1789 were to set the foundations of a new
political culture, the first step toward implementing it
was the administrative reorganization of the country, a
plan that required the destruction of preexisting provincial and local loyalties. As a consequence, in January
1790 the National Assembly voted to re-create France as
a conglomerate of eighty-three *départements*, rational
geographical divisions designed to promote the whole
(the French state) rather than the constituent part (the
département). This new map included the *département*
of the Basses-Pyrénées, a territorial division that exists
to this day, joining Iparralde to the neighboring
province of Béarn (with a new administrative capital in
the non-Basque town of Pau).

THIS REORGANIZATION left Basques as a minority in
the *département*. Following Darnton's thesis,[45] we
might consider the redrawing of the French map as a
concerted effort to imprint the symbolic force of the Revolution. By creating a new *geographical* and *political*
reality, the French revolutionaries intended to create
and foment a new *social* and *cultural* reality; according

"Live in Euskal Herria Festival: The People's Euro Rock against the World Company, Arrosa (Nafarroa Beherea), July 2, 3, 4, 1999." This annual music festival draws groups from all over Europe. It celebrates global diversity against the imposition of uniform globalization. *Photo: Koldo Mitxelena Kulturunea archives.*

to this plan, the people of Iparralde, for example, would gradually stop thinking of their identity in terms of their province or Basqueness (however limited that may have been) and would instead begin to think of themselves as French citizens. This was the first step in creating an *imagined community*, to use Benedict Anderson's term,[46] or an *invented tradition* whereby, according to Eric Hobsbawm, "a set of practices, normally governed by overtly or tacitly accepted rules and of a ritual or symbolic nature ... seek to inculcate certain values and norms of behaviour by repetition, which automatically implies continuity with the past."[47]

ALREADY BY 1790, it had become apparent that the wishes of the Basque provinces ran counter to those of the increasingly powerful National Assembly. Bowing to what seemed inevitable, the provinces of Iparralde had recognized the political authority of the new governing body, but their last hope of preserving at least a sense of what had previously existed rested in the possibility of creating a single Basque *département*. This, however, was not forthcoming. The result of the formative year of political change, for most Basques of Iparralde at least, was the dissolution of the distinct nature of the Basque identity, be it political, social, or cultural. From March 1790 on, according to the official division of the French political orbit, the distinctive existence of a Basque territory disappeared. The Basques of Iparralde were now officially French citizens.

THE CONSOLIDATION OF THE REVOLUTION AND ITS EFFECTS ON IPARRALDE

In 1790, a formal constitution was proclaimed, followed in 1791 by the creation of the Legislative Assembly, a unicameral central decision-making body whose establishment fulfilled many of the original ideals behind the

---

cahiers first presented before the Estates General two years previously. The momentum generated by these changes propelled further events, as the hitherto *evolutionary* nature of the Revolution took a decidedly *revolutionary* turn. In August 1792, the office of the monarchy was suspended, leading to the establishment of a National Convention with, for the first time, established political parties as we know them today. Of the two parties, the Girondins and the Jacobins, it was the latter, the more extreme of the two in its desire to forge a new political, social, and cultural order, that increasingly promoted the idea of a unitary and indivisible French republic. This Jacobin ideal, beginning with the proclamation of the First Republic in September 1792, has subsequently permeated French politics to the present day.

WITH THE proclamation of the First Republic, Jacobin power grew steadily through a combination of a politically intelligent philosophy—in Jacobin terms, you were either a *patriot* (good) or *aristocrat* (evil), an ideological creation of binary opposites that represents a classic piece of Enlightenment rationalism—and the use of political violence to terrorize those people who did not adhere to their plans for the emerging French state. Following the execution of Louis XVI in January 1793, the modern French republic was born and the power of the Jacobins reached its apex. From 1793 to 1794, when Revolutionary fervor was at its most zealous, Jacobins began to talk of purging the state of all "aristocrats" (or counter-revolutionaries). This period, during which suspected enemies of the new French state were sought out and executed on what, for the time, was a mass scale (with at least 12,000 victims in approximately one year), is commonly known as the

Early twentieth-century French railroad poster advertising the coast of Lapurdi. Iparralde was marketed for its proximity to Hegoalde. Note the references to Donostia and Hondarribia (St. Sebastien and Fontarabie in French).
Photo by permission of Koldo Mitxelena Kulturunea archives.

Reign of Terror. (The contemporary term "terrorism" derives its etymological roots from this appellation.)

The use of violence to symbolically purge the country of those elements viewed (rightly or wrongly) as enemies of the state seemingly carried little of the Enlightenment principles of freedom and democracy. However, as Darnton notes, the policing of Enlightenment categories was crucial to their successful implementation.[48] As such, political violence by the French state during this period symbolically echoes the Enlightenment representation of oral culture as brutish or backward, as something to be eliminated through the use and dissemination of a literate culture based on *modern* languages.

IN IPARRALDE, the Terror was directed principally against the Church, prompting a violent response on the part of the Basque clergy, with guerrilla priests openly defying state decrees. Perhaps the most serious incident associated with the severe French state policy toward Iparralde at this time, however, was the deportation of 3,000 Basques from several border towns in the spring of 1794. As Jacob states, the primary reason for the deportation seems to have been the desertion of Basque conscripts from the French army (an incident that would be repeated in generations to come),[49] yet other factors also played a part: More than anything else, Iparralde was viewed by Paris as a weak point in its state-building aspirations, especially given the potential of the rural clergy to foment dissent among the Basque population. The deportees were eventually allowed to return that same fall, but fewer than half those deported survived the involuntary exile. Those who did survive returned to find their property in the hands of French "patriots" (a factor contributing to later emigration from the region). A revenge of sorts was carried out in

1796, when a clandestine armed Basque group operating in Lapurdi assassinated a "Monsieur Mundutegi," one of the architects of the deportation, in his hometown of Ustaritze (Ustaritz).

Between 1789 and 1795, the French Revolution inexorably altered life in Iparralde. During those years, the revolutionaries effectively sought to force Enlightenment reason on the populace as a whole. The logic of Enlightenment thought—a general philosophy composed of rational binary opposites—taken to a political extreme culminated in the period known as the Reign of Terror. Although this was eventually superseded in 1795 by yet another form of political organization known as the Directory (the first post-Revolution regime of the French state), the damaging effects of these changes for the majority of Basques in Iparralde would prove impossible to undo.

The central ideal of Revolutionary France was that of overhauling the Old Regime and its feudal values. Yet while much of the French kingdom had, indeed, operated under such a system, Iparralde had enjoyed a distinctively *non-feudal* status. The *Biltzar*, for example, was probably a more democratic institution than any of the Revolution's incarnations.

JACOB'S conclusion is especially pertinent: "[T]he Revolution did real violence to Basque institutions and social values. Despite its fraternal intentions, the Revolution served to destroy a highly participatory Basque political culture through abolition of the *fors* and suppression of the Labourdin Bilçar and the Estates of Navarre and Soule."[50]

As a consequence of this political sea change, a new *culture* emerged that offered Basques a modern political identity as French citizens. While Iparralde quite clearly rejected this concept at the time, the seeds of future change had been sown.

This moment, a couple of decades at the close of the eighteenth century, in many ways marked the birth of modernity. For during this time the foundation of modern social and political organization, in the shape of the modern nation-state, was laid down in the shape of Revolutionary France. We might conclude, then, that the very foundation of modernity implied denying a specifically Basque cultural or political identity.

Before examining the more lasting consequences of these changes, we should also take note of the extension of French Revolutionary values outside the French political orbit and, in particular, the effect of this on Hegoalde.

Lesson three

REQUIRED READING

James E. Jacob, *Hills of Conflict: Basque Nationalism in France* (Reno, Las Vegas and London: University of Nevada Press, 1994), pp. 16–38.

Helen J. Castelli, "Response of the Pays Basque to the Convocation of the Estates General in Pre-Revolutionary France," in William A. Douglass, Richard W. Etulain, and William H. Jacobsen, eds., *Anglo-American Contributions to Basque Studies: Essays in Honor of Jon Bilbao* (Reno: Desert Research Institute, 1977), pp. 93–105.

Robert Darnton, *The Great Cat Massacre and Other Episodes in French Cultural History* (New York: Vintage Books, 1985), pp. 191–213.

LEARNING OBJECTIVES
1. To understand the Enlightenment concepts of reason and uniformity, and how they impacted the political culture of the French Revolution.
2. To comprehend broadly the course of events from 1789 through the accession of Napoleon, and how the Basques of Iparralde responded to these changes.
3. To examine the nature of the modern French state at its birth, its underlying values, and the implications of these ideas for Iparralde.

WRITTEN LESSON FOR SUBMISSION
Document Question 1
Carefully examine the following two documents. What do both documents tell us about Revolutionary attitudes toward the concepts of nation and nationality? What, if any, are the differences between the two in these documents? What, in your opinion, would be the immediate consequences of the opinions stated in the documents for Iparralde in the late eighteenth and early nineteenth centuries?

Extract from the Declaration of the Rights of Man and the Citizen (1789):
The representatives of the French people, organized as a National Assembly ... have determined to set forth in a solemn declaration the natural, inalienable, and sacred rights of man, in order that this declaration, being constantly before all members of the social body, shall remind them continually of their rights and duties; in order that the acts of the legislative power, as well as those of the executive power, may be compared at any moment with the objects and purposes of all political institutions and may thus be more respected; and, lastly, in order that these grievances of the citizens,

*based hereafter upon simple and uncontestable princi-
ples, shall tend to the maintenance of the constitution
and redound to the happiness of all. Therefore the
National Assembly recognizes and proclaims ... the following rights of the man and the citizen:*

1. *Men are born and remain free and equal in rights.
   Social distinctions may be founded only upon the
   general good ...*
2. *The principle of all sovereignty resides essentially in
   the nation. No body nor individual may exercise any
   authority which does not proceed directly from the
   nation ...*
3. *Liberty consists in the freedom to do everything
   which injures no one else; hence the exercise of natural rights of each man has no limits except those
   which assure to the other members of the society the
   enjoyment of the same rights. These limits can only
   be determined by law ...*
4. *Law can only prohibit such actions as are hurtful to
   society. Nothing may be prevented which is not forbidden by law, and no one may be forced to do anything not provided for by law ...*
5. *Law is the expression of the general will. Every citizen has a right to participate personally, or through
   his representative, in its formation. It must be the
   same for all, whether it protects or punishes. All citizens, being equal in the eyes of the law, are equally
   eligible to all dignities and to all public positions
   and occupations, according to their abilities, and
   without distinction except that of their virtues and
   talents ...*
10. *No one shall be disquieted on account of his opin-
    ions, including his religious views, provided their
    manifestation does not disturb the public order
    established by law ...*

11. *The free communication of ideas and opinions is one of the most precious of the rights of man. Every citizen may, accordingly, speak, write, and print with freedom, but shall be responsible for such abuses of this freedom as shall be defined by law ...* [51]

Extract from the Law of II Thermidor (1794):
The National Convention, after having heard the report of its legislative committee, decrees:
1. *From the publication date of the present law onwards, no public act shall be written in anything other than the French language, anywhere that constitutes territory of the Republic ...*
2. *From the month following the publication of the present law onwards, no law, including even common signature, shall be registered if it is not written in the French language ...*
3. *All public employees and officials, all government agents that, from the publication date of the present law onwards, might say, write or sign, in the exercise of their duties, hearings, verdicts, contracts or any other general proceedings, conceived in languages or tongues different from French, shall be brought before a reformatory police tribunal of their residence, condemned to six months in prison and removed from office ...* [52]

4 · The French Revolution (II)

ALTHOUGH DURING its initial phase the French Revolution had a greater impact on Iparralde than it did on Hegoalde, the Revolutionary tide ultimately engulfed Europe as a whole, including the Spanish kingdom. As such, we will explore here the export of Revolutionary ideals—in the main through aggressive military expansionism—and how this sowed the seeds of political change in Napoleonic France's neighbor to the south. It is important to note the general framework of this change, in particular the role that violence played in the beginnings of the modern state. Euskal Herria, together with the rest of Europe, was engulfed by violent change during the period between the end of the eighteenth and the beginning of the nineteenth century. In this chapter, we will examine the impact of Enlightenment ideals, the French Revolution, and the Napoleonic Empire on the provinces of Hegoalde.

THE BASQUE ENLIGHTENMENT

Enlightenment ideals penetrated certain sectors of Hegoalde's society at the close of the eighteenth century. Generally speaking, these sectors were confined to the more liberal coastal zones of Bizkaia and Gipuzkoa that had developed strong protoindustrial and commercial economic infrastructures, most especially in Bilbo (Bilbao) and Donostia (San Sebastián). Those modernizing elements of the Basque population, the ascendant middle classes, were receptive to ideas that promised a political influence corresponding to their economic power. Yet the most obvious expression of these new enlightened concerns was the creation in 1766 of the Real Sociedad Bascongada de Amigos del País (Royal

Basque Society of Friends of the Country) in Azkoitia (Azcoitia), Gipuzkoa.

The Royal Basque Society of Friends of the Country originated in a series of meetings between Basque nobles, clerics, and military and commercial leaders, and emerged with the dual intent of promoting technical and commercial research as well as providing a modern framework for developing specifically Basque business connections throughout not only the Basque Country proper but also the Spanish empire. Among the society's initiatives was a scientific research center, the Seminario Patriótico de Vergara (Patriotic Seminary of Bergara), founded in Bergara (Vergara), Gipuzkoa. Through research conducted in the Bergara laboratory, the brothers Juan José and Fausto Elhuyar—whose family originated in Hazparne (Hasparren), Lapurdi— discovered a new metal, wolfram or tungsten, which has the highest boiling point of any metallic element. This discovery revolutionized the science of metallurgy in the eighteenth century and beyond, leading to the new metal's use as a filament in lighting, electrical wiring, and the production of steel alloys. The society also contributed significantly to the dissemination of Enlightenment thought in Spain, as one of its prominent members, Manuel Ignacio de Altuna, was a friend of the Enlightenment thinker Jean-Jacques Rousseau and introduced the French philosopher's ideas to the Castilian kingdom.

ACCORDING TO William A. Douglass and Jon Bilbao, "it is evident that the young idealists who founded the society, in their altruistic concern with the Basque economy, represented a departure from the highly personal economic outlook of the traditional Basque entrepreneur"; they also note that the founders "were motivated in large measure by a concern with ethnic group

Jean-Jacques Rousseau. Manuel Ignacio de Altuna, was a friend of the Enlightenment philosopher. As a result of this friendship the new ideas sweeping Europe in the eighteenth century would arrive promptly in the Basque Country.
Bust by Jean-Antoine Houdon, Louvre.

loyalties."[53] The society remained the preserve of the educated and wealthy few: For the majority of Hegoalde's inhabitants, the ideas associated with the Enlightenment, especially those that challenged ecclesiastical authority, were for the most part too threatening to their traditional society.

REVOLUTIONARY INCURSION INTO HEGOALDE

In February 1793, the French Convention declared war on Great Britain, the Netherlands, and the Spanish kingdom. In July and August of that year, French forces swiftly occupied much of Gipuzkoa and northern Nafarroa, attacking several towns during their advance (the razing of houses being the preferred tactic). From the late fall of 1793 through the winter of 1793–94, the French forces entrenched themselves in a ring of territory in these two provinces. That same fall of 1793, the *Junta* of Gipuzkoa met in an attempt to forge an agreement with the occupying forces, whereby the province would enter into an accord with the French state that would secure its "independent" status within a loose form of union.

THIS WAS rejected by Paris, which instead imposed a direct form of union with Gipuzkoa, annexing the province as a protectorate of the French republic soon after and disbanding the Gipuzkoan *Junta*. Thereafter, several Gipuzkoan priests were imprisoned and a guillotine installed in Donostia, provoking a mini exodus of Gipuzkoans (and many Bizkaians from the areas near the province's border with Gipuzkoa) westwards into Bizkaia. Yet the occupying French forces also found willing collaborators, especially among the enlightened elite of Donostia.

The protectorate status of Gipuzkoa within the French republic would last two years. The winter of 1794–95 brought food shortages to the nascent republic and a rise in social unrest. Contending with food riots and a renewed offensive on the part of monarchists, the Convention was forced to curb its foreign offensives. As such, by the Peace of Basle in 1795, the French republic concluded an agreement with the Spanish kingdom that returned Gipuzkoa to the Castilian political orbit.

THIS PROMPTED several calls from Madrid to abolish the Basque *foruak*, punishing Gipuzkoa for its traitorous defection to the French republic. The response of King Carlos IV's prime minister, Manuel Godoy, was hesitant. Although official policy had been one of increasing centralization throughout the eighteenth century, he needed the support of the Basque economic elite to shore up the state economy.

SPANISH CENTRALIZATION

Throughout Europe, the exportation of French Revolutionary ideals sparked a response among Old Regime powers. In most cases, predictably, the radical changes imposed by the French were rejected, but there was also an ironic mimicking of some Revolutionary innovations. In the aftermath of the war with the French republic, for example, the Spanish kingdom sought to impose further measures of political centralization (a policy, we should remember, that originated through the influence of the former French monarchy). As such, in the decade after 1795, several measures were adopted by Madrid that sought to undermine Basque foral rights. Interestingly, the strategy adopted to further the cause of political centralization took a decidedly cultural twist: Stanley Payne mentions, for example, the publication of several historical tracts that sought to downplay the historical importance of the *foruak*.[54]

Napoleon Bonaparte was a Corsican born to Genovese parents. He rose to fame in the late 1790s as a brilliant young general in the Revolutionary army. His own personal vague connection to France proper may well have encouraged him to become French through battlefield exploits in the name of his adopted mother country. *Engraving from Richard Sutphen (ed):* Old Engravings and Illustrations I.

This official state assault on traditional Basque privileges was followed by a series of decrees increasing tax and draft levies in the four provinces of Hegoalde. Of the four, it was Nafarroa that felt the weight of the assault the most. Payne reminds us that it alone retained "a fully articulated medieval constitution, with an executive administration (though not independent sovereignty), its own judiciary, and a Cortes of limited legislative power."[55] As a result, like Nafarroa Beherea to the north in relation to developments in France, the effects of state centralization were most acutely felt in the medieval Basque kingdom than in any other of Hegoalde's provinces.

THE BASQUE REACTION

The most virulent response to the proposed changes occurred in Bizkaia. A small town notary, Simón Bernardo Zamacola, proposed to Madrid the creation of a new free port alongside Bilbo (to be known as the Port of Peace after Godoy's nickname, the "Prince of Peace"). The new facility, if adopted, would obviously reduce the trade coming through Bilbo, and the plan thus provoked a heated protest in 1804 among those whose livelihoods depended on the major Basque port. The uprising, known as the *zamacolada*, was a broad-based riot including several cross-class interests, and it demonstrated to the central authorities the depth of feeling among Basques against royal interference in what they considered their internal affairs. It was swiftly quelled with the help of several thousand troops, and many of the ringleaders were shipped to colonial penal institutions or banished from Bizkaia.

IN 1805, MADRID made further reprisals by abolishing the mayoralty of Bilbo and the *corregimiento* (the monarchy's administrative representative authority in the provinces) of Bizkaia, to be replaced by the offices of *alcalde mayor* (principal mayor) and *commandante general* (military commander), respectively, the former being completely subordinate to the latter. It was a clear policy, on the part of the Spanish crown, to advance central rule into the foral territory of the Basques. The changes provoked by the *zamacolada* thus left Bizkaia under de facto Spanish military authority after the right of assembly in the province had been abolished.

NAPOLEONIC ASCENDANCY

In 1795, the first post–French Revolution regime, the Directory, had come to power in France as a means of stabilizing and consolidating the changes brought about in the heady period between 1789 and 1794. Although the Directory was also brought about as a means of curbing the Revolutionary excesses of 1793–94, it could not relinquish the heavy hand of violence that marked the origins of the French state. Indeed, in many ways the country turned from outright terror to a kind of "liberal authoritarianism" still heavily reliant on the use of state force.

ACCORDING TO Howard G. Brown, "the use of massive repression during these years—and not the Terror—permanently altered the state's role in society ... [and] a systematic use of military means of repression was the key to whatever success the Directory had in restoring order."[56] These tactics were embraced also by Napoleon on his ascension to power in 1799. By the late 1790s, the French populace had tired of the constant political, social, and economic upheavals affecting the country, but the moderate (though authoritarian) Directory could not produce the kind of leadership needed to steer the new French republic to stability. Instead, a new kind of leader would emerge, not from the ranks of

Enlightened intellectuals, but from the military. Ironically, the man to secure stability in the nascent French state, the model political organization for most of the next two hundred years, was neither French nor a paragon of Enlightened libertarian values.

NAPOLEON Bonaparte was a Corsican born to Genovese parents. He rose to fame in the late 1790s as a brilliant young general in the Revolutionary army, the institution that in late Revolutionary France perhaps best seemed to embody, in the popular imagination, the values of the Revolution. Napoleon's ascendancy owed much to the fact that the Revolution had grown stale and no leaders had emerged to carry on the mantle of the earlier ideologues. The leaders of the Directory mistakenly believed that Napoleon could be used as a figurehead to guide the French state through its first post-Revolutionary phase. In 1799, Napoleon, challenging their authority, forced a new constitution whereby ultimate decision-making authority rested with a body known as the Consulate. Not by chance, Napoleon appointed himself First Consul.

Not only did the political culture at the birth of the modern French state recall Bourbon absolutism, then, but it would also serve as a model for twentieth-century dictators to come. In 1804, this was more than apparent as Napoleon crowned himself Emperor of the French. With the establishment of the Napoleonic empire came the Civil Code (renamed the Napoleonic Code in 1807), a new legal system that, among other elements, codified property rights so that inheritance would be equally divided among elder male children. The French legal system thus ran counter to the Basque practice of retaining small farmsteads (*baserriak*) intact through primogeniture, an inheritance system that allowed for only one heir to take over the family property. The wider

consequences of the Civil Code will be discussed in the
following chapter.

At about the same time that Napoleon was consolidating his power, there emerged a solitary voice in Paris
to defend specifically Basque interests. Born in 1749,
Dominique-Joseph Garat had been, together with his
older brother Dominique, one of the first Revolutionary
deputies for the province of Lapurdi. He subsequently
served in the Revolutionary government as Minister of
Justice and later as Minister of the Interior, as well as
becoming France's ambassador to Naples in 1798.
Under Napoleon, he served with distinction as a senator
and was later appointed a count of the empire. Between
1803 and 1809, he approached the French emperor several times with plans to create a separate Basque federation (including the seven provinces); though it would
function as a satellite of the French empire, the federation he proposed would be constructed along the lines
of traditional Basque popular assemblies and would
defend and encourage the use of Euskara. It was a bold
plan and not unrealistic, given Napoleon's heavy-
handed "alliances" with other distinct cultural group-
ings, such as the Confederation of the Rhine. However,
the French emperor was ultimately unreceptive to the
proposals, and Garat died in his birthplace, Ustaritze, in
1833 with his plan for a Basque federation unrealized.

IN 1802, NAPOLEON began a new aggressively expansionist phase. In the following years, he conquered
most of Europe, falling only to the combined forces of
the other European powers in 1815. Taking Revolutionary principles, by force, throughout the rest of
Europe—including the Spanish kingdom—Napoleon
left a profound legacy that, as we shall see, was crucial to
developments in Hegoalde.

The Napoleonic invasion of Spain in 1808 led to the
occupation and near destruction of Hegoalde. This led
to widespread poverty and indebtedness as the rural
populace sought to rebuild their shattered economy.
Engraving by Thomas Bewick.

THE NAPOLEONIC INVASION OF HEGOALDE
In 1808, a new king, Fernando VII, assumed the throne
of Spain. He was more alert (if not exactly sympathetic)
to the importance of Basque particularities than was his
predecessor, Carlos IV. As such, he made sure, on his
accession, to swear the traditional oath of loyalty to the
foruak. But the peaceful reassurance brought about by
his declaration was short-lived: Soon after, Napoleon, in
a general attempt to shore up his southern flank and
more particularly to curb the smuggling that was
affecting the protected status of the French economy,
invaded the Spanish kingdom.

As the invasion took place, the French emperor sought the abdication of the Spanish monarch, in favor of a handpicked French candidate for the post: his brother, Joseph Bonaparte. During the summer of 1808, Napoleon called an assembly in Baiona (Bayonne), to which he invited several influential figures within the Spanish kingdom, including Basque representatives. His plan was to gain support for the creation of a new noble class supportive of the royal candidacy of his brother. At the meeting, the separate delegations of Araba, Bizkaia, Gipuzkoa, and Nafarroa coordinated their efforts in an attempt to convince the French that the centralizing tendencies of their state had little chance of success in a political culture long used to specific rights and liberties. Amazingly, considering the nature of the French empire, not to mention events just a few years previously in Iparralde, Napoleon agreed to their demands. The new Spanish constitution of 1808 thus guaranteed the *foruak* of Hegoalde while at the same time installing Joseph Bonaparte as king.

THE BAIONA meeting and resultant constitution did not mark a definitive end to conflict in the peninsula, however, for the overwhelming majority of the population were not willing to accept the imposition of a puppet sovereign by Napoleon. During the summer of 1808, sporadic popular outbursts against the French occupying forces were brutally suppressed, leading to the outbreak of an insurgent war in which Hegoalde would play a prominent role. By 1809, the French effectively took on the role of occupying forces in hostile territory, with garrisons stationed in strategic centers. Soon after, acts of repression by the occupying French, with the compliance of local collaborators, increased, inflaming the local population even more, and a major war developed in Hegoalde.

By the end of 1809, in a tactic that would be adopted more than once in future generations, small, insurgent guerrilla bands had started organizing. (The term "guerrilla" was coined in 1812 to refer to the peasants—most of them Basque—fighting the French.) Making effective use of the rugged terrain from which they came, these armed units would ultimately prove decisive in the struggle against the French imperial forces. As Renato Barahona notes, the only response that the French could find was the increasing use of terror against the hostile local population (a response that had already been employed within the French state itself).[57] By 1811, the tide was beginning to turn. The Basque guerrillas effectively controlled the countryside, having developed a successful politico-military organization. Toward the middle of 1812, the French, hemmed into the principal urban centers of Hegoalde, were quite clearly losing the war, and between the summer of 1812 and the spring of 1813 Napoleon's forces gradually withdrew.

DESPITE ITS successful conclusion for the majority of Basques in Hegoalde, the war inevitably brought with it harsh social and economic repercussions. Throughout the region, farms had been deserted by a population fleeing the harsh reprisals of the French. This led to widespread poverty and indebtedness as the rural populace sought to rebuild their shattered economy.

At a wider level, too, there were important changes. In 1812, the Spanish opposition to French occupation proclaimed the Constitution of Cádiz. Prepared by Spanish liberals taking advantage of the absence of the monarchy and influenced in great part by both Enlightenment rationalism and the French Revolution, the constitution (ironically, given the ostensible opposition to the imposition of Napoleonic rule) called for a centralized state with limited popular representation. This was the first attempt to forge the modern Spanish state, and, as Robert P. Clark observes, it "created the next threat to the freedom of the Basque provinces."[58] From the outset, the Spanish constitution met with resistance in Hegoalde, as the Basque provinces sought to reaffirm their local rights and privileges. This struggle would, in many ways, serve as the driving political theme in Hegoalde from the conclusion of the Spanish War of Independence in 1813 through to the present day.

Although the Reign of Terror came to an end in 1794, violent upheaval continued to be a feature of Basque life, in both Iparralde and Hegoalde, well into the first two decades of the nineteenth century. To cite one example, Enlightenment thought, the French Revolution, and the Napoleonic wars radically transformed Basque rural society through the destruction of its infrastructure and the beginnings of a migratory process that would mark a significant social and demographic change for Euskal Herria in the nineteenth century. The period after 1815, for the majority of Basques, was one of hardship as they sought to rebuild their rural economy. For other Basques, those of the liberal enclaves in Bilbo and Donostia, for example, the period marked the first step in a modernizing process that would bring positive social, economic, and even political changes later in the nineteenth century.

Lesson four

REQUIRED READING

Renato Barahona, *Vizcaya on the Eve of Carlism: Politics and Society, 1800–1833* (Reno and Las Vegas: University of Nevada Press, 1989), pp. 21–30.

Stanley G. Payne, *Basque Nationalism* (Reno: University of Nevada Press, 1975), pp. 33–37.

Howard G. Brown, "From Organic Society to Security State: The War on Brigandage in France, 1797–1802," *The Journal of Modern History* 69, no. 4 (December 1997), pp. 661–95.

LEARNING OBJECTIVES

1. To examine post-Revolutionary developments in France and their immediate implications for Euskal Herria.
2. To understand how both the French Revolution and the ascendancy of Napoleon would also have lasting effects on Hegoalde.

WRITTEN LESSON FOR SUBMISSION

1. In his article about the law-enforcement policies of the Directory, "From Organic Society to Security State," Howard G. Brown concludes that "the late Republic's war on brigandage and communal responses to it were decisive in replacing an *organic society* with a *security state*" (p. 695; italics added). If this was indeed the case—and feel free to critically evaluate this opinion—to what extent did the French Revolution and Napoleonic empire deviate from Enlightenment ideals?
2. What, in your opinion, were the most profound changes brought about in Euskal Herria as a result of the French Revolution? Consider especially Basque society and culture before and after the Revolution and its aftermath.

5 · Iparralde, 1815–70
The birth of the modern state

ITH THE benefit of hindsight, we might consider
W the French Revolution and Napoleonic ascendancy
as a bridge between the absolutism of the kingdoms of
France and Spain and what would definitively emerge in
the nineteenth century as the modern French and
Spanish states. Europe after 1815 was a changed continent as well as a continent in change, and this momentous shift, from Old Regime to modern society, would
have a profound impact on the everyday lives of
Basques. Indeed, we cannot consider Basque culture and
society in the nineteenth century without first understanding the political, economic, and cultural structure
under which it existed.

According to David Held, the emergence of the
modern state was due to three general factors: the effective use of violence (be it in the waging of external warfare or internal repression), the successful development
of economic resources (always channeled toward the
benefit of the central state economy, whether domestic
or foreign), and the achievement of political legitimacy
among the majority of the population (often as a result
of the first two factors, and always as a means of providing the state with loyalty and resources).[59] Taking
this argument into account, we might consider the following questions: To what extent can we speak of a
specifically *Basque* culture amid the emergence of the
French and Spanish states? What impact did the rise of
these states have on Basque society? What were the differences between the emergent French and Spanish
states, and did these differences (if indeed there were
any) imply varying fortunes for the Basques of Iparralde
and Hegoalde?

THE DIFFICULT INVENTION OF FRANCE

Between the final defeat of Napoleon and the creation of the Third Republic in 1870, the French state went through a series of incarnations as it struggled with the difficult task of post-Revolutionary political adjustment. Between 1815 and 1830, the French monarchy attempted to reestablish its authority along Old Regime political and institutional lines, but attempts to turn back the clock of history proved futile, and in 1830 a liberal monarchical state emerged as a kind of compromise between Old Regime and Revolutionary ideals. Louis Philippe, the new monarch, was proclaimed "king of the French" rather than "king of France," and the Revolutionary tricolor flag was reinstated. In many respects, the "July Monarchy," as it was called, represented the final triumph of the French middle classes (the *bourgeoisie*) in exerting their political muscle, one of the key original ideals of the French Revolution.

THE NEW political arrangement, however, only served to exacerbate the differences between alternate visions of what really constituted France, and through the nineteenth century this debate underpinned much of the political, social, and cultural foundations of the new state. At the same time, through the 1830s and 1840s (and in common with other countries in western Europe), the French state was beginning to experience the first throes of modernization and industrial change, further underscoring the cleavages between old and new. From the mid-1830s on, a series of industrial disputes broke out, with workers demanding better labor conditions and the protection of traditional crafts in the face of increasing competition from machine-based industries. The 1840s witnessed years of tremendous economic hardship throughout much of Europe, with a series of poor harvests in the still overwhelmingly

The revolutionary ideal of liberty was portrayed by a romantic heroine. However this figure came sword-in-hand so the revolutionary ideal of freedom was thus enforced by more traditional methods of violence. *From* Croquis Révolutionnaires *by Pilotell, ca 1871.*

---

agriculturally based economies leading to food shortages and clamors for political, social, and economic
change.

In 1848, Paris once more erupted in revolutionary
fervor. Louis Philippe, implicated for many years in various cases of corruption, was forced to abdicate, and the
Second Republic was proclaimed. For a brief time
during 1848 and 1849, the French state was consumed
by an idealism resonant of 1793–94, but this idealism
frightened the new power brokers of the state: bourgeois
property holders. Consequently, the uprising, provoking
a conservative reaction among these middle-class property holders against the progressive nature of the new
regime, was ruthlessly suppressed. With the Second
Republic still in place, Louis Napoleon Bonaparte,
nephew of the former French emperor, emerged victorious in presidential elections as an emblem of his
uncle's greatness. His electoral triumph would ultimately doom the Second Republic, however: In 1851,
Bonaparte seized personal power, and the Second
Empire was instituted with Napoleon III as its self-pro-
claimed leader the following year.

NAPOLEON III's reign was largely noteworthy for a
domestic policy that began with aggressive authoritarian measures (strict political censorship and intimi-
dation of political opponents, for example)—an expression of the conservative reaction against the 1848–49
uprising—yet gradually relaxed into a more moderate
regime as he sought popular support in the wake of several disastrous forays into external warfare during the
1860s. However, an inglorious end awaited Napoleon III:
His empire crumbled in the ruinous war with Prussia in
1870, a painful event in the historical imagination of the
modern French state and one that would serve as an

---

essential reference point in the invention of France by subsequent generations.

IPARRALDE IN THE CONSOLIDATION OF THE FRENCH STATE

Despite the turmoil associated with the beginnings of the modern French state, what was clearly emerging (although in heavily contested form) was a vision of France as not merely a functional conglomerate of its citizenry, but rather as a nation to be adored and defended. As such, a key component of the state-building process (perhaps *the* key component) was the development and cultivation of French nationalism. For Ernest Gellner, nationalism "is in reality the consequence of a new form of social organization, based on deeply internalized, education-dependent high cultures, each protected by its own state."[60] Thus, in his classic turn of phrase, "it is nationalism which engenders nations, and not the other way round."[61] This idea implies that the twin processes of political state building and economic modernization *required* a social and cultural expression, an ideology even, to consolidate their success. This expression would be fulfilled by French state nationalism.

FRENCH NATIONALISM had already been employed, with varying degrees of success, during the Revolution, and this model of nationalism served as the basis of nineteenth-century state policy. In general terms, following Benedict Anderson's argument, we might say that the French nation had to be *imagined* or articulated through discursive practices such as state education and even military service.[62]

In the opinion of Geoff Eley and Ronald Grigor Suny, "[The] need to constitute nations discursively, through the processes of imaginative ideological labor—that is, the novelty of national culture, its manufactured or invented character, as opposed to its deep historical rootedness—is probably the most important point to emerge from the more recent literature. Moreover, in principle there is little difference in this respect between the 'historic' nations (which enjoyed either the reality or the remembrance of autonomous statehood between the fifteenth and the eighteenth centuries, like England, France, or Hungary) and the so-called history-less peoples [the Basques, for example] (which did not)."[63]

TO WHAT EXTENT, then, did Iparralde become an integrated part of the French state during this initial period, from 1815 to 1870? Despite the Revolution and the beginnings of the state-building process with its concomitant French nationalism, the Basques of Iparralde retained much of their culture through the first half of the nineteenth century. Everyday life still revolved around family, *baserri*, Church, and village, and day-to-day communication was still conducted in Euskara.[64] Furthermore, a new wave of Basque migration from Hegoalde was actually strengthening cross-Pyrenean ties at this time. Through the nineteenth century, seasonal workers from Nafarroa migrated to Iparralde—women from the Baztan valley came each spring to weed grainfields, and the men came in the early winter to plough fields in preparation for the new crops—and the sandal factories of Maule (Mauléon) in Zuberoa also offered temporary employment to Nafarroans.

In many ways, however, life changed dramatically for the Basques of Iparralde during this period. The implementation of the Civil Code, for example, forced *baserriak* to be broken up among heirs (contrary to Basque family inheritance custom), and consequently many Basques could no longer afford to farm them, provoking

a wave of emigration beginning around the mid-1820s.
(Migratory patterns will be discussed in greater detail in
Chapter 10.) Despite this, for the most part the Basques
of Iparralde gladly accepted the restoration of the French
monarchy as a step toward stability in an incipient state
that had been beset by violence and warfare for an entire
generation. In effect, this would allow the French state to
begin the process of extending the *idea of France* in
Iparralde, of transforming Basques into Frenchmen.

POLITICS
State influence in Iparralde in the period after 1815
quickly came to be represented by an electoral system
that, despite the idealistic promises of the Revolution
and Napoleon, concentrated political and economic
power in the hands of the new French middle class:
former aristocrats who had successfully negotiated their
change of name if not status, property holders, mer-
chants, civil servants or state employees in general, and
members of the "liberal" professions such as doctors
and lawyers. This class, which was relatively small in
number, adhered swiftly to the new ethos of Frenchness,
and increasingly exercised its economic and political
muscle over those sectors that constituted the majority
of the Basques of Iparralde: small rural property holders,
baserritarrak, shepherds, and rural artisans, for
example.

AT THE SAME time, the Church still exercised a powerful hold over the rural population of Iparralde.
Consequently, and increasingly throughout the nineteenth century, Basques found themselves caught
between the demands of their spiritual and economic
masters when the time came to define political allegiances. For the most part, the inhabitants of Iparralde,
remembering the violent excesses of the Revolution,

Charles Philipon was prosecuted for drawing King Louis-Philippe as a pear ("poire" French slang for "fool"). In court the artist demonstated the likeness in a series of sketches. He was acquitted. Criticism of the monarchy paved the way for the new French middle classes to assume power.

which they associated with extreme republicanism, tended to favor more conservative political options. (It should be noted, however, that voting restrictions were still abundant for much of this period—in 1829, for example, Iparralde recorded only 158 voters, a number rising to just 514 by 1841. Between 1848 and 1851, with the proclamation of the Second Republic, voting rights were extended throughout the country.)

INTERESTINGLY, despite the conservative political tendencies of Iparralde during this period, Michel Renaud was elected on a Radical Republican / Progressive Catholic ticket for Donibane-Garazi (Saint-Jean-Pied-de-Port) in 1848, and gradually this ideology—an egalitarian republicanism welded to social or progressive Christian ideals—began to take hold in certain areas of Iparralde, such as Donibane-Garazi, Iholdi (Iholdy), and Donapaleu (Saint-Palais) in Nafarroa Beherea and the entire province of Zuberoa—that is to say, in those regions clinging most forcefully to their past traditions and Basque culture. After 1851, however, with the establishment of the Second Empire, Renaud was dismissed from office and the movement suppressed. A new political chapter then began in Iparralde with the creation of the Etcheverry dynasty. The Etcheverry family, from Baigorri (Saint-Etienne-de-Baigorry) in Nafarroa Beherea, had become successful and prosperous members of the new middle class through banking and financial interests. The first Etcheverry was elected to public office on a Conservative ticket in 1848, and several others successively emerged to dominate the politics of Iparralde until the early years of the Third Republic in the 1890s.

CULTURE

From the early 1830s on, several laws were passed regulating state education as a means of extending the use of
the French language and, by definition, encouraging the
disparate peoples of the French state to think of themselves as French citizens. After 1830, knowledge of
French orthography was mandatory for anyone holding
public office (railroad, postal, and customs officials, tax
collectors, civil servants, elected officials, and even
tobacconists!), and a law of 1833 made knowledge of the
French language obligatory for schoolteachers. The education system quickly became, then, as Manex Goyhenetche dramatically puts it, "an ideological instrument of the French State."[65] Yet as late as the 1850s,
there remained a pressing need for teachers with sufficient knowledge of the language to ply their trade in
Iparralde. Indeed, in 1866, the number of individuals
regularly using Euskara as their primary language
would be at least 95 percent of the population (out of a
total population of just under 124,000).[66] We might
fairly conclude, then, that by 1870, French nationalism
as expressed through educational institutions had failed
to convince the Basque population of its Frenchness.
Indeed, it is quite likely that by the late 1860s, as much
as half of the population of the French state, some
7.5 million people (probably even more), had little to no
knowledge of French.

IF STATE SCHOOLING had failed to install French patriotism among the Basques of Iparralde, then that
other cornerstone of the inventing process, military
service, likewise enjoyed little success. Conscription was
introduced into the French state in 1798, and various
laws thereafter regulated the period of service: six years
in 1818, eight in 1824, and seven in 1855. It would
appear, according to Weber's observations, that Basques

From the early 1830s on, several laws were passed regulating state education as a means of extending the use of French. From this time French would be the language of success while other tongues were relegated to the stable. *From Thomas Hugo:* Bewick's Woodcuts, *London 1870.*

---

were renowned for their aversion to this particular form of state intrusion. As a border people, they had a natural escape route toward their kinsmen in Hegoalde, and this was an option utilized to its full extent throughout the nineteenth century. Those escaping the exigencies of the state also exercised an option to flee further afield, especially to the emigrant Basque communities of Latin America.

IF ONE FIGURE in the cultural life of Iparralde during the first half of the nineteenth century stands out, it is J. Augustin Chaho. Born in Atharratze (Tardets), Zuberoa, in 1811, Chaho pursued a career as a writer,

propagandist, radical politician, and proto–Basque
nationalist. In a series of works in the 1830s and 1840s,
Chaho, who ran for office on the same ticket as Renaud,
called for the unification of Euskal Herria through a confederation of the Basque provinces. As a correspondent
covering the first Carlist War (discussed in the following
chapter), he immediately sympathized with the traditionalist Carlist cause, despite his socialist sympathies.
His justification for this "unholy" alliance was that
Carlism defended the original independence of the
Basques. With Napoleon III's rise to power, however, he
was forced into exile for his part in the 1848 uprising in
Baiona (Bayonne) and settled in the Araban capital of
Gasteiz (Vitoria) in 1851. Three years later, he returned
to Baiona, where he died in 1858.

EVEN THOUGH the French state experienced a
number of difficulties in finding political stability
during this initial period, a specific ideological outlook
had emerged as to what should constitute France. From
the mid-eighteenth century on, a French political culture had been developing that prioritized the dilution of
different cultures, through cultural assimilation, into
one uniform vision. This could best be achieved, subsequent French political regimes believed, through state
institutions. As such, observes Pierre Birnbaum, "The
French nation-state, rejecting the legitimacy of specific
cultures, has long considered cultural pluralism as illegitimate in the name of positivist and universalist state
norms which would not themselves constitute a proper
cultural model."[67]

Through the mid-nineteenth century, however, and
even later, as Marie-Pierre Arrizabalaga demonstrates,[68]
little substantially changed in Iparralde to alter the pre-
Revolutionary society and culture of the Basques. To be
sure, the state, through its policies of national integra-

tion, had begun to make inroads into Basque society, but at mid-century these were relatively limited. Through the first half of the nineteenth century, for example, the economic base of Iparralde remained that of agriculture, and demographically we can even speak of population gains. The persistence of a more traditional lifestyle in Iparralde was aided in no small measure by the decidedly conservative turn in state-level political culture after 1815. This, allied to the unstable nature of central political authority, allowed the distinct political culture of Iparralde (a conservative bastion dominated by a Basque-speaking rural clergy) to remain relatively free from state interference.

From the 1850s on, this would begin to change, although only gradually at first. The railroad, the nineteenth century's most potent symbol of modernization and progress, arrived in Iparralde in 1855, when the Paris–Bordeaux line was extended to Baiona; the remaining thirty-five kilometers to Hendaia (Hendaye), sponsored by the all-powerful Etcheverry political dynasty, were completed in 1864. Beginning in the 1850s, a cautious but steady growth in industry—composed in the main by small-scale confectionary and footwear production—took place with a concomitant population shift: between 1851 and 1866, the rural-village population of Iparralde declined by 10 percent.

FOR THE FRENCH state, these developments would be tremendously significant. A declining rural Basque population was good news for Paris, signaling as it did the first step in challenging the influence of the Church, which enjoyed an allegiance from the majority rural population of Iparralde. Yet the full effects of this trend, already under way in the 1850s, would not be felt until well into the twentieth century. Through most of the nineteenth century, we might accurately conclude that the French state continued to evince a weak level of national-state integration from Iparralde. The Basques were not yet Frenchmen.

Lesson five

REQUIRED READING

Eugen Weber, *Peasants Into Frenchmen: The Modernization of Rural France, 1870–1914* (Palo Alto: Stanford University Press, 1976), pp. 41–49, 67–94.

SUGGESTED READING

Marie-Pierre Arrizabalaga, "The Stem Family in the French Basque Country: Sare in the Nineteenth Century," *Journal of Family History* 22, no. 1 (January 1997), pp. 50–69.

Ernest Gellner, "Nationalism and Modernization" and "Nationalism and High Cultures," in John Hutchinson and Anthony Smith, eds., *Nationalism* (Oxford: Oxford University Press, 1994), pp. 55–63, 63–70.

David Held, "The Development of the Modern State," in Stuart Hall, David Held, Don Hubert, and Kenneth Thompson, *Modernity: An Introduction to Modern Societies* (Oxford: Blackwell, 1996), pp. 56–87.

LEARNING OBJECTIVES

1. To measure the consolidation of the French state in the aftermath of the Revolutionary and Napoleonic eras.
2. To understand the extent to which a specifically Basque culture and identity survived this initial period of French state building.

WRITTEN LESSON FOR SUBMISSION

1. To what extent is David Held's argument about the emergence of the modern state valid in relation to France between 1815 and 1870? What are the *strengths* and *weaknesses* of Held's argument, with particular regard to this period?

2. What, in your opinion, was the biggest single change in the society and culture of Iparralde between 1815 and 1870, and what makes it so significant?

6 · Hegoalde, 1814–39
The Birth of the Modern State and Euskal Herria (II)

WHILE FRANCE is often cited as an exemplary case of successful or strong state building (even though this proved difficult through much of the nineteenth century), the process in Spain provides a contrary example, and events there were even more complicated than those in its northern neighbor. Between 1814, with the restoration of Ferdinand VII to the throne (and consequently the return of Bourbon absolutism), and 1868, with the fall of the monarchy, the modern Spanish state went through a series of transformations in its search for political hegemony over the disparate inhabitants within its borders, as was occurring in France during the same period. In contrast to the French experience, however, the state-building process in Spain encountered stiff and often violent resistance from many of these diverse peoples.

Of particular significance to this investigation of Basque culture and identity in relation to the French and Spanish variants is the emergence during this period of the threatened *foruak* as a key symbol of Basque particularism amid an increasing trend toward Spanish state uniformity. The primary question we should consider here is to what extent a specifically Basque identity was expressed through the defense of the *foruak*. As we have seen, the first concerted efforts to dismantle the foral system took place in the eighteenth century, with several Bourbon attempts at centralizing political authority in Madrid. However, in the nineteenth century, amid rapid economic transformation and social restructuring, it was middle-class Spanish liberals who took up this same cause and extended the idea to promote cultural uniformity as well. As a consequence, a political readjustment took place, whereby the majority of the people in Hegoalde embraced a broad political, social, and cultural defensive cause known as Carlism.

THE BOURBON RESTORATION AND HEGOALDE, 1814–33
Just as the French state wavered between different types of political regime throughout the nineteenth century, so did its Spanish counterpart. In 1814, Fernando VII assumed the Castilian throne and immediately set about trying to reimpose a strict form of absolutist rule. Although he recognized the foral system of Hegoalde, his ultimate political designs rested with the eighteenth-century Bourbon philosophy of political centralization. In 1818, he modified a key feature of Basque foral liberties by demanding compliance with Spanish military service among the inhabitants of Hegoalde. Although the Basque provinces renegotiated this decree to recompense the crown financially rather than through actual service, it was clear that despite the struggles of the previous two decades foral liberties remained under assault.

COMING so soon after the upheavals of the previous generation, such change was precipitous. The extreme measures of Fernando VII provoked a middle-class backlash that ultimately resulted in the fall of the royal government, and the Liberal Triennium of 1820–23 was subsequently established. The Liberal Triennium marked the temporary triumph of the constitutionalists of 1812 (see Chapter 4), and though it ultimately fell to military pressure, it served to establish the political context of the Spanish state-building process. From Madrid, there existed two possible routes to the creation of a modern state: monarchical, absolutist, and centrist, or liberal, constitutionalist, and centrist.

Nineteenth-century factory in Bilbo. Rivers supported both industrial and domestic needs thus demonstrating their importance in the modern economic development of Euskal Herria.
By permission of Editorial Iparaguirre, S.A. archives.

The reaction of Hegoalde to the brief interlude of liberal rule was muted. Having already suffered some degree of foral readjustment under Fernando VII, the Basque provinces had grudgingly become accustomed to the dominant centrist policies of Madrid. The case of Nafarroa merits special mention, however, for (like its extension to the north in relation to France) it enjoyed a special position within the Spanish political orbit. With its own legislative and judicial system, the province enjoyed not just a series of regional rights and privileges, but something approximating an independent or home-rule status. In response to the establishment of the Liberal Triennium, there emerged in Nafarroa several small groups actively opposed to the constitutionalist regime. Under clerical guidance, these groups came to dominate rural areas of the province and encouraged violent resistance to the mandate of Madrid.

WITH THE reestablishment of absolutist political authority in 1823, these groups disappeared, yet they left behind a legacy of peasant organization aimed at defying central political authority. In a short time, this defiance would resurface with more vigor, for the return of monarchical rule to the Spanish state did not guarantee that Basque regional privileges would remain untouched from Madrid; the opposite, in fact, proved to be the case. In the decade that followed, Fernando VII continued in his attempt to maximize central political power, leaving Hegoalde vulnerable to legal and administrative reform from the Spanish capital. In 1829, the *Cortes* (parliament) of Nafarroa met for the last time, as a royal decree that year ordered that laws emanating from Madrid be applied universally throughout the kingdom. The years 1830–33 witnessed a series of delaying tactics by the Basque provinces in an attempt to stave off the centralizing policies of the crown. The tense situation was temporarily resolved by the death of Fernando VII in 1833. Ultimately, however, this only worsened the general political climate: the realm was plunged into a succession crisis that quickly enveloped the whole country, plunging modern Spain into a bloody civil conflict that had important repercussions in the Basque provinces.

THE FIRST CARLIST WAR, 1833–39

The Carlist wars explain much about the problems associated with state building in modern Spain. They were not simply dynastic struggles; if they had been, it is likely that they would not have taken on such ferocious aspects. Just as the English or American civil wars were not merely about political or constitutional issues, so the Carlist conflicts embraced a whole series of grievances and oppositions that were more congruent with the general question of how people thought of themselves. In other words, the Carlist struggles are as revealing for what they tell us about primary identity in the nineteenth-century Spanish state as they are for explaining the dynastic problems of the Spanish crown.

How, THEN, should we define these civil conflicts? Following Xosé Estévez, we might initially consider them in these ways:

1. In a general sense, this was a struggle between supporters of Old Regime society, particularly of strict adhesion to the Church and religious principles, and those who favored the progress associated with liberal constitutionalism.

2. Most obviously, this was also a dynastic struggle, between the wife and daughter of Fernando VII, María Cristina and the infant princess María Isabel (the future Isabel II), and his younger brother, Don Carlos María Isidro.

3. A major, though more subtle, component of the struggle was a social and economic one: the clash between a wealthy, educated elite and a poorer, illiterate peasant mass.

4. Intimately connected to this was a notable conflict between urban and rural segments of the population.

5. Finally, and probably the most debatable point that we might consider, is the view that the Carlist wars

Late nineteenth-centiry factory scene, Bilbo. Manufacturing and commercial actvity dominated the river
system of Bilbo and other Basque towns. At this time a
skyline dominated by smoking chimneys was the sym-
bold par excellence of sophistocated modern industrial
development.
By permission of Editorial Iparaguirre, S.A. archives.

---

represented, in however modified a form, a struggle
between defenders of a specifically Basque identity
and those who favored primary allegiance to the idea
of a modern Spain.[69]

WHAT IS immediately evident is that the Carlist wars
were an expression of serious structural divisions—political, social, economic, and cultural—that
explain much about the precarious state of modern
Spain in the nineteenth century.

Both Carlist wars, although ostensibly Castilian dynastic struggles, were principally conducted in the Basque provinces. Between 1833 and 1835, the Carlist forces in support of Don Carlos, who attracted the majority of Basques, assembled and sporadically engaged in open conflict with their liberal foes.

WITHIN THE Carlist ranks, there emerged a brilliant and charismatic leader, Tomás Zumalacárregui from Ormaiztegi (Ormáiztegui) in Gipuzkoa, who organized the Carlist forces—mostly composed of peasant guerrilla bands, following the historical precedent of the Basque resistance to Napoleon's troops—into an effective military unit. After 1835, the expanded force, under the leadership of Zumalacárregui, went on the offensive, but divisions among the national leadership weakened the Carlist cause. Specifically, Zumalacárregui argued for a tactic of swift attacks, from the northern Carlist stronghold of Nafarroa and rural Gipuzkoa through Gasteiz (Vitoria) and south toward Madrid, while Don Carlos and his advisors argued for the capture of Bilbo (Bilbao), the foremost bastion of liberalism in Hegoalde, as more important symbolically to the cause. The latter tactic was ultimately favored, and in the prolonged siege of Bilbo in 1835, Zumalacárregui was killed. Thereafter, the Carlists, bereft of their charismatic leader, plagued by internal divisions and grave tactical errors, and confronted with a following increasingly tired of battle, slid toward defeat. In 1839, the Carlist leader Rafael Maroto signed the Treaty of Bergara, which ended the war.

While the signing of the treaty served to end the war, it also acted as a springboard to constitutional change, for its first article, penned by the victorious liberal general Baldomero Espartero, called for the issue of the *foruak* to be referred to Madrid for constitutional reconsideration. If the foral system had been under threat prior to

1833, it now seemed more than likely that it would not survive the postwar era in its prewar condition.

CARLISM AND BASQUE NATIONAL IDENTITY

Was the central issue of Carlism mainly a dynastic or a religious one? There seems little substance to the argument that peasant masses would rise up in defense of a remote figure they barely knew. The religious argument, then, would appear to have a more fundamental basis. As we know, Euskal Herria remained a repository of strict ecclesiastical loyalty; the religious adherence of Basques had proved the most difficult hurdle for those attempting change, from Enlightenment liberals to Napoleon's armies. However, the rural peasantry was aware of the benefits they had enjoyed in a tax-free region, where goods had generally been more affordable than in other parts of the kingdom, and Don Carlos theoretically promised to maintain this system. Therefore, there might be a case for saying that popular Basque support for the Carlist dynastic cause stemmed from very practical considerations. Yet it is also important to consider other factors: the frustrations (whether social, economic, or cultural) felt by predominantly rural communities amid the increasing power, wealth, and influence of the middle-class elite; and the notion of foral difference as a symbol of protonational identity.

STUART HALL argues that although national identities are not literally imprinted in our genes, we do consider them to be essential to our natures.[70] Thus, he states, "national identities are not things we are born with, but are formed and transformed within and in relation to *representation*."[71] Adapting this argument to the question of a specifically Basque identity emerging through the Carlist struggles, we might argue that the mass adherence of Basques to the Carlist cause

symbolized, if not an expression per se of Basque identity, then, at the very least, an expression of an identity
intimately linked to the *foruak*, with these privileges
understood (rightly or wrongly) as specific to the
Basque provinces. In this way, the foral discourse of the
Carlist cause served as a field or system of cultural representation, from which Basques in the nineteenth century increasingly drew a notion of identity (alongside, of
course, identities based on gender, occupation, and
farmstead, village, community, or province of origin,
etc.). Estévez argues that identification with the *foruak*
implied an adherence to existing social and economic
conditions, for good or bad—that is, that the Basque
peasantry, for all that the foral system offered them in
terms of stability and other benefits, was also tied to the
way things had always been, or at least to what was
thought to be traditional. In other words, any change,
for better or for worse, would have been difficult to
implement; the peasant defense of the Carlist cause was
vehement precisely because of this attachment to the
past. In many ways, the Carlist rebellion served to ignite
an almost existential flame within the Basque populace
as they sought to defend what they believed was their
very being.

WITHOUT DOUBT, the distinctive political and
administrative framework of Hegoalde suffered a
severe setback during the first half of the nineteenth
century as the first steps were taken from Madrid to
implement a modern state. Yet the resistance to this
centralizing initiative found a specific political or ideological expression in Carlism that, although suffering
defeat in its confrontation with the state, gave rise to a
means of expressing specifically Basque grievances. That
said, Carlism is a difficult and complex movement to
understand for its myriad of contradictions. Why, for

example, would rural Basque peasants rise up against middle-class liberalism to defend, effectively, the rights of their rural overlords?

IN CONTRAST to the situation in Iparralde, where ideological unity was never established amid the upheaval of the Revolution, the cementing of a Carlist ideology into the social and cultural fabric of the majority rural Basque populace would prove highly problematic for the state-building ambitions of Madrid. Yet the division among Basques in Hegoalde as to what should constitute their political future also became increasingly evident, and this division led to violent confrontation. With great difficulty, modern Spain was being born, and the problems it was experiencing would remain unresolved for some time to come.

Lesson six

Note: Chapters 6 and 7 should be considered jointly. The reading lists and learning objectives that appear below and the written assignment in Lesson 7 all refer to the material covered in both Chapters 6 and 7.

REQUIRED READING (FOR CHAPTERS 6 AND 7)
Stanley G. Payne, *Basque Nationalism* (Reno: University of Nevada Press, 1975), pp. 37–56.
John F. Coverdale, *The Basque Phase of Spain's First Carlist War* (Princeton: Princeton University Press, 1984), pp. 11–28, 257–83, 284–308.

SUGGESTED READING (FOR CHAPTERS 6 AND 7)
José Alvarez-Junco, "The Nation-Building Process in Nineteenth-Century Spain," in Clare Mar-Molinero and Angel Smith, eds., *Nationalism and the Nation*

in the *Iberian Peninsula* (Oxford and Washington, D.C.: Berg, 1996), pp. 89–106.

Stuart Hall, "The Question of Cultural Identity," in Stuart Hall, David Held, Don Hubert, and Kenneth Thompson, *Modernity: An Introduction to Modern Societies* (Oxford: Blackwell, 1996), pp. 596–618.

LEARNING OBJECTIVES (FOR CHAPTERS 6 AND 7)

1. To examine the nature of nineteenth-century Carlism.
2. To measure the extent to which the *foruak* emerged, in the nineteenth century, as a key symbol of Basque identity.
3. To critically examine the origins of modern Spanish state building.

7 · Hegoalde, 1840–76
The birth of the modern state

IN THE 1830s, the Spanish state began its problematic journey to modernity. From this time on, the political and constitutional history of the country would develop into a long struggle between the forces of tradition and those of modernity, between regional and central authority, and between plural and uniform visions of cultural identity. The first Carlist War of 1833–39 marked the beginning of a long period of political conflict and transformation that would severely rupture not only Hegoalde but the entire state. At its end, the majority of the Basques of Hegoalde found themselves on the losing side of a civil war.

THE INTERWAR PERIOD, 1840–68
The immediate consequence of the first Carlist War for Hegoalde was a restructuring of the foral system, the two most important aspects of which were perhaps the abolishment of the *pase foral*, the de facto Basque veto on royal decrees, and the definitive transference of the Spanish customs border to the French frontier, which ended Basque tax exemptions. Foral privileges would be maintained by the Basque provinces, but only insofar as they did not transgress the limits of Spanish constitutional unity. In effect, this led to a system whereby politically and administratively the Basque provinces were gradually incorporated into the Spanish state, while retaining a good deal of their economic privileges (at least in Araba, Bizkaia, and Gipuzkoa) and some local rights. For Nafarroa, the change involved more of a constitutional shift: in particular, a law of 1841 deprived the province of its special legislative and judicial rights, converting the medieval kingdom into an autonomous com-

ponent of the Spanish state. (Considering the fate of Nafarroa Beherea during the early years of the French Revolution, which not only lost its independent status but was also subsequently incorporated into the *département* of the Pyrénées-Atlantiques, the defenders of Nafarroan independence might have had good reason to breathe a sigh of relief.) In the three decades that followed, the political situation in Hegoalde stabilized as Basque society faced a new upheaval in the form of tremendous economic and social change (discussed in Chapters 8 through 10).

In Madrid, the period between 1840 and 1868 was characterized on the one hand by the consolidation of central political authority with the backing of military power, and on the other by a series of internal struggles among the new power brokers. The weak birth of the modern Spanish state made the search for some kind of consensus the overriding theme in Madrid; however, this would prove increasingly difficult.

IN 1840, THE regency of María Cristina, in effect since Fernando VII's death in 1833, came to an end when she was forced to abdicate amid pressure from the liberal oligarchy of Madrid. General Baldomero Espartero took control of the country, but stability was not forthcoming. Dominated by soldier politicians such as Espartero, Ramón María Narváez, and Leopoldo O'Donnell, and lacking general consensus, even among its liberal ranks (quite apart from the opposition of conservative, traditionalist, and regional Carlist factions), modern Spain embarked on a series of foreign military adventures to deflect attention from domestic problems and to solidify a Spanish national consciousness. As we have already noted (in Chapter 5), this tactic was also being employed by Napoleon III to the north. Indeed, the policy of foreign military endeavor, which at this

Basque author Bernardo Atxaga's works have acquired
international fame. His principal books are now routinely translated into English, as well as many other
languages.

time coincided with the first throes of nineteenth-century European imperialism, was (and perhaps still is) a classic ploy of both the Old Regime and the modern liberal state in their attempts to foster a sense of *national unity*.

Domestically, the period also witnessed the creation of the Guardia Civil (Civil Guard) in 1844—a paramilitary police force specifically designed to defend and extend the idea of the state throughout the country, particularly at the village level—and the 1856 law that centralized the administration of public education as a conscious attempt to promote and extend the use of Castilian throughout the country. Nominally, of course, modern Spain was still a monarchy, with Isabel II (born in 1830) as its queen. By mid-century, she was old enough to occupy her position in earnest, but she too added to the instability of the country as a whole by repeating many of the mistakes made by her mother, María Cristina, during her time as queen regent. In particular, Isabel II found it impossible to come to any kind of political understanding with the more progressive and modern wing of Spanish liberalism. This failure on the part of the monarchy to adapt to the changing nature of nineteenth-century political culture increasingly forced these progressive elements into plotting against them.

WHILE THE public face of Basque politics, dominated as it was by a liberal elite loyal to Madrid (reaping the economic benefits of the foral changes that allowed them state protection for their business interests), outwardly displayed a picture of calm and order, for the majority of the people in Hegoalde foral grievances remained a festering issue. As long as the Carlists found a suitable social and economic niche in Basque society, there remained little need for confrontation with the central authorities, and for much of the period this was, indeed, the case. However, economic changes taking place during and after the 1850s began to ignite new grievances. Furthermore, the aggressive foreign policy of the Spanish state in the 1850s and 1860s received little support from the Basques and led to an ever-growing hostility toward yet further state imposi- tions. As Robert P. Clark observes, "in 1859 and 1860, while Spain was engaged in a war in North Africa, the Basques moved so slowly in supplying troops and money to the war effort the war was over before their troops were introduced into combat."[72] When yet another political system—that of a constitutional demo- cratic monarchy—was introduced in the Spanish state in 1868, Carlism (and by extension the majority of the Basque population in Hegoalde) suddenly found a wealth of reasons to suspect the intentions of Madrid. The scene was set for a renewed round of confrontation.

LIBERAL REVOLUTION AND THE FIRST REPUBLIC, 1868–73

In September 1868, progressive and revolutionary lib- eral sectors in Madrid, in conjunction with important elements among the armed forces, overthrew the gov- ernment and forced Isabel II to leave the country. From 1868 to 1869, a provisional government ruled the country while it drew up a new monarchical constitu- tion.

ONCE THIS constitution had been implemented (in 1869), a new candidate for the Spanish throne was found, Amadeo of Savoy. Yet this constitutional monarchy was doomed to failure as soon as it was implemented: Amadeo arrived in his new kingdom in 1870 but ruled officially for only two years, from 1871 to 1873, when he was forced to abdicate as the most radical sectors within Spanish liberalism seized the opportunity to proclaim the First Spanish Republic. This proved to be too radical of a turn, however, and led to both a renewed Carlist uprising and, ultimately, a more conservative model for Spanish state modernization.

THE SECOND CARLIST WAR, 1873–76

Unlike its predecessor of the 1830s, the 1870s variant of Carlism did not seek to defend but to reestablish Old Regime political culture. By the 1870s, significant political, social, and economic changes had taken place so that Carlism had become a political ideology firmly rooted in nostalgia and mysticism. Even the diffusion of Carlist ideology was complicated by the changed nature of Basque society. For example, during the second war certain urban sectors (principally lower-middle-class elements whose wealth had been founded prior to the industrial development beginning in the mid-nineteenth century, together with the first wave of rural Basque migrants to the new industrial centers) fought alongside the traditional social base of Carlism, the rural peasantry. Much like those who had fought during the first war, these groups generally shared a sense of alienation amid an ever-changing society. Their adversaries, the liberals, drew their support from the new aggressive industrial bourgeoisie, financiers, and the more affluent sectors of the urban middle classes, together with the emerging liberal intelligentsia. The common thread among the latter sectors was their orientation toward Madrid as a focus of their combined aspirations.

LATE-NINETEENTH-CENTURY Carlism was based more on conservative and religious principles than it was on dynastic favoritism. Through the 1860s, an ideology was gradually refined, and a Carlist political party, organized in part by the new pretender Don Carlos

María de los Dolores, competed in Spanish elections. However, especially after 1868, Carlism increasingly viewed its future outside the electoral process. In particular, a spectacular electoral defeat in 1872 paved the way for Carlists to adopt a more direct form of political action. In the spring of 1872, Don Carlos led an unsuccessful military uprising, yet events in Madrid—especially the drift toward republicanism—reinvigorated the cause just as it seemed all was lost. Through 1873, the Carlists enjoyed several spectacular successes in the Basque provinces, but, as in the 1830s, they could not extend their power beyond the rugged Basque countryside, a terrain ideally suited to their favored guerrilla tactics.

As RAYMOND Carr notes, it could be argued that a separate Carlist state—with its own administration, postal system, electronic telegraph, newspapers, and even arms center in Eibar, Gipuzkoa—existed de facto in the rural Basque heartland, if only briefly in 1874.[73] Yet what was perhaps the very strength of Carlism, its strong connection to local community, was also its undoing: Carlist forces had neither the skill, the resources, nor the desire to fight beyond their own environment. Thus Bilbo (Bilbao), still the prize for Carlism in the 1870s as it had been in the 1830s, would remain forever out of reach. In late 1874, the liberal and military alliance of Madrid once more proved overwhelming, and the Carlist fighters were forced into retreat. By the end of the year, the Bourbon monarchy was restored in the Spanish capital, marking the death knell of Carlism. A few small insurgent Carlist units continued to fight, though increasingly aware that it was a losing battle.

By 1875, the reinvigorated Spanish state, personified by the new monarch, Alfonso XII (son of Isabel II, who had been restored to the throne the previous year), had

GLOBEOL
Da fuerza.

Larraza   Carmelo   Germán   Vidal   Aguirrezabala   Legarreta   Sesúmaga   Travieso
Sabino   Acedo   Oufiabeitia

ATLETICH CLUB DE BILBAO - Campeón de España 1922-23

Athletic de Bilbao, winners of the King's Cup in 1923 and champions of Spain. Sporting success was important for those that argued in favor of a specifically Basque identity.
By permission of Editorial Iparaguirre, S.A. archives.

concentrated its efforts on suppressing the Basque / Carlist insurrection in the north. In total, 155,000 Spanish troops confronted the remaining 35,000 Basque volunteers. By the end of that year, the Carlist retreat was all but complete, and in February 1876 the Carlist forces formally surrendered. Thereafter, the pretender Don Carlos fled the Spanish state, and it seemed, to the liberal powerbrokers in Madrid at least, as if the Old Regime had been finally defeated.

This time, there was little debate and no negotiation. From now on, modern Spain would be constructed on a

uniform centralist model. As punishment for their
adherence to the Carlist cause, the Basques of Hegoalde
were deprived definitively of the *foruak* by a law of
July 21, 1876. For the Basque liberal hegemony, however, a vestige of foral privilege would live on in the economic sphere, an important source of their power and
influence: An agreement known as the *conciertos
económicos* (economic pacts), whereby the Basque
provinces retained the right to negotiate their economic
obligations to Madrid every seven years, was all that
now remained of the regional rights. As Clark points
out, it seemed that the scene had been set for the stabilization and consolidation of the modern Spanish
state.[74] By agreeing to the *conciertos económicos*,
Madrid theoretically diffused any possible lingering
regionalist sentiment, while at the same time creating a
solid basis for industrial development and the consolidation of political and administrative power within a
centralized government.

JUST AS the Basques of Iparralde formally became
French citizens (for Paris, at least, if not in their own
minds) in 1792, so the Basques of Hegoalde were transformed into Spanish citizens (likewise, at least on
Madrid's terms) after 1876. The official birth of the
modern Spanish state came at the cost of much violence,
many lives, and little negotiation (again, as in its French
counterpart). After 1876, the political reality of Spain
was that of a country controlled by a liberal elite organized into the symbolically democratic division of two
political parties, who essentially shared the same vision
of what the modern state should be; a military and paramilitary police force whose presence had been constantly invoked to solidify and defend the state against
popular uprising throughout the nineteenth century;
and a monarch, Alfonso XII, who ostensibly represented

the reincarnation of Bourbon hegemony in the Castilian kingdom, but who in reality was no more than a figurehead for the grand design of the liberal elite. In reality, this modern constitutional monarchy served as a front for preserving and extending the interests of Spain's political and economic oligarchy—the agrarian aristocracy and industrial bourgeoisie.

AFTER 1876, A significant change also took place in Spanish political culture. With the introduction of the Restoration Monarchy, there emerged a clear ideology associated with the need to *create* the modern Spanish state: Spanish nationalism. As Adrian Shubert notes, the two watchwords of this ideology were *centralization* and *homogeneity*.[75] The problematic diffusion of this ideology, unacceptable to many Spanish citizens at the turn of the century and beyond, would lead to the central political and cultural problem of contemporary Spain—the difficult definition of what it actually means to be Spanish. As we will see, the Carlist conflicts of the nineteenth century bequeathed a significant legacy for the modern Spanish state: the so-called *national problem* that would consume Spanish state political culture well into the late twentieth century.

By the early 1870s, then, the Basque Country found itself formally divided between two modern European states. In both cases, the birth of the modern state came at a tremendous cost to Euskal Herria; both the French Revolution and the Carlist wars caused significant human and material damage. When considering the birth of the modern state in Europe, therefore, we should be wary of assuming that its democratic modern face implies a pacific beginning. This was most clearly not the case, and in fact it was quite the reverse. The French and Spanish states emerged through the calculated use of political violence when necessary. As such,

The Big Beñat is a popular burger, especially in Iparralde. It was used as the symbol of the 2000 Korrika, or
non-stop relay race in favor of Euskara, to epitomize a
specifically Basque response to globalization or
McDonaldization.
Photo: Koldo Mitxelena Kulturunea archives.

the modern culture of the nation-state, or statist nationalism, implied a severe and violent political change. At
the same time, from about the mid-to-late nineteenth
century, two other significant, and in many ways violent,
forms of changes would come to affect Euskal Herria,
with the economic and social transformations of the late
nineteenth and early twentieth centuries.

Lesson seven

WRITTEN LESSON FOR SUBMISSION (FOR CHAPTERS 6
AND 7)
Document Question 2
Carefully examine the following two documents. Both
texts offer glimpses of early nineteenth-century Basque
culture and identity from an outsider's perspective. The
first is a poem by the English Romantic William
Wordsworth. The second is a fragment of a work by the
English writer George Borrow, composed after a journey
through the Spanish kingdom in the 1830s. What does
each text tell us about the nature of Basque society? To
what extent do you think they accurately portray this
society? Taking into account some of the theoretical
issues that you have come across, and using specific
information from the texts below, how would you define
Basque identity during the first half of the nineteenth
century?

Document 1
William Wordsworth, extract from "The Oak of Guer-
nica" (1810):
Oak of Guernica! Tree of holier power
Than that which in Dodona did enshrine
(So faith too fondly deemed) a voice divine

Heard from the depths of its aërial bower—
How canst thou flourish at this blighting hour?
What hope, what joy can sunshine bring to thee,
Or the soft breezes from the Atlantic sea,
The dews of morn, or April's tender shower?
Stroke merciful and welcome would that be
Which should extend thy branches on the ground,
If never more within their shady round
Those lofty-minded Lawgivers shall meet,
Peasant and lord, in their appointed seat,
Guardians of Biscay's ancient liberty.[76]

George Borrow, extract from *The Bible in Spain* (1843):
In person the Basques are of middle size, and are active
and athletic. They are in general of fair complexions
and handsome features, and in appearance bear no
slight resemblance to the Tartar tribes of the Caucasus.
Their bravery is unquestionable, and they are consid-
ered as the best soldiery belonging to the Spanish crown.
... They are faithful and honest, and capable of much
disinterested attachment; kind and hospitable to
strangers. ... But they are somewhat dull, and their
capacities are by no means of the highest order. ... No
people on earth are prouder than the Basques, but theirs
is a kind of republican pride. They have no nobility
amongst them, and no one will acknowledge a superior.
The poorest carman is as proud as the governor of
Tolosa. "He is more powerful than I," he will say, "but I
am of as good blood; perhaps hereafter I may become a
governor myself." They abhor servitude, at least out of
their own country; and though circumstances frequently
oblige them to seek masters, it is very rare to find them
filling the places of common domestics; they are stew-
ards, secretaries, accountants, etc.[77]

8 · Industry
Social Change in Euskal Herria (I)

IF THE KEY political development affecting Basque culture and society in the nineteenth century was the
birth of the modern nation-state, the principal economic
change was the industrial transformation of Bizkaia,
Gipuzkoa, and, in more modest form, Lapurdi beginning in the middle of the century. The interior Basque
provinces of Araba, Nafarroa, Nafarroa Beherea, and
Zuberoa changed little in their principal economic
endeavor, agriculture, during this time. It might thus be
argued that the modernization of the three maritime
provinces did more to imbalance what we might consider the social or cultural unity of Euskal Herria than
any political changes.

Although, as we have seen (in Chapter 1), there had
been significant *pre-industrial* industrial development
in Euskal Herria, the spectacular transformation witnessed during the late nineteenth century (especially in
Bizkaia) was almost without precedent, even within
Europe as a whole. Without Bizkaia's rich seam of iron
ore, the *second* or *mature* industrial revolution of the
late nineteenth century (or the maturing of the first
Industrial Revolution, as some commentators describe
it), could not have taken place in the way it did. Indeed,
we might venture as far as to say that the rising economic giants of western Europe, Great Britain and
Prussia (later Germany), depended to a great extent on
this small Basque province. Yet interestingly—though
perhaps not surprisingly—the industrial development
of Bizkaia remains hidden from much of the general his-
toriography surrounding this second wave of industrialization. Measured as a province of the Spanish state,
Bizkaia is historically forgotten amid the "miserable

Desierto - Detalle „Altos Hornos"

Late nineteenth-century iron forging in the Altos Hornos factory, Bilbao. Nineteenth-century factory work was arduous and precarious with few safety measures. Note the sparse nature of the workers' clothing and especially their flimsy shoes.

By permission of Editorial Iparaguirre, S.A. archives.

---

performance," as Joseph Harrison terms it,[78] of the Spanish economy as a whole during the nineteenth century.

BIZKAIA

The key to Bizkaia's industrial boom of the late nineteenth century (with its concomitant massive social upheaval) was the invention in 1856 of the Bessemer process, which allowed for the relatively cheap and significantly more efficient production of steel using high-grade nonphosphoric iron ore. What previously had taken almost a day to achieve (the creation of steel from iron) now took a matter of minutes. Almost overnight, the low-phosphorous "red ore" of Bizkaia became a viable, indeed highly attractive, commodity for emerging industrial countries like Prussia (later Germany) and, especially, Great Britain. Although similarly large deposits of this ore could be found in the north of Sweden, it was Bizkaia that ultimately became a principal source of British industrial development. According to Eduardo Jorge Glas, the iron deposits around Bilbo enjoyed three principal advantages over those of rival areas: They were especially rich in metallic content; they were ideally located next to a coastal outlet; and the ore could be extracted cheaply from open-shaft mines.[79]

ASIDE FROM the necessary primary resource and the technology to exploit it, what were the other key factors in Bizkaia's spectacular economic rise? Initially, it was foreign (principally British) capital that stimulated industrial development in the province. In exchange for Basque iron, Great Britain supplied Bizkaia with Welsh coal, which served to underpin industrial production in the Basque Country. However, the first beneficiaries of the boom—in the main, several mine-owning Bizkaian families—were also shrewd enough to reinvest their profits in the local economy, stimulating, for example, successful banking and financial concerns. The definitive passing of the customs frontier to the Basque coast in 1876 was likewise of crucial importance, for Bizkaian economic interests now came under Spanish state tariff protection, allowing British capital investment into the region but keeping out competitive products. Finally, Bizkaia enjoyed a ready source of cheap labor,

principally people from the poorest regions of the
Spanish state (this phenomenon will be examined in
more detail in Chapter 10).

THE GENERAL effect of the booming iron and steel
industry was to encourage smaller industrial concerns making use of Bizkaia's principal product: the
ingot. Consequently, a plethora of factories producing
steel tubes and pipes, corrugated iron, building materials, and boilers emerged in Bizkaia during the late
nineteenth century. These smaller concerns were continuously at the mercy of the larger iron and steel interests, however, and this was increasingly true with the
progressive monopolization of these interests. In 1885,
for example, the three largest iron and steel works—
La Vizcaya, San Francisco, and Altos Hornos de Bilbao—
created the first Iron and Steel Syndicate to avoid potential competition from other regions of the state, and
thereafter managed to coordinate and control production so as to avoid lowering the basic price of their primary products: iron ore and the steel ingot. Although
the syndicate was broken by the exit of La Vizcaya in
1888, a new agreement was established in 1897 that
would ultimately serve as the basis for the more formal
union of the big interests. In 1901, La Vizcaya merged
with the other great iron and steel concern, Altos
Hornos de Bilbao, as well as with a smaller concern,
La Iberia, to form Altos Hornos de Vizcaya, the monopo-
listic heavy industrial concern that came to define
Bizkaian industrial might (and later decline) through
the twentieth century.

Bizkaia's moderate growth between the 1840s and
1870s was replaced, then, by a spectacular economic
boom for some and radical and violent economic and
social transformation (in Bilbo in particular) for many,
with the effects of this change traveling also to

Gipuzkoa. This was heavy industrial development on the classic nineteenth-century British scale, and with the transformation emerged a model Victorian industrial capitalist society. To use Eric Hobsbawm's succinct appraisal, "the (British) industrial revolution had swallowed the (French) political revolution,"[80] so that, by the later nineteenth century, it was industrial capitalism that more than any political ideology defined the social order as well its general beliefs and values. In particular, industrial capitalism legitimized reason, science, progress, and liberalism at the expense of more traditional social values.

GIPUZKOA

As with Bizkaia, water played a key role in the industrialization of Gipuzkoa. However, where Bizkaia's industrial development centered on the economically strategic port location of Bilbo, that of Gipuzkoa emerged in and around the abundant river valleys that dissected its interior. From rivers like the Oria, Deba, and Uriola, small industrial concerns progressively harnessed a source of energy that would sustain Gipuzkoan modernization from the late nineteenth century on. In many respects, Gipuzkoan industrial development during this period served a subsidiary role to that of Bizkaia.

COMPARATIVELY speaking, it was both "light" and small-scale, with the emergence of such concerns as paper mills, cement works, and metallurgical plants of differing specializations. (This would work in Gipuzkoa's favor in the late twentieth century, as it is likely that it saved the province from some of the harsher consequences of industrial decline experienced by Bizkaia.) By the early twentieth century, the principal industrial products of Gipuzkoa were arms from the Deba valley, bicycles and sewing machines from Eibar, metallurgical

output from Legazpi (Legazpia), and paper from
Errenteria (Rentería).

While local industry in Gipuzkoa never experienced
the same dramatic boom as that of Bizkaia, it did
steadily consolidate through the late nineteenth and
early twentieth centuries. Like industry elsewhere, it
benefited from the introduction of electric power, population increases, and the investment of industrial capital. In general, however, the Gipuzkoan market
remained local and its industry maintained a close connection to its preindustrial roots: For example, many
factories in Gipuzkoa continued to use charcoal and
hydraulic power instead of coal and electricity. And
many of the industrial workers in Gipuzkoa were *baserritarrak* who continued to run their small farmsteads
while coping with the more regimented timetable of the
factory.

LAPURDI

After 1815, the formerly renowned shipbuilding
industry of Baiona (Bayonne) suffered a major decline,
with the state officially withdrawing its interests in 1835.
Thereafter, only a modest collection of private holdings
remained. With Baiona's port activity restricted, the city
was progressively disconnected from the major French
communications routes. It was not until 1855 that the
Paris–Bordeaux railroad line was extended to Baiona,
and development toward the interior came even later,
with the opening of a Baiona–Donibane-Garazi line in
1898, extended to Baigorri in 1899. Changes in communications thus proceeded slowly and unevenly.

HEAVY INDUSTRY as such, certainly on the Bizkaian
scale, was never forthcoming in Lapurdi, but the
province did follow a pattern of more modest industrial
endeavor (together with tourism, a new and increasingly

Collection Gorce, édit., Paris

69. BAYONNE — La Gare Maritime

Freighter unloading, Baiona
In the 1920s Iparralde enjoyed a thriving merchant
marine based on the exports of canned fish.
*Photo by permission of Koldo Mitxelena Kulturunea
archives.*

lucrative business explored in Chapter 10) that might be
compared to nineteenth-century economic development
in Gipuzkoa. In Baiona, a modest iron-forging industry
emerged, which between 1914 and 1928 employed 1,800
workers. This in turn encouraged additional development, such as the production of cement and railroad
sleepers, from the early 1880s on. These developments

led to a regeneration of the city's port through imports of iron from Bizkaia and exports of mining posts to Great Britain. Mention should be made also of the renewed trade in contraband goods out of the port of Baiona, principally in the direction of Hegoalde, which also did much to encourage maritime development in Lapurdi.

THE EARLY twentieth century also saw the emergence of a fish-canning industry in coastal Lapurdi. In 1914, a factory was established in Ziburu (Ciboure), which was soon producing 200,000 boxes of canned fish annually. Its success provoked the creation of a rival factory in Donibane-Lohizune (St. Jean-de-Luz) and several smaller outlets through the 1920s. By the end of that decade, at least one thousand people were employed in the industry, which brought with it regeneration of the fishing industry, in a modernized and expanded form, through the first three decades of the century. The interior of Lapurdi tended to retain an economic reliance on agriculture, as in Nafarroa Beherea and Zuberoa. A small-scale footwear industry (following a preindustrial artisan tradition) did develop in the late nineteenth century in the town of Hazparne, but the lack of a railroad connection hampered further industrial development in the rural hinterland, making the Hazparne case an example of the general difficulties experienced by the interior zones of Iparralde in effectively embracing the modernizing process.

ARABA AND NAFARROA

After 1876, with the implementation of a new Spanish political system and the aforementioned transformation of relations between Madrid and the Basque provinces, the interior provinces of Hegoalde experienced a progressive economic stagnation, highlighted by their maritime neighbors' spectacular growth. The majority population of the two provinces, from peasants and small farmers to rural notables and wealthy landowners, overwhelmingly rejected modernization in all its forms, and the economies of Araba and Nafarroa remained tied to the land; indeed, industrial change in the two provinces would not take place until the 1950s and 1960s.

THROUGH THE course of the nineteenth century, the Nafarroan population actually declined, in marked contrast to the increases being experienced in Bizkaia and Gipuzkoa (discussed more thoroughly in the following chapter). Industrialization in the ancient kingdom was especially difficult, given its more limited natural industrial resources and the detrimental effects of the Law of 1841, which extended the customs border of the Spanish state to Nafarroa's northern frontier with Iparralde. Throughout its history, Nafarroa had developed an economy integrally connected with that of Nafarroa Beherea and Iparralde in general, but the state-imposed frontier broke this natural economic union between north and south. Furthermore, unlike Araba, Bizkaia, and Gipuzkoa, Nafarroa had no *concierto económico* (the pacts that guaranteed a degree of economic autonomy for three of the four provinces in Hegoalde) to rely on. Finally, the dominant Nafarroan political class—the archetypal *caciques* (local political bosses) of the Spanish state's rural hinterland—drew their economic power from the land, and it remained in their interests to maintain the economic status quo. The lack of economic growth for the majority of the province's inhabitants brought conflict, as in the fertile southern zone of Erribera (Ribera), or emigration, as experienced in the high country of northern Nafarroa.

NAFARROA BEHEREA AND ZUBEROA

Throughout the nineteenth and well into the twentieth century, the interior provinces of Iparralde maintained a more traditional, agricultural economy based on small-scale family farmsteads. That said, some changes did take place in both provinces. Nafarroa Beherea experienced, together with Lapurdi, the moderate growth of a chocolate-producing industry throughout the nineteenth century. There was even a modest increment in the production of iron nails in several small mountain communities such as Banka (Baigorri) and Mendibe (Uharte-Garazi) in Nafarroa Beherea and Larrañe (Larrau) and Ligi-Atherei (Licq-Athérey) in Zuberoa. The principal nonagricultural economic activity of Zuberoa was the production of footwear, centered in the provincial capital, Maule-Lextarre (Mauléon-Licharre), with a smaller outlet in Atharratze-Sorholüze (Tardets-Sorholus). Between 1890 and 1914, the Zuberoan capital enjoyed an efficient growth that converted it into a provincial manufacturing center of some renown, but scarcely on anything approaching a truly industrial scale.

IF A DUAL society of sorts had been historically evolving in Euskal Herria, with progressive coastal sectors and traditional interior zones, then the industrial transformation of the late nineteenth century served to exacerbate this social division. Industrialization, at least in Bizkaia and Gipuzkoa, played a key role not only in radically reshaping Basque society, but also in forging a new kind of political and cultural reality that, perhaps more even than the Carlist struggles, indelibly altered the day-to-day life of Euskal Herria. Yet away from the industrial zones (sometimes only a matter of several kilometers distant), much of the traditional Basque lifestyle persisted: Most people were engaged in agricultural endeavors and would live and die in the parish of their birth. The contrast could not have been greater.

Lesson eight

REQUIRED READING

Eduardo Jorge Glas, *Bilbao's Modern Business Elite* (Reno and Las Vegas: University of Nevada Press, 1997), pp. 74–107.

Joseph Harrison, "Heavy Industry, the State, and Economic Development in the Basque Region, 1876–1936," *The Economic History Review*, second series, 36, no. 4 (November 1993), pp. 535–51.

LEARNING OBJECTIVES

1. To understand where, how, and why industrialization took place in Euskal Herria during the nineteenth century.
2. To analyze the immediate consequences of this transformation.

WRITTEN LESSON FOR SUBMISSION

1. To use Eric Hobsbawm's dichotomy, what similarities might there have been between the (French) political revolution and the (British) industrial revolution, and in what ways did they differ? In what ways did they both contribute to the modernizing process?
2. In your opinion, what effects might this industrial transformation have had on a specifically Basque identity? To what extent might these changes have aided French or Spanish state building?

9 · Tourism
Social Change in Euskal Herria (II)

TOGETHER WITH the spectacular rise of heavy industry, the second major element of economic transformation in Euskal Herria during the late nineteenth century was tourism. Just as Bilbo (Bilbao) transformed itself into one of the principal loci of Europe's industrial revolution, so Miarritze (Biarritz) and, later, Donostia (San Sebastián) emerged as major European centers of the new leisure industry. In the nineteenth century, a complex network of hotels, lodges, inns, guides, guidebooks, maps, and interpreters was established to serve the newly wealthy middle classes in their pursuit of leisure, the former preserve of monarchs and aristocrats. Tourism was a direct product of industrial capitalism: Not only did it draw its clientele from the industrial bourgeoisie, but the tourism industry in general would never have developed without major technological changes, such as the development of efficient railroad systems. The earliest tourist destinations were stylish spa towns such as Vichy, Spa, Baden-Baden, and Karlsbad, and the development of such centers encouraged, in Eric Hobsbawm's words, "fashionable gatherings justified by the excuse of drinking some disagreeable mineral waters or immersing oneself in some form of liquid under the control of a benevolent medical dictator."[81] Increasingly, these visits took the form of a long term of residence, be it summer or winter.

Nineteenth-century tourism operated as both an economic and a social or cultural practice. From an economic perspective, the newly empowered bourgeoisie found it necessary to display their wealth as a means of securing social prestige and status. Late-nineteenth-century middle-class European society was one of conspic-

uous consumption, and just as material possessions
defined this status, so, increasingly, did the display of
the nonaristocratic rich and professional middle classes
enjoying "free time" away from the pressures of the
workplace. Time thus became an important bourgeois
status symbol. Chris Rojek and John Urry observe of the
tourism phenomenon that, "tourism as practice and discourse involved the clear specification of time (the week
and the fortnight) and space (the specialized resorts and
spas). It particularly involved the centrality of clock-time
to its organization."[82]

TOURISM ALSO revealed an underlying cultural symbolism. The metaphor of mobility associated with
nineteenth-century tourism was equally applicable both
to the newly empowered and confident middle classes
and to their political culture as expressed by the nation-
state. The bourgeoisie, like the state, was rich and powerful, and keen to set out and dominate its surroundings. Through the nineteenth century, the railroad was
building the nation-state, and the pioneer explorers of
this new form of transport were the middle classes, who
exported their urbane culture (such as the latest fash-
ions of Paris or Madrid) to their provincial countrymen.
In the case of the tourist industry in the Basque
Country, an extra ingredient could be added to the bourgeois tourist experience: the fact that coastal resorts
such as Miarritze and Donostia offered a glimpse (however rudimentary) of another world, a strange, mysterious culture reflected by an incomprehensible language. Without having to venture out of Europe, in
other words, tourists in Euskal Herria were afforded the
experience of *orientalism*, described by Edward Said as
the creation by urbane nineteenth-century Europeans of
an "exotic other" (peasants speaking archaic languages,

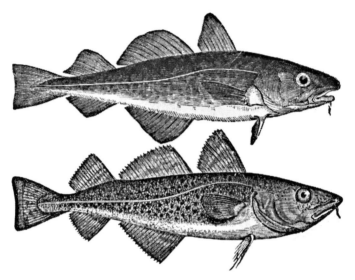

After the decline of whaling Basque seafarers sought new catches. The pursuit of cod, in particular, led them (together with others) to open up new sea born routes across the Atlantic.

Illustration from Jim Harter (ed): Animals.

_____

for example) by which they could measure their own progress and success.[83]

B Y THE LATE nineteenth century, then, for middle-class European culture, rural Basques were becoming a relic of Europe's primitive past. A similar process was taking place in the Scottish Highlands, a remote corner of Great Britain, where the burgeoning tourist interest was the product of two key develop-

ments: the Romantic movement and royal patronage.
The effects of tourism to the region were multiple,
including the Anglicization of many Highland Scots
(with a concomitant loss of their language, Gaelic) and
improved communications routes that ultimately
extended the idea of the British state to this region.

Linda Colley observes, in reference to nineteenth-
century tourism in the Highlands: "Far less industri-
alised and urbanised than South Wales, Lowland Scotland or England, their people were less likely to be
infected with radical ideas, and far more willing, perhaps, to know their place and keep to it. Visiting these
regions, patrician tourists enjoyed the comforting illusion that they had travelled back in time, to when their
world was still safe."[84]

THE EFFECTS of tourism in the Basque Country were
similar in many ways. For the civilized classes, the
Basque people remained exotic outsiders to the notions
of progress and modernization. For example, a 1926
guidebook for Anglo-American visitors to Iparralde
observed that "the heart of the Basque province should
only be approached with reverence ... [for] as we go further inland, we are coming to a part of the world of great
antiquity and full of secrets, in which there has been
living for centuries a mysterious race which has never
allowed itself to be permeated or corrupted by any other,
which speaks a tongue of its own, a mother-tongue, of
which only very distant connections are to be found
throughout the entire world."[85]

The development of the modern tourist industry was,
therefore, aside from its economic effects, just as significant as that of heavy industry in provoking significant
social and cultural change in Euskal Herria. Like its
more infamous counterpart, tourism encouraged the
dislocation of traditional, mostly coastal, communities

and the disruption of traditional lifestyles. In a short
space of time, from mid-century on, a whole new form of
employment opened up for the rural poor—jobs with
fixed wages and hours, without the harsh conditions of
farmwork, that also carried an aura of glamour and
sophistication (though this was rarely more than an illusion). For example, 46.8 percent of Miarritze's inhabitants were employed in rural endeavors in 1856, a
number that had fallen to 16.4 percent by 1891; over the
same period, the number of those employed in the hotel
trade rose from just under 15 to 75 percent.

IPARRALDE

In 1854, Empress Eugénie, wife of Napoleon III, began
visiting Miarritze as a summer escape from the rigors of
court life in Paris. This prompted a trend among subsequent French heads of state, and as a result, up to the
outbreak of World War I in 1914, the town gradually
acquired a reputation as a fashionable destination for
the rich and powerful. With the extension of the Paris–
Bordeaux railroad line to Baiona (Bayonne) in 1855, the
journey from the state capital to Miarritze was cut down
to fifteen hours (and this was cut further when the line
was extended to include the coastal towns of Lapurdi in
the mid-1860s).

B Y THE END of the 1850s, Miarritze, with a population
scarcely reaching 2,500, was welcoming close to
10,000 visitors each year, accommodating its guests with
a casino, spa facilities, and a series of hotels constructed
along the oceanfront. Political upheaval—the Franco-
Prussian War of 1870–71 and the subsequent proclamation of the Third Republic—did nothing to affect the
town's dramatic economic growth; indeed, the town
enjoyed its golden age in the period 1872–1914. By 1879,
the number of annual visitors had climbed to 17,000,

and this topped out in 1913, on the brink of war, at 40,000.

The growth of Miarritze as a resort town in turn promoted growth among its neighbors, Angelu (Anglet), Donibane-Lohizune (St. Jean-de-Luz), Ziburu (Ciboure), and Hendaia (Hendaye)—so much so, in fact, that by the late nineteenth century the coastal stretch between Miarritze and Hendaia had become Europe's premier coastal resort area. Visits by Europe's high society, the affluent middle classes, and the continent's royal families transformed coastal Lapurdi from a region of traditional small rural and fishing communities into the playground of Europe's rich and powerful. By the turn of the century, an established pattern of tourist migration had been established, with the French and Spanish middle classes dominating during the summer months and the English arriving in the winter. Angelu, a small town between Baiona and the more fashionable Miarritze, remained a less-developed resort than either of its two neighbors. Donibane-Lohizune, until that time a traditional fishing village, opened its first hotel specifically directed toward the summer tourist trade in the early 1880s.

THE ADJACENT town of Ziburu also served as a location for medicinal bathing centers. Although Hendaia boasted a lengthy beachfront, its development was, in many ways, more restrained: The Hendaia railroad station, geared principally toward traffic destined for and coming from the Spanish state, remained several kilometers from the beachfront and a tramway connecting the two was only built in 1900. Of the less populous coastal towns, Getaria (Guéthary) developed a small resort industry, whereas Bidarte (Bidart) and Urruña (Urrugne) remained predominantly fishing and rural centers.

HEGOALDE

While Bilbo led the way in the Spanish state's development of heavy industry, Donostia became the predomi-
nant leisure resort for Spanish high society. Throughout
its history, Donostia had served principally as a fishing
and garrison town and as an administrative center for
Gipuzkoa. The coming of the railroad, however, marked
a key change. In 1864, the Madrid–Irun line was completed, linking the Gipuzkoan capital to both Madrid
and Paris. As was the case with Miarritze, royal
patronage proved also to be a critical factor in the transformation of Donostia into a tourist destination, encouraging the dominant classes—aristocrats, politicians, and
the ascendant bourgeoisie—to ape their betters by traveling to the coastal town. Isabel II visited Donostia for
the first time in 1845. Three years later, the queen
regent, María Cristina, decided that the refreshingly
cool Basque coastal air would be better suited to her del-
icate son, the future monarch Alfonso XIII, during the
oppressively hot summers in Madrid,[86] and from that
date on, Donostia became the summer residence of the
Spanish monarchy and its entourage.

IN AN ECONOMIC boom equal to that of Bilbo in terms
of the changes it effected, Donostia transformed itself
from a city of fishermen and small business interests
into a major leisure center, at the same time remaining
the administrative and commercial capital of Gipuzkoa.
Suddenly, all along its waterfront a host of hotels
appeared, followed by the construction of a casino over-
looking the bay and a specifically tourist-oriented
esplanade hugging the coastline. By way of entertain-
ment facilities, visitors could partake of theaters or the
naturally sheltered beaches and bathing houses. By the
early twentieth century, the city had begun to attract an

42 SAN SEBASTIAN. — Caseta de baños. — Ll.

Bullocks moving bathing houses on a beach, Donostia.
Nineteenth-century tourism was the preserve of the
wealthy. Hardship was avoided at all costs and modesty
was paramount
By permission of Editorial Iparaguirre, S.A. archives.

international clientele, and this added an air of glamour
to Donostia's already established tourist industry.

AT THE MOST intense moment of European bourgeois
opulence and confidence (the two decades before
the outbreak of World War I in 1914), Donostia stood
alongside Miarritze as one of Europe's premier resorts.
Yet at the same time, it remained a repository of traditional Basque society. Literally a stone's throw from the

elegance of the waterfront, one could find the old quarter and port, home to Basque-speaking fishermen, craftsmen, and petty traders. Although modernization radically transformed the Gipuzkoan capital, it could never quite obliterate what had come before. As was the case in Bilbo, the clash between these two worlds—in many ways, a violent clash—would profoundly influence the political and social trajectory of the city well into the twentieth century.

THE SPECTACULAR growth of the tourist industry in Iparralde leveled out after World War I (1914–18), but tourism remained a successful endeavor for proprietors of tourist facilities. As the French franc suffered a series of reverses in the aftermath of war, foreign visitors (especially from the United States and the Spanish state) took advantage of favorable exchange rates to visit the coast of Lapurdi. Through the 1920s, annual visitors to Miarritze, which remained a magnet for European and North American high society, stabilized somewhere between 25,000 and 35,000. Tourism actually expanded into the interior regions of Iparralde, such as Donibane-Garazi (St. Jean-Pied-de-Port) in Nafarroa Beherea and Azkaine (Ascain) and Kanbo (Cambo-les-Bains) in Lapurdi, which developed as spa resorts, through the first three decades of the twentieth century. However, the world economic decline after 1929, coupled with the political tensions of Europe in the 1930s, served to undermine tourism to Iparralde. The tourist industry recovered to some extent after World War II, but the region never regained the status that it had previously enjoyed.

In Hegoalde, Donostia experienced sustained growth in the development of its leisure industry between the late 1880s and the late 1920s, although the period saw a gradual chang in clientele: Whereas in its glamorous heyday the city had attracted royalty and the extremely wealthy, by the 1930s summer visitors to the city (probably more numerous than ever) were principally drawn from the middle classes. As Miarritze declined, to some extent, as a tourist center through the mid-twentieth century, Donostia continued to thrive as an important leisure center.

What might we generally conclude from the development of tourism in Euskal Herria at this time? How is it related to our quest for a specifically Basque history? We might argue that the very emergence of tourism as a cultural practice marked the consolidation of the modern industrial capitalist society dominating the Basque Country toward the end of the nineteenth century. While many of those engaged in providing tourist amenities were local people who had forsaken traditional occupations (in fishing or agriculture, for example) in pursuit of a better income and a generally more comfortable lifestyle, the growth of tourism also represented the encroaching ideology of the state in Basque society and culture. As Rudy Koshar observes, "both tourism and nationalism are grounded in the idea of opposition to the everyday desire for authenticity."[87]

FOR THE bourgeois *parisien* or *madrileño* visitors to the Basque coast, the practice of tourism involved not only an affirmation of their own material success—part of the universal middle-class experience—but it also involved a *national* quest. They were, in effect, materially conquering an outpost of their empire and in this way imagining or inventing their nation-state. The very Basqueness of the resort towns, while essential to their appeal as tourist destinations, caused them to remain relegated in the imagination of the French and Spanish nation-states to a small, safe, and exotic fringe of the overall national experience.

Lesson nine

REQUIRED READING

John K. Walton and Jenny Smith, "The Rhetoric of Community and the Business of Pleasure: The San Sebastián Waiters' Strike of 1920," *International Review of Social History* 39, part I (April 1994), pp. 1–31.

Chris Rojek and John Urry, *Touring Cultures: Transformations of Travel and Theory* (London and New York: Routledge, 1997), pp. 1–19.

SUGGESTED READING

Rudy Koshar, "'What ought to be seen': Tourists' Guidebooks and National Identities in Modern Germany and Europe," *Journal of Contemporary History* 33, no. 3 (July 1998), pp. 323–40.

LEARNING OBJECTIVES

1. To understand tourism as a cultural practice.
2. To examine the development of a Basque tourist industry between the late nineteenth and early twentieth century.
3. To critically assess the tourist industry in Euskal Herria in terms of what it tells us about national identity.

WRITTEN LESSON FOR SUBMISSION

1. Chris Rojek and John Urry comment that, "despite the strong cultural associations in the West between tourism and personal enrichment and social enlargement, we are not able to immunize ourselves from the wider cultural conflicts of everyday life" (*Touring Cultures: Transformations of Travel and Theory*, p. 19). Critically examine this claim in light of the

information about Donostia provided in John K. Walton and Jenny Smith's article "The Rhetoric of Community and the Business of Pleasure: The San Sebastián Waiters' Strike of 1920." As far as you can tell, to what extent did visitors to Donostia pursue *personal enrichment* and *social enlargement*? To what extent did they *immunize* themselves from what was going on around them?

2. From the information provided by Walton and Smith, what do you see as the most profound changes that took place in Donostia as a result of the tourist boom? What, in your opinion, does the conflict that Walton and Smith highlight reveal about the problems associated with the tourist industry in the Basque Country?

10 · Migration and urbanization
Social Change in Euskal Herria (III)

BETWEEN THE end of the first Carlist War in 1839 and the first quarter of the twentieth century, a great portion of Euskal Herria experienced a demographic change that altered considerably the fabric of Basque society. Five interrelated trends took place during this period:

1. Population growth in the three maritime provinces.
2. Population stabilization or even decline in the four interior provinces.
3. Increasing urbanization in the maritime provinces.
4. Increasing (urban) immigration into Hegoalde from non-Basque provinces of the Spanish state.
5. Increasing (rural) migration out of both Iparralde and Hegoalde, principally to the Americas.

Basque society therefore became *less homogeneous* and *more urban* during the nineteenth century, a change that explains much about social and political trends in Euskal Herria during the twentieth century.

Table 10-1 lists population figures (based on rough estimates) for five of the seven Basque provinces and for Euskal Herria as a whole during the nineteenth to early twentieth century, and gives us a basic idea of population trends during the period.

At a glance, then, we can see that population trends as a whole were quite uneven, especially after the mid-nineteenth century, when Bizkaia and Gipuzkoa began to grow at a significantly faster rate than the other provinces. Nafarroa retained a large population (in comparison to the other provinces), but in real terms practically stagnated through the nineteenth century, much like Araba. Iparralde's overall population grew through

Region	Early 19th C.	Mid-Late 19th C.	Early 19th C.	20th C.
Araba	70,000	98,000	93,000	97,000
Bizkaia	116,000	169,000	235,000	350,000
Gipuzkoa	121,000	163,000	182,000	227,000
Nafarroa	200,000	280,000	300,000	312,000
Iparralde	100,000	115,000	126,000	120,000
Euskal Herria	607,000	825,000	936,000	1,106,000

Table 10-1

the first half of the century, but then actually went into decline, principally through the effects of outward migration.

POPULATION GROWTH

The three maritime provinces of Euskal Herria—Bizkaia, Gipuzkoa, and Lapurdi—were the primary source of Basque population growth in the period from the beginning of the nineteenth century to the early years of the twentieth, due principally to the location of heavy industry, tourism, and urban areas in this region. Without doubt, the most spectacular population growth during the period took place in Bizkaia. Even before the industrial boom of the late nineteenth century, Bizkaia had experienced a substantial growth between 1787 and 1857, from 116,000 to 169,000 inhabitants. If growth through the first half of the nineteenth century had been noteworthy, through the late nineteenth and early twentieth centuries it was extraordinary.

By the early years of the twentieth century, Bizkaia, the third largest Basque province in terms of population

Early twentieth-cenbtury tourist poster advertising the
"Ilbarritz" rose garden in Miarritze, together with the
Grand Hotel and Casino. After a day spent taking the
spa waters or on the beach, visitors could stroll in the
grounds before trying their luck gambling in the
evening.
*Photo by permission of Koldo Mitxelena Kulturunea
archives.*

one hundred years previously, was now far and away the most populous region of Euskal Herria. Gipuzkoa likewise experienced substantial growth, though not in as dramatic a fashion. Indeed, through the first half of the nineteenth century, it actually trailed Araba in population-growth rates, and it also lost some of its population in the initial wave of Basque industrial migration to Bizkaia. However, growth rates picked up with the onset of Gipuzkoa's own industrialization, and its population grew steadily thereafter, especially from the early twentieth century on.

EXACT FIGURES for Iparralde are hard to calculate, as it remained subsumed by its *département*; however, given its modest industrial growth, the emerging tourist industry, and the general interior-coastal shift within the three provinces, we might reasonably conclude that the growth rates of Lapurdi maintained a steady increase through the period.

POPULATION STABILIZATION AND DECLINE

As a concomitant trend to the population increases of the maritime provinces, Euskal Herria's interior zone experienced both stabilization (in other words, no growth) and decline in its population. This was the result of a lack of industrial development (with a continuing reliance on agriculture) and, precisely because of this industrial deficiency, the impact of a rising migratory flow out of the region (to both the maritime provinces as well as outside Euskal Herria altogether). Whereas the interior provinces of Hegoalde—Araba and Nafarroa—tended toward stabilization (with only minor fluctuations in population-growth rates), the interior provinces of Iparralde—Nafarroa Beherea and Zuberoa—began, from about the mid-nineteenth

century, a process of depopulation that would continue
until late into the twentieth century.

AT THE TURN of the nineteenth century, Nafarroa had
been the most populous Basque province and had
been one of the most densely populated areas of the
Spanish kingdom. Thereafter, however, in the absence
of a significant influx of people and with a steady emigration rate, which continued throughout the century,
Nafarroa's growth rate was minimal. Araba experienced
the second-highest growth rate in Hegoalde through the
first half of the nineteenth century, but thereafter stabilized, as it did not develop any significant industrial
base. Both provinces (together with Gipuzkoa) would be
the principal sources of the first waves of migration to
the industrial regions of Bizkaia during the mid-to-late
nineteenth century.

Despite modest increments in the population-growth
rate through the first half of the nineteenth century, the
number of inhabitants in Nafarroa Beherea and Zuberoa
began to decline beginning in the mid-nineteenth century. Indeed, in the period between 1876 and 1901, the
population of Iparralde as a whole declined by some
6.7 percent, a figure that was magnified considerably in
the rural interior provinces.

This population decrease was not due to a declining
birth rate, for this rate increased during the same period
(producing a relatively youthful population with little
opportunity for economic gain). Rather, the reasons for
the population shift of these provinces included the
increasing difficulties experienced by those people
employed in the agricultural sector, the lack of any
industrial development in the rural hinterland, the
availability of steady and more remunerative work in
both coastal Lapurdi and outside the region (Paris being

---

a natural and favored destination), and an emerging trend toward overseas migration.

URBANIZATION

Although there was a consistent rural-urban shift in Iparralde throughout the nineteenth century, the greater scale of urbanization in Hegoalde, above all in Bizkaia and Gipuzkoa, made for a distinct separation—socially and economically—between the cities and towns of these two provinces and their Basque neighbors to the south, east, and north. Table 10-2 shows population figures for four Basque towns from the late eighteenth through the early twentieth century.

The figures demonstrate that from the mid-nineteenth century on, Bilbo suddenly began to grow at an incredible rate, doubling its population in successive generations (a feat equaled later in the twentieth century by Donostia), while Baiona, although experiencing modest growth during the same period, began to level out by the turn of the twentieth century. Iruñea grew only slowly through the nineteenth century, leveling out (much like Baiona) around 1900.

DURING THE first half of the nineteenth century, there was little urbanization of note in Iparralde. The only significant urban area, Baiona, was still in effect attempting to recover from the destruction of its maritime industry during the French Revolutionary and Napoleonic wars, and despite some small industrial development, the city managed at best to maintain a population of between 20,000 and 25,000. However, during the second half of the century, a more significant pattern of urbanization took place. The interior regions of Iparralde lost 15 percent of their population between 1851 and 1876 and a further 6 percent between 1876 and 1901, with coastal Lapurdi and Baiona gaining,

Town	Late 18th C.	Early 19th C.	Mid- 19th C.	Late 19th C.	Early 20th C.
				Approx.	
Baiona (Bayonne)	**9,452** (1779)	**18,992** (1806)	**25,758**	**26,000** (ca. 1850)	**27,601** (1901)
Bilbo (Bilbao)	**10,943** (1797)	**10,243** (1842)	**15,000** (ca. 1850)	**32,734** (1877)	**83,306** (1900)
Donostia (San Sebastián)		**10,000** (ca. 1840)	**10,000** (ca. 1850)	**21,355** (1877)	**41,200** (1900)
Iruñea (Pamplona)	**14,066** (1786)			**22,896** (1860) **26,663** (1887)	**28,886** (1900)

Table 10-2

respec-tively, population increases of 59 and 26 percent during this latter period (1876–1901). In the case of Baiona, we might add that this increase included the annexation of the town of Santespiritu (Saint Esprit) on the north bank of the Atturi river in 1857, adding a further 8,000 inhabitants to its population. The growth of the tourist industry along the coast of Lapurdi added to the general trend toward urbanization, as the rural youth of Iparralde (especially from the more remote areas of Zuberoa and Nafarroa Beherea) migrated to towns such as Miarritze (Biarritz), which had 18,260 inhabitants by 1911, Donibane-Lohizune (St. Jean-de-Luz), and, of course, Baiona.

Basque farmers display their cattle, Donibane-Garazi, Nafarroa Beherea, late nineteenth century. The buying and selling of livestock at market marked a significant moment on the rural calendar.
By permission of the "Les Amis de la Vieille Navarre" Association archives.

IMMIGRATION

The principal factors driving immigration to the Basque Country in the late nineteenth century were the industrial development taking place in Bizkaia and Gipuzkoa and, to a lesser extent, the emergence of the tourist industry along the coast of Lapurdi. The initial wave of migration to the mining and industrial areas in and around Bilbo came from rural areas of both the province of Bizkaia itself as well as Araba, Gipuzkoa, and Nafarroa. This intitial wave, however, was soon followed by a massive influx of people from the rural areas of northern Castile (and towns such as Valladolid and Palencia) as well as the poorest quarters of the Spanish state (with migrants from León, Galicia, Asturias, and Aragón paramount among them). The masses that flooded into the mining areas west of Bilbo's Nerbioi river—progressively creating a *greater* Bilbo—soon came, within a generation in fact, to form a classic nineteenth-century proletariat in the heart of Euskal Herria's industrial region. This region was scarcely prepared to receive such an influx. Living and working conditions were harsh, and the immigrant population quickly found itself constituting an industrial working class located socially between two other (predominantly Basque) sectors: the urban bourgeoisie and the rural peasantry. This, as we will later see, would define much of the political trajectory of twentieth-century Basque society.

EMIGRATION

The story of Basque migration overseas is lengthy and complex, and space precludes a more detailed discussion of the Basque experience in the New World. For the purposes of this study, however, it is important to examine the reasons behind Basque emigration in the nineteenth century and the multiple effects of this demographic change.

FOLLOWING William A. Douglass, we might highlight two broad types of influence that shaped nineteenth-century Basque emigration: *structural givens* (the intrinsic nature of Basque society and culture) and *time specifics* (aspects of Basque society and culture specific to the nineteenth century).[88]

1. *Structural givens:*
   a) Rural Basque society's stem-family household system, based on *primogeniture*, the tradition of naming one sole heir. This system meant that disinherited family offspring were often forced to seek a living away from the family farmstead. As such, at least since the fifteenth century, the system had encouraged migration to urban areas within the Basque Country as well as overseas.
   b) Environmental conditions. Climate, terrain, and soil type through much of Euskal Herria were not especially conducive to sustaining large populations. Where this was the case, traditional village-based economies tended to remain intact, effectively maintaining a finite population level and forcing some inhabitants to seek a living elsewhere.
   c) An emigratory tradition in Basque society. Although obviously time-specific at its inception, we might argue that (as a result of the foregoing reasons, for example) Basque society and culture actively encouraged a kind of self-imposed migratory pattern, be it the tradition of sending children to serve the Church or encouraging them to seek adventure and material gain overseas.

2. *Time specifics:*
   a) Political-administrative changes. The dismantling of the foral system had severe consequences throughout Euskal Herria. In Iparralde, after the introduction of the Civil Code, many rural families were forced to sell their farmsteads, as they could not survive economically without their traditional communal land. Furthermore, the transferring of the customs frontier to the border proper between the French and Spanish states destroyed the formerly lucrative Baiona–Iruñea trade and much of the

A French Customs Official inspects the wares of a Basque peasant woman at the entrance to Donibane-Garazi, Nafarroa Beherea, late nineteenth century. Cross-border trade between Iparralde and Hegoalde, legal or otherwise, was an integral part of the Basque economy. *By permission of the "Les Amis de la Vieille Navarre" Association archives.*

---

region's prosperity. The imposition of military service by both states, which in many cases required seven years, also served to create many emigrants among those unwilling to accept such conditions.
b) Economic changes. The French Revolutionary and Napoleonic wars devastated the maritime commerce of Lapurdi, forcing a major restructuring of its economy throughout the nineteenth century. With the general process of modernization, small artisan-

based concerns (often run in conjunction with the
family farm) were forced out of business. Nineteenth-
century industrialization also played an important
role in attracting rural Basques to the urban environment, as did the development of tourism.

c) Opportunity. In the 1830s, the newly formed independent republics of Latin America began to seek
immigrants in their own state-building processes.
Iparralde became a small, but important, source of
these immigrants. It is highly likely that, proportion-
ately, migration from Iparralde was greater than that
from Hegoalde in the nineteenth century; estimates
of the number of emigrants leaving the three
northern Basque provinces during this period vary
from 50,000 to 100,000. Whatever the actual figure,
the number of inhabitants leaving Iparralde represented perhaps as much as half of all French state
emigration during the century, and was thus a
remarkably high rate for such a small portion of the
overall population. The principal destinations for the
migrants were Argentina and Uruguay, whose capitals, Buenos Aires and Montevideo, counted in 1842
12,000 and 14,000 French immigrants, respectively,
the majority of whom were Basque. There was also a
smaller, but consistent, migration from Iparralde to
both Mexico and Chile during the 1830s. However,
from about mid-century on, the principal focus for
migrants from Iparralde gradually shifted to the far
west of the United States. Migration to Latin America
tapered off after World War I, but continued to the
United States up until the late twentieth century.

As García-Sanz Marcotegui and Arizcun Cela point
out, Nafarroan emigration began in the 1840s after
the first Carlist War.[89] A network of agencies operated throughout the province during the nineteenth

century, encouraging the growth of a Nafarroan
migratory pattern, with ready ports of exit in Bilbo
and Pasaia (Pasajes), Gipuzkoa. By the end of the century, it is likely that Nafarroan emigration to Latin
America was contributing significantly to the stag-
nant nature of the province's overall population.

THE DEMOGRAPHIC trends of the nineteenth century
indicate an increasing division between the seven
provinces of Euskal Herria. In Bizkaia and Gipuzkoa, the
population rise was, to say the least, remarkable. In
Nafarroa and Araba, population figures tended to level
out, whereas in Iparralde we might actually point to a
region of increasing depopulation, at least from the last
quarter of the century on (Nafarroa Beherea and
Zuberoa lost between 20 and 25 percent of their population during the third quarter of the century, for
example), except in those towns of the coastal stretch of
Lapurdi that benefited from both a rural-to-urban shift
and the positive economic and demographic effects of
tourism. We might argue plausibly that trends in Iparralde were the mirror opposite of those in Hegoalde
during the same period.

What were the effects of this population transformation on Basque identity? Without doubt, the population
exchange of the late nineteenth century altered Basque
society to a great extent. William A. Douglass and Jon
Bilbao conclude that quite possibly as many as 200,000
Basques migrated to the New World over the course of
the nineteenth century.[90] If so, this is a remarkable
figure given the total pre-industrial-boom population of
somewhere in the region of 800,000 inhabitants.
Whereas through the mid-nineteenth century the
majority of Basques had been *euskaldunak* (Basque
speakers), their numbers fell relative to the massive

influx of non-Basque immigrants. Similarly, the same period witnessed the rupture of a great deal of traditional Basque society, especially through the emigration of rural Basques. Thus, two cornerstones of what might have constituted a specifically Basque identity—language and a traditional lifestyle—were increasingly under threat from the late nineteenth century on. At the same time, possibly, a *new* form of Basque identity was emerging, be it urban and industrial or even global, through the new network of migrants overseas.

Lesson ten

REQUIRED READING

William A. Douglass, "Factors in the Formation of the New-World Basque Emigrant Diaspora," in William A. Douglass, ed., *Essays in Basque Social Anthropology and History* (Reno: Basque Studies Program, 1989), pp. 251–67.

John K. Walton, Martin Blinkhorn, Colin Pooley, David Tidswell, and Michael J. Winstanley, "Crime, Migration and Social Change in North-West England and the Basque Country, c. 1870–1930," *The British Journal of Criminology* 39, no. 1 (1999), pp. 90–112.

Angel García-Sanz Marcotegui and Alejandro Arizcun Cela, "An Estimate of Navarrese Migration in the Second Half of the Nineteenth Century (1879–1883)," in William A. Douglass, ed., *Essays in Basque Social Anthropology and History*, pp. 235–49.

SUGGESTED READING

Daniel Alexander Gómez-Ibáñez, *The Western Pyrenees: Differential Evolution of the French and Spanish Borderland* (Oxford: Clarendon Press, 1975), pp. 95–133.

LEARNING OBJECTIVES

1. To survey the demographic transformation of Euskal Herria between the mid-nineteenth and early twentieth centuries.
2. To understand the reasons for the changing nature of Basque society during this same period.
3. To analyze what effect this change might have had on Basque identity.

WRITTEN LESSON FOR SUBMISSION

1. Why do you think most rural Basques favored overseas migration instead of the internal option, to the industrial zones of Euskal Herria? What does this tell us about the nature of rural Basque society?
2. Critically assess the changing nature of Basque identity in the nineteenth century. Which of the three main social upheavals discussed so far—political, economic, or demographic—had the most impact on changing the nature of Basque identity, and why? Substantiate your answer with specific examples.

11 · Spain's first transition
Spanish nationalism and socialism in Hegoalde

THE EXPERIENCE of Euskal Herria during the period between the 1870s and 1930s is marked indelibly by the consolidation of the modern centralized liberal states as the supreme form of political organization and state culture as the primary focus of national identity. Both states, France and Spain, faced competition from other sources of political, social, and cultural identity, although it was probably more difficult for Madrid, given the existence in Hegoalde of a more complex society of multiple industrial and rural classes. Beset further by colonial problems, the Spanish state ultimately failed in its designs to imprint a Spanish national identity on its Basque citizenry. We will now examine the political and cultural consequences of the wider social, economic, and demographic transformations explored in previous chapters. In particular, we will discuss the construction of a Spanish national identity by the modern liberal state in Spain during the late nineteenth and early twentieth centuries. The attempt to implement a modern liberal state, it is argued here, marks Spain's *first transition* (distinct from the more well-known *transition to democracy* beginning in 1975, which will be discussed later).

Relative to the nineteenth century, this was initially a period of stability, as a model liberal state, replete with constitutional monarchy and two-party democracy, was established. However, much of this stability was illusory—in effect, the *image* of a democratic society was created. The illusion was exposed after 1898, when Spain's disastrous involvement in a colonial war with the United States resulted in the loss of Spain's remaining overseas empire. Thereafter, the Spanish political system gradually broke down, leading to the imposition of military rule in 1923.

THE BASQUE response to the birth of the modern liberal Spanish state reflected the complex social structure of Hegoalde. The large industrial and financial concerns of Bilbo (Bilbao) together with the affluent bourgeoisie of Donostia (San Sebastián) and rural oligarchs tended to support the system. However, the industrial working classes and progressive bourgeois elements embraced socialism as an alternative vision of what modernity should imply. The rural peasantry retained an affiliation with Carlism but gradually switched allegiance through the period to Basque nationalism. This was an ideology that also increasingly appealed to lower-middle-class elements alienated by the escalating changes associated with modernization in Basque society.

THE RISE AND FALL OF RESTORATION SPAIN, 1876–1923

With the victory of the liberals in the second Carlist War (discussed in Chapter 7), a new political system was created: The Bourbon monarchy was restored with the accession of Alfonso XII in 1874, and in 1876 a two-party political system (composed of liberals and conservatives) was implemented by the most powerful political leader of the era, Antonio Cánovas de Castillo. However, this was a symbolic front. The real power in the state rested in a sort of consensus between the various political, social, and economic elite groups within the country. As such, while the two political parties took turns in governing the country through a well-established pattern of election rigging, they were essentially composed of the same power base: a landed elite who exercised political authority through a powerful network of bossism (*caciquismo*) and brokered deals with poten-

Workers leaving the biscuit factory of Errenteria, Gipuzkoa, early twentieth century. The first wave of industrial immigration to Euskal Herria was "local." Here we can see Basque immigrants (notice the boinas or berets), probably from rural Gipuzkoa and Nafarroa, working in this important industrial town.

By permission of Editorial Iparaguirre, S.A. archives.

---

tial challengers to their authority such as the armed forces and the industrial bourgeoisie.

THE SPANISH state after 1876 imposed a more centralized system than ever before. This took the form of both unofficial constructs (such as *caciquismo*) and official policies. State education, for example, became particularly important in creating a Spanish national identity. A uniform educational system was introduced

that promoted Castilian as the official language of the
state and actively discriminated against the country's
other languages. "Liberalism's stress on education and
culture," observe Helen Graham and Jo Labanyi, "was
integrally linked to emergent ideologies of nationalism,
through which the ascendant bourgeoisie sought to inte-
grate the rest of the population within the national territory into its own project."[91] The dominant ideological
thrust of the state was exemplified by the scholar
Marcelino Menéndez y Pelayo, a protégé of Cánovas and
author of the three-volume *Historia de los heterodoxos
españoles* (History of Orthodox Spaniards), published
between 1880 and 1882 and widely disseminated
throughout both the educational system and society as a
whole. According to Carolyn P. Boyd, his vision of
Spanish national identity "depended on an unresolved
mixture of essentialist and historico-cultural arguments:
on the one hand, Spaniards formed a 'race' or 'caste'
intrinsically inclined towards religious orthodoxy; on
the other hand, their religious and cultural unity had
been won dearly and against great odds."[92]

THE SYSTEM established by Cánovas thrived through
the 1880s, but toward the end of the decade internal
problems began to plague the state. Politically, the insti-
tutionalization of *caciquismo* had eroded any hopes of
creating civic authority in the Spanish state. Madrid was
quite clearly fixing elections through the compliance of
the Ministry of the Interior, civil governors (the government's provincial representatives), and local powerbrokers, backed up by the paramilitary threat of the Civil
Guard. At the rural level—where *caciquismo* functioned
most clearly—this was increasingly alienating the
majority population. During the late 1880s, a series of
agricultural crises further led to increasing social discontent among the peasantry. At the same time, two

regions of the state—Catalunya and Euskal Herria—
were greatly prospering (leading to an escalating belief
among some in their distinct identities), even though
their industrial working classes still had to endure
squalid living and working conditions. This in turn led
to a wave of industrial protest through the 1890s from
both anarchists in Barcelona and socialists in Bilbo.

DURING THE 1890s, then, the Spanish state was
increasingly dividing along both social (class) and
cultural (nation) lines. The traditional response to
crisis—deflecting public opinion away from domestic
problems by means of foreign adventure—would once
again surface as a tactic in Restoration Spain. Between
1810 and 1825, the Spanish empire had lost all of its
former possessions in Latin America, except Cuba and
Puerto Rico. During the early 1890s, stirrings of discontent were now also apparent in these remnants of the
empire, together with increasing anticolonial activity in
Spanish-controlled Morocco. The state response was
swift and direct. By the mid-1890s, troops were actively
engaging separatist rebels (as they were viewed from
Madrid) from Cuba to Morocco and the Philippines,
which provoked a wave of popular Spanish nationalism.
In 1898, the United States entered this conflict on the
separatist side in both Cuba and the Philippines. This
proved to be decisive, for by the summer of that year
Spain had lost its American empire.

After 1898, Restoration Spain gradually imploded as
Spanish identity was called into question from a number
of fronts. The disaster of military defeat aggravated the
social, political, and economic crises that had beset the
country through the late 1880s and 1890s, and consequently, during the first two decades of the twentieth
century, the country drifted into an abyss of conflict

Old Regime guard duck. Premodern symbols were
ridiculed by the nation-building countries of
Europe in the nineteenth century as superstitious,
lethargic and stupid.
From Grandville's Scènes de la vie privée et publique
des animaux, *1866.*

defined by a corrupt political system, increasing social tensions, and an erratic postcolonial economy (discussed in greater detail in Chapter 13). Modern Spain effectively remained a country with the framework of symbolic liberal institutions superimposed onto a predominantly Old Regime society, and furthermore its most dynamic and modern centers were located in regions with strong local (national?) identities. Out of this turmoil emerged divergent views as to how to resolve the *problem* of modern Spain.

SEBASTIAN BALFOUR highlights three broad visions "of the nation-state and of Spanish nationalism" that emerged during this time as alternatives to the Restoration system: The non-nationalist Catalan bourgeoisie conceived of a conservative federal vision of the state that would redistribute political power into the hands of regional economic elites and envisioned a unified Spanish identity that recognized its local variations; republican and socialist interests favored a centrist model of political organization hostile to regional identities, and a national identity celebrating the innate qualities of the Spanish masses; finally, the increasingly dissatisfied Spanish military returned to an older model of Spanish nationalism that emphasized a sense of Christian mission and Castilian warrior values in an authoritarian model of state reorganization.[93] Geoffrey Jensen argues, however, that both liberal and authoritarian models existed within Spanish military nationalism, but observes that, "like their civilian counterparts, liberal and conservative versions of Spanish military nationalism were overwhelmingly Castile-based."[94]

Amid the turmoil, a revolt broke out among disenchanted war veterans and anarchists in Barcelona in 1909 that signaled the beginning of the end for Restoration Spain. The violent response of the state only

confirmed what for many had become increasingly
obvious: the transition in Spain had failed. Still in
recovery from the ravages of the colonial wars, the
country remained neutral throughout World War I and
even enjoyed a modest (though short-term) economic
recovery. By war's end, the crisis was even more pronounced as Madrid's liberal elite were now bitterly
fighting among themselves over a lasting solution for
the country. From 1917 on, the armed forces were
actively agitating against the state. Coupled with
socialist and anarchist hostility (inspired by the Russian
Revolution of 1917), and regional discontent in the form
of growing Catalan and Basque nationalist movements,
MADRID WAS increasingly powerless to act. To compound matters, Spain embarked on yet another
disastrous colonial adventure, this time in North Africa,
beginning in 1914. By 1921, Spanish forces were bogged
down in hostile terrain, faced with an aggressive and
astute enemy composed of North African Rif tribesmen,
and retained little enthusiasm for what seemed like a
meaningless endeavor. The inevitable defeat that followed was viewed with horror by the armed forces.
Between 1921 and 1923, they called for Madrid to take
responsibility for its actions in North Africa, and when
this was not forthcoming, they rose up against the government. In September 1923, the Captain General of
Barcelona, General Miguel Primo de Rivera, assumed
the leadership of the country in the name of God, the
fatherland, and the army.

POLITICAL CULTURE IN POST-1876 HEGOALDE

If one word captures the experience of Hegoalde during
the Restoration era it is *change*. We might reasonably
consider the period between 1876 and 1923 as one of
radical social transformation on an almost unprece-

dented scale. In 1876, Hegoalde was still an overwhelmingly rural, agricultural, and Basque-speaking society. According to statistics for 1867, 83 percent of the 180,000 inhabitants of Bizkaia spoke Basque, whereas the figures for the remaining provinces of Hegoalde were as follows: 95 percent of 179,000 in Gipuzkoa, 11 percent of 95,000 in Araba, and 20 percent of 300,000 in Nafarroa. Politically, Hegoalde was governed by a liberal elite confined to urban enclaves on the Bizkaian and Gipuzkoan coasts, with their main (though muted) rural-based opposition to be found in the smoldering ideology of Carlism. By 1923, a considerable shift had taken place, transforming this society into a more socially and politically complex unit. In particular, it had become more urban, Spanish-speaking, and politically plural. If liberalism still dominated the elite political culture in 1923, its principal rivals were socialism and Basque nationalism.

WHAT WERE the political ramifications of these social and economic transformations? In the immediate aftermath of the second Carlist War, liberal power in Hegoalde was consolidated through the establishment of the *conciertos económicos* (economic pacts) that guaranteed a degree of fiscal autonomy for the liberal Basque industrial bourgeoisie. There followed a spectacular economic growth, assuring massive benefits for the ruling politico-economic elite while creating a large underclass of increasingly disaffected industrial workers. In keeping with the times, this was a classic industrial society of *haves* and *have-nots* where the benefits to those with power and influence were tremendous in relation to those who did not exercise such economic or political muscle. From the early 1890s on, the ruling Basque elite—in particular, those whose wealth had been built on profits from iron and steel concerns—further benefited from an increasingly strict government policy of economic protectionism, and in 1897 the major industrial families of Hegoalde created a liberal monarchist political party, La Unión Liberal (Liberal Union), to protect and consolidate these ties with Madrid. As a consequence, while the Basque industrial elite settled into a comfortable pattern of political dominance espousing an ideology that has been described by Manuel González Portilla as "Spanish economic nationalism," the newly emerging working classes began to organize.[95]

SOCIALISM IN HEGOALDE

According to E. P. Thompson, "class happens when some men, as a result of common experiences (inherited or shared), feel and articulate the identity of their interests as between themselves and as against other men whose interests are different from (and usually opposed to) theirs. The class experience is largely determined by the productive relations into which men are born—or enter involuntarily. Class-consciousness is the way in which these experiences are handled in cultural terms: embodied in traditions, value-systems, ideas, and institutional forms. ... [C]lass is a relationship, not a thing."[96]

THIS DEFINITION of the *meaning* of class, with its emphasis on the cultural and fluid nature of the phenomenon, is especially pertinent to the emergence of an industrial proletariat (working class) in and around Bilbo at the end of the nineteenth century.

In the space of a few years, the left bank of the Nerbioi river, which runs from the center of Bilbo to its ocean outlet, became the new home for several thousand immigrants. As we have already noted, they were, in the main, migrants from the poorest rural areas of surrounding provinces, such as Araba and Gipuzkoa, as

This image, taken in the 1980s, reflects a long tradition
of industrial protest in urban Basque areas.
Photo: Iñaki Uriarte.

---

well as from provinces outside Euskal Herria, including
Burgos, Santander, La Rioja, and León, and their
working and living conditions were harsh, with twelve-
hour workdays and high incidences of alcoholism,
tuberculosis, and smallpox. The shock of this transformation, in both an occupational and a social sense, was
tremendous. Yet despite the fact that the vast majority of
the newcomers were illiterate peasants, already during

the first wave of non-Basque immigration there was some initiative toward the development of class consciousness through group organization. As Cyrus Ernesto Zirakzadeh points out, in 1868 a group of workers in Bilbo formed one of western Europe's earliest chapters of the First International or International Working Men's Association, founded in 1864 by Karl Marx as a collective organization for the expression of socialist and anarchist ideals.[97] Similarly, in 1870 another group of workers constituted a Bilbo section of the anarchist collective La Federación de los Trabajadores de la Region Española (The Federation of Workers of the Spanish Region), followed by similar groups in the Araban capital of Gasteiz (Vitoria) in 1870 and in Zumarraga, Gipuzkoa, in 1872.

In 1888, Spain's socialist party, clandestinely in existence since 1879, acquired legal status (together with its union, the Unión General de Trabajadores, or General Workers Union [UGT]) as the Partido Socialista Obrero Español (PSOE; Spanish Socialist Workers Party).[98] In 1890, the UGT held its second annual congress in Bilbo, attracting 5,000 participants from throughout the state. That same year, socialist councilmen were elected for the first time in both Bilbo and the Bizkaian mining town of San Salvador de El Valle. Between 1890 and 1911, there were five general strikes and 169 minor protests in Bizkaia alone, organized in the main by the socialists.

BASQUE SOCIALISM drew its support from among the immigrant workers of Bilbo's left bank. At its birth, it was revolutionary and Marxist in character and quickly addressed the so-called *national question*, a debate that consumed most of Europe's socialist movements of the time. Both its early militant leader, Facundo Perezagua Suárez, and Perezagua's more moderate, *evolutionary* successor, Indalecio Prieto, rejected all notions of Basque difference; national or regional differentiation, especially among the working classes, was viewed as a bourgeois attempt to keep the proletariat divided. As such, socialist thought in plurinational Spain never acquired the kind of sophisticated compromise sought by the Austro-Marxists.[99] And though the Basque socialist thinker Tomás Meabe claimed that *Basqueness* should only be measured in international terms, as all nations were effectively oppressed by the capitalist system, socialism emerged in a decidedly *statist* context in Euskal Herria. Basque socialism was, furthermore, hostile to the power of the Church (defended by the emerging Basque nationalist movement), as demonstrated by Prieto in 1911, when, on being elected as a provincial deputy, he characterized himself as "anticlerical and a non-Catholic."[100]

THE BOURBON Restoration was an attempt on behalf of the state to impose modernity on Spanish society. The transition was attempted through a construction of the framework of a liberal state, with certain institutions functioning better than others. However, nineteenth-century liberalism's political, social, and economic framework did not manage to engage the state's citizens. Furthermore, Spanish liberalism bequeathed the modern state a brand of nationalism that would undergo several transformations through the twentieth century. In this sense, it is important to remember the links between liberal and authoritarian regimes in modern Spain. As Jensen notes, "liberals *did* promote a form of [Spanish] nationalism that would serve the twentieth-century authoritarian Right—whether fascist, traditionalist or a combination of both."[101]

The immediate ramifications of the social changes under way in Hegoalde during the same period were

twofold. First, there was a consolidation of hegemonic
liberal and Spanish nationalist political and economic
power among the Basque industrial elite. Through the
auspices of the Liberal Union, the elite families of
Hegoalde (principally based in Bilbo) promoted a pro-
government and constitutional monarchist politico-
cultural ideology, together with economic policies based
on the encouragement of Spanish military adventure to
stimulate the Basque iron and steel industry. Second,
there emerged a powerful socialist movement that drew
the majority of its support from the predominantly
immigrant working classes. Importantly, socialism in
the Basque Country remained *Spanish* (more than
Basque or internationalist) in its politico-cultural orientation, although it rejected much of the framework of
Spain's first transition. There was still another challenge
to the hegemony of Spanish liberalism, however, and
one that drew its inspiration from more traditionalist
sectors of Hegoalde's society: Basque nationalism.

Lesson eleven

REQUIRED READING

Cyrus Ernesto Zirakzadeh, *A Rebellious People: Basques,
Protests, and Politics* (Reno and Las Vegas: University
of Nevada Press, 1991), pp. 54–62.

Tom Nairn, "Internationalism and the Second Coming,"
in Gopal Balakrishnan, ed., *Mapping the Nation*
(London and New York: Verso, 1996), pp. 267–80.

SUGGESTED READING

Shlomo Avineri, "Marxism and Nationalism," *Journal of
Contemporary History* 26, no. 3–4 (September 1991),
pp. 637–57.

Carolyn P. Boyd, *Historia Patria: Politics, History, and National Identity in Spain, 1875–1975* (Princeton: Princeton University Press, 1997), pp. 65–98.

Geoffrey Jensen, "Military Nationalism and the State: The Case of *Fin-de-Siècle* Spain," *Nations and Nationalism* 6, no. 2 (April 2000), pp. 257–74.

Sebastian Balfour, "The Loss of Empire, Regenerationism, and the Forging of a Myth of National Identity," in Helen Graham and Jo Labanyi, eds., *Spanish Cultural Studies: An Introduction* (Oxford: Oxford University Press, 1995), pp. 25–31.

LEARNING OBJECTIVES

1. To trace the emergence of the modern liberal state in Spain.
2. To examine the nature of Spanish nationalism and its role in the consolidation of the modern Spanish state.
3. To examine the rise of socialism in Hegoalde.

WRITTEN LESSON FOR SUBMISSION

1. We have encountered the term "nineteenth-century liberalism" several times up to this point. Using specific examples from the Spanish case, to what extent do you think that this ideology conforms to the definition of a *nationalist* ideology?
2. Why do you think that socialism was so hostile to the question of Basque national difference when, seemingly without reservation, it proclaimed itself *Spanish*?

T HIS EXPLORATION of the history of Euskal Herria has so far centered on the extent to which we can really speak of a specifically Basque identity. Our argument has been restricted in the main to a social, cultural, and more speculative political interpretation of a distinctively Basque history. Toward the end of the nineteenth century, however, a clearer picture emerged, whereby the inhabitants of Euskal Herria were increasingly called on to politically define their national status. As discussed in the previous chapter, at least two versions of Spanish nationalism emerged during this period.

First, we can point to a classic nineteenth-century liberal vision that implied a central uniform state political culture sustained by a monocultural ideology celebrating Castilian imperial strength. In Hegoalde, Spanish liberalism drew its support from the industrial bourgeoisie. Principal among the political parties associated with this variant of Spanish nationalism was the Liberal Union, centered in Bilbo (Bilbao), but we should also point to the existence of more conservative and traditionalist parties, which tended to dominate in the remaining provinces of Hegoalde. Controlled and sustained by landed interests, these parties consolidated their hold on much of Basque rural society by forcing the peasantry (the majority of whom were tenants of the powerful landowners), through the insistence of local powerbrokers known as *jauntxos*, to vote for them. There are two clearly defined periods of Spanish nationalist / liberal dominance during the Restoration period: The *caciquismo* of Antonio Cánovas de Castillo from 1876 to 1898 (see Chapter 11), and, after 1906, the more

pragmatic yet still right-wing Spanish nationalist dominance of Antonio Maura (discussed in greater detail in
Chapter 13).

The second instance of politically defined national
identity to emerge in Hegoalde at the end of the nineteenth century was socialism. Like socialist movements
elsewhere in Europe, that of the Spanish state eschewed
internationalism (beyond the symbolic realm, that is—
"The International" was still sung at meetings and ban-
ners proclaiming the Marxist slogan "Workers of the
world unite" were carried at demonstrations) by cultivating a sense of Spanish working-class solidarity.
Indeed, most socialists in fin-de-siècle Europe—with
some notable exceptions, such as the Austro-Marxist
Otto Bauer and James Connolly of Ireland—tended to
eschew any pretensions to *national* allegiance as well,
while at the same time creating state-oriented political
parties.

SOCIALISM IN Hegoalde initially drew its strength
from the large number of immigrant workers who
had settled on the left bank of Bilbo's Nerbioi river and
in smaller industrial towns such as Eibar in Gipuzkoa.
In terms of national identity, they had little reason to
associate themselves with their adopted homeland.
Exploited by their Basque employers, they retained a
sense of their original regional identities. Indeed, these
same employers were keen to cultivate such regional differences among the immigrant workers, so as to prevent
any sense of solidarity among the proletariat. Socialism
thus incorporated a sense of Spanish nationalism—
though one celebrating the valor of the Spanish masses
rather than imperial greatness—as a means of uniting
the workers. Within this context, yet another political
ideology emerged—that of Basque nationalism, which

rejected the social and cultural implications of Spanish liberalism and socialism.

THE ORIGINS OF BASQUE NATIONALISM

José Luis de la Granja Sainz lists three historical factors in the origins of Basque nationalism.[102] Let us critically examine these ideas:

1. *Remote Precursors*. Between the fifteenth and nineteenth centuries, several writers constructed historical myths claiming a distinct or unique quality to Basque culture. The elements of this myth-making varied from a mysticism associated with the Basque language to ruralism and egalitarianism as essential aspects of Basque culture, and an original Basque independence. This was hardly a phenomenon unique to the Basque Country, for throughout Europe scholars and clerics were assiduously inventing "national traditions." In England, for example, myths created during the same period to sustain a sense of English national identity included three main cornerstones: ethnic homogeneity (the undeniable existence of an English-speaking *English* race), ruralism (the countryside as repository of the positive values associated with being English), and an island mentality (the English as natural seafarers and adventurers). On close inspection, these images prove to be pure invention: It is impossible to speak of an English race on an island dominated by wave after wave of immigration, from Celts and Romans through Germanic tribes such as Angles, Saxons, and Jutes, to Vikings, Normans, Huguenots, Jews, and so on. Furthermore, the English countryside served as little more than the rustic backdrop to the invention of England, a country forged on urban-based industrial development and wealth. Finally, it is Great

The San Francisco neighborhood, a principal immigrant quarter of Bilbo, early twentieth century. Here newcomers had to contend with soldiers stationed in the barracks (to the right), making this one of Bilbo's tougher and livelier areas. To this day, San Francisco is the destination for immigrants to the city.
By permission of Editorial Iparaguirre, S.A. archives.

Britain, not England, that is an island, and, moreover, until the sixteenth century there were scarcely any English seafarers of note. Indeed, as Jeremy Paxman argues, "the English were a land-loving people and the sea which surrounded them was, as John of Gaunt put it, more a moat than anything else."[103]

2. *Nineteenth-Century Antecedents*. During the nineteenth century, three general ideas greatly influenced
   the emergence of Basque nationalism: Romanticism,
   foralism, and Carlism. Building on an already established invented tradition, Romantic writers of the
   nineteenth century centered notions of Basque difference on the possession of the *foruak*. A foralist ideology (i.e., one favoring the preservation of foral
   rights) thus emerged at about the same time as
   Spanish liberalism's first attempts to create modern
   Spain. We might conclude that foralism appeared as a
   kind of original response to proto–state-building in
   Spain, just as Basque nationalism later emerged
   during the initial stages of the modern liberal
   Spanish state. The clash of Carlism and liberalism
   was physically played out in the two Carlist wars of
   the nineteenth century. Without doubt, Basque
   nationalism drank heavily from the mythical well of
   Carlism.
3. *The Industrial Revolution*. As we have seen, the social
   and cultural changes wrought by the economic
   changes of the late nineteenth century profoundly
   altered Basque society, at a pace that was violently
   swift by any standard. In the space of a generation,
   Hegoalde—more specifically, Bizkaia / Bilbo and to a
   lesser extent certain areas of Gipuzkoa—was transformed from a generally homogeneous (socially and
   culturally speaking) to a profoundly plural society.
   Whereas the two variants of Spanish nationalism
   both fed off industrial progress (though in different
   ways), Basque nationalism initially came to represent
   the reactionary clamor against industrial modernity.

These were the general historical factors leading to the
emergence of Basque nationalism, but what of specific

ideological instances? If Carlism (discussed in greater detail in Chapters 6 and 7) provided Basque nationalism with one ideology from which to draw inspiration, the second important ideological source of Basque nationalist rhetoric was a traditionalist foralism associated with two groups: In 1877, La Asociación Euskara de Navarra (Basque Association of Nafarroa) was created by activists who wished to promote Basque cultural unity as a means of regaining the foruak. The group counted among its members the writers Juan Iturralde y Suit, Hermilio Olóriz, and Arturo Campión. Through the 1880s, it promoted a series of folkloric gatherings aimed at fostering and promoting a sense of Basque cultural unity. The group never arrived at the idea of Basque independence, preferring to foster a sense of Basque unity loosely tied into a Spanish framework.

SIMILARLY, in Bizkaia a group of foral traditionalists led by Fidel de Sagarmínaga established La Sociedad Euskalerria de Bilbao (Basque Country Society of Bilbo) in 1879, along much the same lines as its Nafarroan counterpart but with a decidedly more political tone. The *euskalerriacos*, as the society's members were known, pursued a program aimed at the restoration of the *foruak* and the union of the four provinces of Hegoalde. While Sagarmínaga cannot be considered a Basque nationalist as such (for he believed in the confederation of peoples within the Spanish state), by 1898 the *euskalerriacos*, under the new leadership of Ramón de la Sota y Llano and the group's principal ideologue, the priest Resurreción María de Azkue, had joined the ranks of Basque nationalists.

Narratiba

PIANO GAINEAN GOSALTZEN
Harkaitz Cano

erein

Harkaitz Cano's Piano Gainean Gosaltzen (Having
Breakfast on the Piano) is a series of essays written
during the author's extended visit to New York. Literary
production in Basque is now at ease in a variety of settings throughout the world.

SABINO DE ARANA Y GOIRI AND THE INVENTION OF BASQUE NATIONALISM

Born in 1865 into a comfortable middle-class Carlist family, Sabino de Arana y Goiri retained familial political sympathies until 1882, when his brother Luis convinced him of the idea that Euskal Herria was the homeland of the Basques—in other words, that Basques only had a right to claim distinct privileges (the *foruak*, for example) by reason of their difference from the rest of Spain. From this time on, Sabino dedicated his life to establishing what in time would become Basque nationalism. Through the 1880s, while studying for a law degree in Barcelona, he dedicated most of his time to investigating Basque history and learning Euskara, arriving in 1892 at the publication of a short romanticist historical text, *Bizkaya por su independencia* (Bizkaia Through Its Independence), the first explicitly Basque nationalist text. The following year, he presented some of the ideas developed in the work to an assortment of foralist sympathizers (including a good number of *euskalerriacos*) in what has come to be known as the Larrazábal Address. From this moment on, Sabino and Luis Arana, together with a small (but steadily growing) number of followers, developed a series of ideas that came to define the early Basque nationalist movement.

WHAT, THEN, were the central tenets of this movement? Early Basque nationalism broadly defined itself by the slogan *"Jaungoikua eta lege zarrak"* ("God and the old laws"—in other words, the *foruak*), and its principal ideology implied a traditionalist critique of the modern liberal Spanish state. What distinguished this ideology from its foralist predecessors and, indeed, marked a more radical departure from strictly traditionalist platforms, was its insistence on independence as the best means of safeguarding Basque interests.

Furthermore, Basque nationalism was born with certain *essentialist* theoretical assumptions.

If nationalism enjoyed a liberal quality (in the general sense of a "liberating" discourse) during its first incarnation between the late-eighteenth-century American and French revolutions and the failed European uprisings of 1848, thereafter it took a decidedly conservative turn.[104] Throughout late-nineteenth-century Europe, nationalist ideologies, whether state or nation variants, tended to celebrate historical traditions and innate qualities of the collective group. The essentialist doctrine of Marcelino Menéndez y Pelayo (see Chapter 11), for example, rested on the assumption that the *essence* of the Spanish nation resided in the quasi-racial and religious differentiating quality of its people.

ESSENTIALISM was based on a prescribed beginning-middle-end historical sequence, in which the particular collective group played a central defining role. In the emergent states of the era, this often took the form of a particular mission intended to benefit the rest of humanity. As such, England (or Great Britain) increasingly struggled with the United States in the promotion of the democratic / capitalist civilizing mission of the Anglo-Saxon race, French nationalism (particularly through the mythologizing of Revolutionary and Napoleonic ideals, explored in more detail in Chapter 24) promoted the country as the liberating nation of the world, German culture fostered a romanticist ethnocultural nationalism as opposed to what it viewed as the artificiality of cosmopolitan construction, and Spanish essentialist nationalism imbued its race with the mission of defending the Roman Catholic faith against all heretics.

Without doubt, romanticism must have served as a general contextual influence on the young Arana, but it would be a mistake to conceive of early Basque nationalism as merely a romantic form of reaction to the evils of modernity. As we have seen, Spanish nationalism had already taken root in a variety of guises well before the emergence of its Basque counterpart. In this age of nationalism, a cultural struggle was under way for the hearts, minds, and, specifically, *identities* of individuals. Basque nationalism emerged in many ways as a response to Spanish nationalism, and as such was a comparatively "normal" development for the time.

WHAT, THEN, were the components of this essentialist Basque nationalism? For Arana, the Basque nation had "existed" as a distinguishable and separate entity throughout history. Its central tenets were, further, to be found in a conglomeration of factors: race, ruralism, religion, and original independence.

1. *Race.* This was a dominant philosophical theme of late-nineteenth-century Europe and North America. Social Darwinism gathered momentum in the United States and Great Britain, for example, as a validation of the entrepreneurial spirit of the Anglo-Saxon peoples. The original conception of Basque nationalism had a significant xenophobic component, directed mainly against non-Basque immigrants to the industrial areas of Bizkaia. Arana branded such immigrants *maketos* (a derogatory term with racist implications) and drew physical distinctions between the newcomers and native Basques. (A parallel of sorts might be drawn with the way in which Spanish nationalism, during the Cuban uprising of the 1890s, demonized white insurrectionists as "traitors" and their black counterparts as "savages."[105]) While Arana used race as a defining factor and was quick to promote the "qualities" of the Basque race over its Spanish counterpart, he never went to the extremes

espoused by the French aristocrat Joseph-Arthur, Comte de Gobineau, who promoted a more explicitly racist creed. For instance, he never envisaged a racial hierarchy in European society and, indeed (as we shall see), was quick to defend non-European (and non-Christian) peoples in their anticolonial struggles against European powers. We should be careful to place this concept of race in its historical context: A cornerstone of essentialist nationalisms, it was, at that time, the normal expression of the virtues of a particular people. Thus, Spanish nationalism celebrated the heroic and bellicose characters of the Castilian people, just as Arana conceived of essentially Basque virtues to distinguish his creed. Arana invented the word *Euzkadi* to denote the Basque homeland as something more closely approximating "the land of the Basques" (in an obviously racial sense), rather than Euskal Herria ("land of the Basque-speakers").

2. *Ruralism.* Mythical appropriation of rural symbolism (as in the English case) was a standard feature of most European nationalisms. It was in the main constructed by urban (and urbane) middle-class thinkers who felt disenchanted by their immediate surroundings. Arana fits this stereotype perfectly. He was born in Abando, a separate town at the time but later engulfed by Bilbo as a neighborhood, and his early writings, as Granja Sainz astutely observes, are replete with references to Bilbo as the location of all modern society's evils: capitalism, industrial development, and Spanish immigration.[106]

By contrast, the countryside in his writings retains the truer essence of Basqueness. Ruralism celebrated the timelessness of the countryside, with its ever-repeating

Sabino de Arana y Goiri, founder of Basque nationalism
The charasmatic and controversial first leader of the
EAJ-PNV used the cult of personality to promote his
political agenda.
*By permission of Abertzaletasunaren Agiritegia. Sabino
Arana Kultur Elkargoa archives.*

cycles of regeneration. In the ruralist imagination, nothing changed; societies were preserved in their original and pure states. Without doubt, this carried with it romantic overtones, but the utopian and dream-like quality of ruralism was as much a product of modernity as of anything else.

COMPARE, FOR example, Adam Smith's and Karl Marx's alternative (though intimately connected) visions of "perfect" capitalist and socialist societies. Smith's classic work *The Wealth of Nations* (1776), perhaps the single most influential treatise to articulate modern capitalism, is full of references to "natural" phenomena (the natural regulation of wages, natural prices, natural liberty, and so on). He used nature as a symbol for strengthening his argument that the economy of a society should be regulated by the "invisible hand" (another utopian rural metaphor) of individual self-interest. Marx, borrowing from previous thinkers such as Jean-Jacques Rousseau, described a naturally "good" humanity estranged or alienated from its sense of self and innate creativity by modern industrial conditions of labor. Unlike the Romantics, however, he did not argue for a return to some primitive paradise, but rather for a utopian restructuring of modern society so that people could find pleasure in working with one another, free of competition or self-interest and for a common good, as in their rural past.[107]

3. *Religion.* A key component of the Aranist conception of nationalism was religion. For Arana, an independent Basque Country, although separating Church and state, should be subordinate to basic religious precepts. In addition to Basque nationalism's main slogan (*"Jaungoikua eta lege zarrak"*), Arana also coined the phrase *"Gu Euzkadirentzat ta Euzkadi Jaungoikuarentzat"* ("We for Euzkadi and Euzkadi for God").

Liberalism was the enemy of Basque nationalism for its struggle against religious authority, and Basque nationalism was thus imbued with a sacramental quality; its particular mission was the salvation of the Basque race through separation from liberal Spain. Religious affiliation was, of course, and remains an intensely strong emblem of national identity in general. It was also a principal factor of Spanish nationalism's most extreme variant, and it has likewise played a defining role in nationalist movements from Ireland to Poland and the Balkans.

4. *Original Independence*. As Granja Sainz notes, the myth of original independence, fostered and promoted throughout Basque nationalism's history, is a historical reconstruction designed to serve specific political ends. According to Arana, the independence of Bizkaia (and later the Basque Country) dated back to its origins, and had been safeguarded throughout history by the *foruak*. With defeat in the first Carlist War in 1839, the Basques had lost this independent status, and thereafter Euskal Herria had been an occupied country. This logic (whether historically accurate or not) promoted within Arana a sense of solidarity with the anticolonial movements that were beginning to emerge in the late nineteenth century. The myth of original independence was integral to many nationalist movements of the nineteenth century, and was particularly strong in well-developed states like Great Britain and France. Such myths served as a bonding element for the ethnocultural community in much the same way that tribal societies share common myths of creation.

IN MANY ways, from among the myriad collective identities to which human beings can lay claim, that of national identity remains the most potent. It could be persuasively argued that a key political change took

The violent transformation of a predominantly rural economy to a heavy industrial base caused a traumatic upheaval in Basque society, forcing many people to emigrate to the New World.
Engraving by Thomas Bewick.

---

place in fin-de-siècle Hegoalde whereby Basques were increasingly forced to choose a specific national identity from three mutually opposing models: an increasingly strident sense of "Spanishness," as promoted and defined by the central state; a more subtle Spanish identity, subsumed within both an international and class framework, offered by socialism; and a (re?)nascent Basque national identity. Indeed, the tremendous pull of national allegiance distinguishes the political history of Europe during the nineteenth century and up to the eve of World War I from that of earlier times. As such, events at the end of the nineteenth century through the beginning of the twentieth were decisive in defining the future shape of Basque history: From the 1890s on, the Basques of Hegoalde would increasingly be forced to define their national identity in consciously political ways.

Lesson twelve

REQUIRED READING

Stanley G. Payne, *Basque Nationalism* (Reno: University of Nevada Press, 1975), pp. 61–86.

Marianne Heiberg, "Urban Politics and Rural Culture: Basque Nationalism," in Stein Rokkan and Derek W. Urwin, eds., *The Politics of Territorial Identity: Studies in European Regionalism* (London, Beverly Hills, and New Delhi: Sage Publications, 1982), pp. 355–73.

Robert P. Clark, *The Basques: The Franco Years and Beyond* (Reno: University of Nevada Press, 1979), pp. 33–55.

SUGGESTED READING

Michael Biddiss, "Nationalism and the Moulding of Modern Europe," *History* 7, no. 257 (October 1994), pp. 412–32.

LEARNING OBJECTIVES

1. To define the national question in Restoration Spain.
2. To examine the nature of Basque nationalism.

3. To think critically about the meaning of nationalism in general as a social, political, and cultural phenomenon.

WRITTEN LESSON FOR SUBMISSION
Document Question 3

CAREFULLY EXAMINE the following two texts. The first is an article written by Sabino de Arana y Goiri for his weekly newspaper, *Bizkaitarra*. The second article was written for the Bilbo-based socialist newspaper *La Lucha de Clases*. Both texts offer politically charged thoughts on the relationship between the Basque Country and Spain at the close of the nineteenth century. With regard to the national question, what are your initial responses to these articles? In other words, what do they tell us about how people conceived of terms and concepts like "nation," "nationalism," "separatism," "identity," etc.? (Feel free to invoke the more general theoretical readings we have come across if you wish.) From this cursory glance, what strikes you as the most important statements that the two documents make, from the point of view of the historian, and why?

Sabino de Arana y Goiri, extract from "Foralism is Separatism," *Bizkaitarra*, April 22, 1894:

Bizkaian nationalism implies the constitution of Bizkaia as a nation absolutely free and independent from the rest. As this policy, in the opinion of the nationalists, matches Bizkaia's claim, namely that it appears through history as neither theoretically nor legally considered a part or a region of the Spanish nation, but a true nation in and of itself, presently and despite this dominated by Spain, it seems that this nationalism is not suggesting that one should separate or dismember a part from the whole but rather, that one should reestablish naturally and fairly a perfectly distinct and natural whole that has been annexed and ruined abnormally and unjustly.

As a consequence, nationalism cannot properly be termed separatism, but inappropriately and only if one accepts that Bizkaia is united to Spain. However, there is also no doubt that the Spanish, either through a lack of knowledge of the history and laws that Bizkaia possesses, or through the sly tactic of convincing the European powers (for what might ensue) that this Bizkaian policy is violating the integrity of the Spanish nation, have to deny nationalism its true name and instead term it improperly separatism, based on the assumption that Bizkaia is by law an integral part of Spain.

At any rate, and since the name does not make the thing, this Bizkaian policy—objectively as old as Bizkaia although subjectively, at least in the minds and hearts of Bizkaians, so new before the public—that is scarcely a year old, seeks, whether termed nationalism or separatism, the complete independence of Bizkaia (this does not mean that Bizkaia has to disregard the other regions of Euskal Herria. No: Araba, Bizkaia, Gipuzkoa, Lapurdi, Nafarroa, Nafarroa Beherea, and Zuberoa are peoples related by the ties of race, language, character, and customs, and according to nationalist policy are called on to form a Confederation ...) maintaining only international relations with Spain that, through natural law, must exist between all nations as human societies inhabiting the same earth, and through special treaties that might be established in the realm of trade.[108]

Extract from "Always Spaniards," *La Lucha de Clases,*
1899:
*In the Basque case, there are no reasons, historical or
otherwise, that might recommend the secession of the
region from Spanish nationality.*

*The Basque provinces have always been Spanish; if
there were a time in which the Basque Country formed
an independent nation, which we flatly deny, this has
been lost in the distance of primitive time, and, after all,
it never had any other basis than that of the independence of Castile, Aragón, and Nafarroa, that is, of princes
and sovereigns.*

*They even enjoyed a privileged position within the
national community. The Basque provinces have
belonged constantly to the Spanish nation for centuries,
without being treated as a conquered country, but on the
contrary being granted exemptions that the other
provinces did not enjoy, a fact that we won't comment
on for we wish these liberties and even greater ones for
all the regions, but that we note only to highlight the
injustice of Bizkaian separatism.*

*A Basque language in obvious retreat and a folklore
condemned to uniformity offer the pretext to claim a distinctive quality with a political calling.*

*This has no foundation as Bizkaian separatism,
which can't think of itself in terms such as the pride of
the country's wealth, but only the desire for notoriety by
four guys and the madness of four idiots.*[109]

13 · Fin-de-siècle Hegoalde
From the first transition to the first dictatorship

B Y THE LATE 1890s, a tripartite political system
existed in Hegoalde that, as we have seen, increasingly concerned itself with defining people's national
identity. We will now examine the fortunes of Basque
nationalism in more detail from the last decade of the
nineteenth century through the military dictatorship of
General Miguel Primo de Rivera, ending in 1930.

During the first two decades of the twentieth century,
Restoration Spain disintegrated, revealing many of the
inherent weaknesses of the modern Spanish state. This
was also a crucial moment in the history of Basque
nationalism, for while the Euzko Alderdi Jeltzalea-Partido Nacionalista Vasco (EAJ-PNV; Basque Nationalist
Party), formally founded in 1897 but in de facto effect
since 1895, would firmly establish itself as a rising political force in Hegoalde, it experienced many of the same
tensions and contradictions that were plaguing the
system it theoretically sought to replace. We might say,
then, that at the very moment Basque nationalism consolidated as a political force, it also revealed a basic
weakness, namely, a difference of opinion over the
essential goal of the movement—autonomy within a different kind of Spanish state or outright independence.

THE BASQUE NATIONALIST PROGRAM, 1893–1903
Basque nationalism was born in a time and place—Bilbo
(Bilbao) of the early 1890s—marked by the rising dual
phenomena of Spanish liberalism and socialism. Under
Sabino de Arana y Goiri's guidance, Basque nationalism
developed through three stages before its leader's pre-
mature death in 1903: Between 1893 and 1898, the
movement passed through its most dynamic and, for

The seafront casino at Miarritze, late nineteenth century. Europe's high society could look out on to the Bay of Biscay for inspiration and luck.
Illustration by permission of Koldo Mitxelena Kulturunea archives.

some, most radical phase (in the sense of its declaredly separatist stance). From 1898 to 1902, it adopted a more pragmatic stance following the integration into its ranks of the foralist *euskalerriacos* led by Ramón de la Sota y Llano. Finally, in 1902–03, during the remaining months of his life, Arana began to conceptualize nonseparatist autonomist nationalism.

1893–98. In 1894, Arana founded a private society, Euskaldun Batzokia (Basque Center), as a meeting place for the followers he had already attracted through *Bizkaitarra* (The Bizkaian), the weekly broadsheet he had begun publishing the previous year. Arana controlled all aspects of this nationalist agitation, acting out of a messianic need to convince his Bizkaian compatriots of the need to rediscover their own past and culture. His society was open only to those with Basque last names, and by 1895 it counted 120 members, mostly young men between twenty and thirty-five years of age. In July 1895, the society created the Bizkai Buru Batzar (Bizkaian Governing Committee), which in effect served as an embryonic political party that was soon known as the Basque Nationalist Party, whose eventual aim was the creation of an independent confederation of Basque states known as Euzkadi. That these organizations were explicitly political was recognized by Bizkaia's civil governor, who quickly closed down the Euskaldun Batzokia and the Bizkai Buru Batzar, before the EAJ-PNV had even been formally created, as "a threat to the Spanish nation." Who, exactly, constituted this threat? Just over a hundred young males principally drawn, like the Arana brothers, from Bilbo's preindustrial middle classes.

Basque nationalism was specifically Bizkaian until 1897, when Arana began to conceive of its transcendence among the other Basque provinces. When the original members of the Euskaldun Batzokia and the Bizkai Buru Batzar regrouped in 1897, then, it was as the *Basque* (rather than Bizkaian) Nationalist Party.

1898–1902. Despite the Spanish state's evaluation of Arana's nationalist group as a threat to its existence, this was hardly the case. Through 1898, Arana mustered, at

best, a couple of hundred followers. When all was said
and done, his utopian goals could not translate into
electoral success. However, in 1898, the *euskalerriaco*
group split between Spanish and Basque nationalists as
a result of changing economic circumstances, which
divided the Bilbo bourgeoisie into those elements
favored by Madrid's economic protectionism (or
Spanish economic nationalism), such as the iron and
steel interests, and those dominated by the economic
oligarchy, such as the shipping industry. Led by Sota,
the Basque nationalist element joined the ranks of
Arana's followers under the provision that they
would have some say in the ideological evolution of the
EAJ-PNV.

FROM THIS moment on, Basque nationalism took on
a dual identity that blended the mystical but
engaging rhetoric of Arana with the pragmatism of Sota.
As a consequence, in the municipal elections of 1899,
five EAJ-PNV candidates were elected to Bilbo's eighteen-
member city council. It was a spectacular success for
such a recently formed party, and confirmed the great
(lasting) strength of the EAJ-PNV: its capacity to capture
a cross-social vote. Where liberalism relied for its political strength on upper-class power and influence, and
socialism on the mass vote of the industrial proletariat,
Basque nationalism appealed to a broad section of
society. Although rooted in the preindustrial and marginalized middle classes, it increasingly attracted the
Basque working classes as well as some members of the
upper-class establishment. This was cultivated by Arana,
who gradually moved toward a more modern political
ideology embracing capitalism after 1898 (in opposition
to many of his early followers, including his brother
Luis).

At the same time, these were the years of Spanish imperial defeat, and the domestic repercussions for "unpatriotic" elements were harsh. Basque nationalists were increasingly subject to acts of violence by mobs of Spanish patriots, as well as being persecuted "officially" through summary fines, closures (the Euskaldun Batzokia was forcibly closed down twice more, in 1899 and 1902), and incarcerations.

1902–03. By 1902, although he had suffered much personally in the process, Arana observed that great progress had been made through departing from the more extreme utopian goals of his earliest ideological formations. As such, from a prison cell and following a combination of the logic of his own personal conversion to capitalism and the pragmatic influence of Sota, he introduced what came to be known as the *españolista* (Hispanicist) evolution, whereby he renounced claims to Basque independence, seeing a more ready solution to his original quest in the gaining of a substantial (regionalist as opposed to nationalist) autonomy. His plans to replace the EAJ-PNV with a new political party, La Liga de Vascos Españolistas (Hispanicist Basque League), went unrealized, however, for he died of Addison's disease the following year.

MAURA AND A NEW VARIANT OF SPANISH NATIONALISM

WITH THE waning of the early Restoration system after 1898, the Spanish state stumbled through a period of uncertainty until Antonio Maura assumed a definitive leading role (a position previously occupied by Antonio Cánovas de Castillo) in 1906. Maura recognized the volatile nature of the Spanish political culture he had inherited and pursued a pragmatic program

Basque nationalist rally, Sukarrieta, Bizkaia, 1917.
Basque meteorogical conditions made umbrellas a nec-
essary component of public demonstrations.
By permission of Editorial Iparaguirre, S.A. archives.

aimed at salvaging the Restoration system. Maura's
objectives were threefold: to maintain the hegemonic
interests of the Spanish establishment through the creation of a modern political party; to eradicate the system
of *caciquismo*, which, although supporting establishment interests, had ultimately undermined Restoration
Spain's authority; and finally, to establish a regional
policy that recognized the value of decentralizing (to
some degree) the administrative system. This was, however, still Spanish nationalism. Maura's basic aim was
the preservation of the Restoration system as the best
guarantor of establishment interests in the country.

ULTIMATELY, this more pragmatic philosophy coincided with the moderation of both the Spanish
socialist movement after 1910 (from which time it opted
in favor of a strictly *evolutionary* rather than *revolutionary* program and allied itself with more moderate
republican factions) and the Basque nationalists during
the later years of Restoration Spain. However, Maura's
conciliatory moves toward Basque nationalism (such as
his support for the Basque nationalist Gregorio de Ibar-
reche's candidacy for mayor of Bilbo) found disfavor
with the Partido Conservador de Vizcaya (Conservative
Party of Bizkaia), led by Fernando Ybarra and created in
1909, and the Partido Liberal de Vizcaya (Liberal Party of
Bizkaia), led by Gregorio Balparda and established in
1910. Both parties dedicated their political programs to
an outright offensive against Basque nationalism.

1903–23. Two months before his death in November
1903, Arana had named Ángel de Zabala (known as Kon-
daño) as his successor to lead the EAJ-PNV. Zabala had
opposed Arana's final evolution toward regionalism
and spent the initial years of his leadership attempting
to hold together the two factions of the party: the

moderates (in the main, descendants of the *euskalerri-acos*), whose program rested on an ambiguous autonomous stance, and the radicals (in the main, descendants of the original members of the Euskaldun Batzokia), who maintained a clearly defined separatist line. It was a struggle that would mark the party through the twentieth century, and one that plagued several other ethnonationalist movements throughout Europe, most notably in Ireland. Between 1903 and 1908, the two factions struggled for control of party policy. In 1906, the EAJ-PNV. ratified its original principles in favor of a conservative and religious political platform. Gradually, however, the moderate (and lay) faction took control, although the radicals retained important figureheads, such as Zabala and Luis Arana (head of the Bizkaian section of the party since 1908), within the party structure. In a curious dichotomy, while the moderates controlled much of the quotidian organization of the party, the radicals controlled the leadership.

D ESPITE these differences, the party grew in strength during the first two decades of the twentieth century, in particular extending its power base outside Bilbo, first to provincial Bizkaia and thereafter to rural Gipuzkoa. Increasingly after 1910, due to a modest growth in the Basque agricultural sector, many leaseholding *baserritarrak* were able to purchase their farmsteads, which then allowed them to reap the profits from their dairy and garden produce. This new-found financial independence released the Basque peasantry from their economic (and therefore political) obligations to predominantly Carlist and traditionalist landlords and *jauntxos*. As a consequence, the rural vote in Bizkaia and Gipuzkoa gradually shifted toward Basque nationalism. In their attempts to extend the electoral base, the Basque nationalist leadership changed the name of the

EAJ-PNV. to Comunión Nacionalista Vasca (CNV; Basque Nationalist Communion) in 1916 as a means of neutralizing the overtly political aspirations of Basque nationalism.

The CNV was the party of the moderate faction, favoring less the religious and traditionalist orthodoxy of Arana and more the pragmatic platform of autonomy. While it made several inroads into Gipuzkoa during the period between 1916 and 1923, it was less successful in Nafarroa and Araba. The majority of Nafarroa's inhabitants retained an affinity with Carlism that Basque nationalism found more difficult to break than that of Bizkaia or Gipuzkoa. Only a small percentage of Nafarroan Carlists switched to Basque nationalism, whereas nontraditionalist sectors of the population—predominantly the middle classes of Iruñea (Pamplona)—increasingly identified with Maura's regionalist-sensitive Spanish nationalism. Araba, with two-thirds of its population still engaged in the agricultural sector, remained (like Nafarroa) a bastion of traditionalism. The principal political force in the province through this period was La Communion Tradicionalista (Traditionalist Communion), as it had been since the beginning of the Restoration system in 1876, with Basque nationalism registering gains, however minimal, in Gasteiz (Vitoria) and Laudio (Llodio), a northern Araban industrial town within the Bizkaian economic orbit.

DESPITE a notable economic resurgence as a consequence of Spain's neutrality in World War I, the problems of Restoration Spain came to a head during the years 1916 and 1917. The government, led by Maura, faced challenges from the military, from the continued direct political action of anarchism, and regionally from Catalunya and Hegoalde. This coincided with the first real electoral impact of the Basque nationalists. Their electoral success was so great, in fact, that in July 1917 the provincial governments of Araba, Bizkaia, and Gipuzkoa agreed to pressure Madrid into ceding autonomy as a recognition of the provinces' previous foral status. (Nafarroa remained absent from the initiative.) This aroused the wrath of the two Basque-founded Spanish nationalist parties, even more than that of Maura. Indeed, his response was more pragmatic. In 1918, he invited into a government coalition representatives of the principal Catalan regionalist party, the Lliga Catalana (Catalan League), thereby deflecting their hostility to central authority and paralyzing the CNV, for without the support of the Catalan party, the CNV could not pursue its autonomist agenda. The party thus settled into a policy of accommodation and consolidation.

THIS DID not please the more radical (and predominantly younger) members of the party. In 1920, several members left, forming a revised version of Arana's original organization two years later. The new party, which adopted the name of the original Basque nationalist party, EAJ-PNV, included among its ranks Luis Arana, Eli Gallastegui (the most charismatic of the young Basque nationalists), known as Gudari, and the former party leader Zabala. Faithful to Aranist ideology, the revamped EAJ / PNV claimed as its principal political demand the independence of Euskal Herria, as opposed to the autonomist stance of the CNV, but departed from Aranist orthodoxy in creating a women's group, Emakume Abertzale Batza (Women's Nationalist Association), an organization that steadily grew thereafter.

In 1923, the EAJ-PNV. worked with other groups in the Spanish state to form the Triple Alliance, a pact between Basque, Catalan, and Galician political groups aimed at promoting a heady ideal of post–World War I Europe:

Euskaldunon Egunkaria, the only all-Basque language newspaper circulating throughout Euskal Herria in the twenty-first century.

the "principle of nations." This was an idea advocated
by United States president Woodrow Wilson during the
Paris Peace Conference of 1918–20, accord-ing to which
democracies based on the nationality principle—that is,
a principle that recognized in some meaningful way distinct national or ethnic differences—were more likely to
preserve the peace in the war-torn continent. Thus,
argued the American president, if the national aspirations of the subject peoples in Europe were granted,
there would be less reason for people to engage in violent conflict. Two days after the signing of the Triple
Alliance pact by Basque, Catalan, and Galician nationalists in 1923, however, Primo de Rivera led a military
coup in Barcelona to maintain another principle of
nationality: that of Spain, one and indivisible.

THE DICTATORSHIP OF PRIMO DE RIVERA, 1923–30
That the military coup led by Primo de Rivera shocked
few people within the country at the time tells us much
about the failure of Spain's first transition state. After
claiming the leadership, Primo de Rivera abolished all
political parties, and in 1924 attempted to create a
Spanish variant of Benito Mussolini's fascist Italy by
forming a statewide movement, La Unión Patriótica
(Patriotic Union). The dictatorship, which paled in comparison to Francisco Franco's later incarnation in terms
of ferocity, tolerated to some degree the existence of an
autonomist Basque nationalism (allowing the publication of cultural works, for example), but it severely
repressed the separatist Basque nationalists, impris-
oning and exiling many.

THE DICTATORSHIP was an authoritarian response to
the severe social and political problems generated
by the failure of the Restoration system, and the new
regime included many members of the Restoration elite

(drawn most obviously from the former regime's more conservative sectors). Primo de Rivera's rule did not, however, solve the problem of modern Spain. With a continuously declining economy causing general dissatisfaction, and with Primo de Rivera himself progressively alienating his political allies, the dictator was a lonely figure by the end of the 1920s. In a relatively short space of time (compared to the decline of Restoration Spain), Spain's first dictatorship proved that traditionalist authoritarianism was not the answer to the country's ills. In 1930, Primo de Rivera abdicated from power, followed by the Spanish king Alfonso XIII one year later, leaving Spain to follow yet another path: that of the Second Republic.

PROSCRIBED in the political sphere, Basque nationalist activity moved into the cultural realm during Primo de Rivera's dictatorship. A precedent for Basque nationalist cultural activity had been established with the creation of two learned societies in 1918: Euskaltzaindia (Academy of the Basque language) and Eusko-Ikaskuntza (Society of Basque Studies). (The implications of these organizations will be discussed in greater detail in Chapter 16.) Cultural activity also assumed more popular forms, such as performances by touring music and dance groups, which traversed the four provinces of Hegoalde promoting traditional cultural endeavors. The aim, of course, was a kind of cultural renaissance among Basques, or a raising of national consciousness. That much of this activity revolved around inventing traditions reflected the precedent (namely, the state-building process) that the cultural activists saw around them. Of the many organizations to flourish during this period, perhaps the most dynamic was the Mendigoizaleak (Mountaineers), which had originally formed the nucleus of the EAJ-PNV's youth wing (created in 1908) and therefore also played a leading role in refounding the party in 1922. Reincarnated as a recreational organization during the dictatorship, the group sponsored hikes to remote mountain summits, where, free from state supervision, members delighted in shouting Basque nationalist slogans and planting the *ikurriña* (Basque national flag). Cultural activity such as this, building on the gains that Basque nationalism had already made prior to Primo de Rivera's coup, would ultimately lead to increased support for the movement.

The Restoration system was built on the twin foundations of placating dominant socio-cultural and politico-economic interest groups at the expense of constructing democratic values and reworking Spain's social problems (as well as resolving past ones). The democratic nature of liberal Spain was an illusion. In reality, the state functioned through a carefully controlled system of patronage and influence. The brooding specter of Carlism—the "dangerous" and "threatening" enemy of the Restoration system—represented Spain's forgotten past, which, as many twentieth-century Spanish regimes were to discover (not necessarily in relation to Carlism, but certainly to unresolved problems of a historical nature), one can push aside but never obliterate the past.

DURING THE first three decades of the twentieth century, Basque nationalism—an ideology invented in Bilbo in the early 1890s—expanded the geographical base of its support, but at the same time fragmented into two easily definable factions. On one side were the dominant moderates: those in favor of working within the existing system to pursue a degree of autonomy reflecting (in their opinion) the level of self-rule enjoyed by the Basque provinces under the foral system. On the other side were those loyal to the original radical aim of Arana: outright independence, expressed through an overt anti-Spanish rhetoric. Where this wing departed from Arana's original doctrine was in regard to religion, which played a lesser role in their conception of Basque nationalism.

Lesson thirteen

REQUIRED READING

Cameron J. Watson, "Sacred Earth, Symbolic Blood: A Cultural History of Basque Political Violence," Ph.D. diss. (University of Nevada, Reno, 1996), pp. 202–50.

Stanley G. Payne, *Basque Nationalism* (Reno: University of Nevada Press, 1975), pp. 87–116.

LEARNING OBJECTIVES

1. To trace political developments in Hegoalde from the birth of Basque nationalism through to the dictatorship of Miguel Primo de Rivera.
2. To understand the reasons behind the successful evolution of the Basque Nationalist Party.
3. To account for the fragmentation of Basque nationalism during this period.

WRITTEN LESSON FOR SUBMISSION

1. What, in your opinion, were the principal reasons for the increasing popularity of Basque nationalism between 1903 and 1923?
2. What, if any, was the common ground between the two wings of Basque nationalism? Do you think there were justifiable grounds for believing that the two factions could ever be reconciled? Explain your answer.

14 · Iparralde, 1870–1914
The Third Republic and the Gallicization of France (I)

IN IPARRALDE during the period between the late nineteenth and early twentieth centuries, the principal opposition to French state authority was clerical. Indeed, at a more general level, church-state relations defined the struggle to create modern France. By deflecting popular identity away from that of the Church, the French state gradually succeeded in creating compliant French citizens out of the Basque peasantry. Without question, the state was aided in its mission by the brutal experience of World War I. For Rogers Brubaker, French nationalism was the product of war: "On September 20, 1792, at Valmy, under fire from the Prussian infantry ... the ragtag French army held its ground to the cry of 'Vive la Nation!' ... [T]he episode has come to symbolize the transformation of war through the appeal to the nation in arms."[110] As a consequence, "from 1792 on ... and justified by the doctrine of the *patrie en danger*,' elements of a xenophobic nationalism at home and an expansionist, aggressive, nationalism abroad, originally missionary and crusading, later imperialist and triumphalist,"[111] emerged in tandem with the rise of the French state. It was a long process, but between the violence of 1792–93 and that of 1914–18, France forged its citizenry.

In this and the following chapter, we will explore the fortunes of Iparralde in a broad historical sweep from 1870 through to 1945. It was an era during which, we might argue, modern France really came of age; consequently, for the first time in their history, the majority of Basques in Iparralde began to think of themselves as French citizens. This moment thus marks the successful *Gallicization* of the French state—in other words, the successful implanting of monocultural French (Gallic) values in the population. If one general question underlies this period of Basque history, it is that of the exact reasons behind this transformation of identity. In order to explain the change, we first need to examine the structure and key moments of the Third Republic in France, the emergence of French nationalism, the effects of war on Iparralde, and the extent to which Basque nationalism filtered into the three northern Basque provinces.

THE MAKING OF THE THIRD REPUBLIC
The Third Republic was more a product of chance than of design. Under Napoleon III, the French empire had engaged in a disastrous war with Prussia in 1870–71 that had left the empire destroyed, and the subsequent abdication of the emperor forced the country into a makeshift constitutional solution. The immediate aim of the ruling classes in 1871, however, was to maintain their former power. This indeed was the basis, together with a need to negotiate peace with Prussia, upon which a newly convened National Assembly met at Bordeaux in 1871. The price of the peace negotiated by the National Assembly was great: The French state lost the predominantly ethnically German provinces of Alsace and Lorraine, taken two hundred years previously by Louis XIV. This geographical loss would prove to be the single most crucial event in defining French foreign policy thereafter, a policy based fairly evidently on the notion of *revanche* (revenge) against the newly created German state.

DOMESTICALLY, the loss of Alsace and Lorraine reinforced an even greater sense among the ruling classes that the geographical integrity of the state should remain paramount. Centralization and

The Oldargi Theater Company performing in Euskara in the 1920s. For Basque nationalism, culture was a substitute for formal politics during the dictatorship of Primo de Rivera.
By permission of Abertzaletasunaren Agiritegia. Sabino Arana Kultur Elkargoa archives.

uniformity thus became more important than ever. Although a not inconsiderable lobby, divided between different candidates, pressured the National Assembly to reinstate a monarchy, the general belief among the political elite was that this was not in the best interest of the state. Some monarchists were considered too close to the Church (viewed increasingly as an enemy of

French state integrity) and others as potentially too
favorable toward the reinstatement of provincial liberties—in other words, toward decentralization. For the
Paris-based political elite, both these connections were
unacceptable. Therefore, through the early 1870s the
National Assembly approved a series of laws that set up
a new republic (a constitution was never written). The
structure of the governing body that was established was
intensely conservative. The President, elected for a
seven-year term of office and eligible for re-election
thereafter, enjoyed extensive personal power, including
the right (with the compliance of the Senate—a bastion
of conservative and even monarchist power) to dissolve
the elected Chamber of Deputies.

The National Assembly was dissolved in 1875, and in
1876 the first general elections were held. However, the
unexpected result, a clear majority for republican interests in the Chamber of Deputies, went against the
wishes of the conservative powerbrokers, and a constitutional crisis ensued. Elections were held again in 1877,
and thereafter the French state embarked on a different
path from that originally envisaged by the political elite.

ACCORDING TO Alfred Cobban, "the election of 1877
can be regarded as the real foundation of the Third
Republic. It was not only a political turning point, it was
a more decisive social revolution than anything that had
occurred in 1830, 1848, or 1871. It was the point at
which rural France repudiated the authority of the notables ... whose influence had kept the great rural masses
of France steadily on the side of social conservatism
whatever political changes might come about."[112]

The election resulted in an overwhelming victory for
the republican lobby, and this meant that the French
ruling classes could no longer hope to re-create *their*

system—Napoleon III's empire—under the mask of a republic.

THE GALLICIZATION OF FRANCE, 1877–1914

From 1877 on, political power in Paris balanced between the Chamber of Deputies on one side and the President and the Senate on the other. Politics in the nascent republic became a contest between the Left and the Right, as both factions were fairly evenly divided. Initially, however, there was general agreement between the two factions on the need to strengthen the state after the turmoil of the last years of the empire and the upheaval of war and defeat. As a consequence of this consensus, it was from the Chamber of Deputies (where the Left and the Right interacted on a regular basis) that modern republican France—indeed, *modern France*—emerged.

Between 1877 and 1881, many of the cultural symbols of present-day France were ratified by the Chamber of Deputies. For example, "La Marseillaise" became France's national anthem and July 14 the national day. Symbols were important for the hearts of the citizenry, but only through education could the state capture their minds, so thereafter the principal domestic focus of the Third Republic became education.

As JAMES E. JACOB observes, "the bulk of France's efforts at nation-building in the early Third Republic took the form of remedial legislation in the fields of education, transportation, church-state relations, and military conscription. Taken together, these policy initiatives represented a deliberate attempt by the state to penetrate a rural society which was, at best, ignorant of the republican state and, at worst, abidingly hostile toward it."[113]

By the 1890s, the monarchists had ceased to be an important political force. Only among certain sectors of the armed forces and the Church did they still enjoy any substantial affiliation. Most conservatives had gravitated toward moderate republicanism during the period. There was cause for optimism among the leaders of the republic, for it now seemed that their political culture was at last making ground. Following the new republic's initial period of consolidation, between the mid-1870s and the mid-1890s, the state then went on the domestic offensive. This offensive involved integrating the most remote rural sectors of the population into the new state, principally through military service and education.

THUS, IN the space of a generation, between the last decade of the nineteenth century and the eve of World War I, observes Herman Lebovics, there was fashioned "an enduring conservative republic ruled by an elite held together in a net made from trade-offs and standoffs among growers and industrialists, bankers and state fiscal offices, free traders and protectionists, clericals and republicans, regional elites and national, that is, Parisian, ones."[114]

Through the early years of the Third Republic, France remained an overwhelmingly rural and socially conservative state. French agriculture even enjoyed a boom during the first decade of the twentieth century that maintained the predominance of the rural economy and kept wider industrial development to a relatively modest scale. We might think of the French state at this time as a kind of rural republic.[115] Republican leaders viewed the installation of state values at the rural level as the key to the success of their regime, and between the late 1890s and the coming of war in 1914 rural integration would be the dominant domestic policy. From 1889, for example, all physically able young French men were required to do military service. Through conscription, the state actively sought to foster a sense of patriotic duty to the French nation; indeed, the armed forces were considered in many ways as "the school of the nation." Rural integration was most evident in the realm of education, where, as we have mentioned, much of the ideology of modern France was truly created.

As EUGEN WEBER states, "the school, notably the village school, compulsory and free, has been credited with the ultimate acculturation process that made the French people French—finally civilized them, as many nineteenth-century educators liked to say."[116]

Through education, the Third Republic would instill the virtues of citizenship as a form of national allegiance to the French state, though this was not necessarily the openly stated purpose of republican educators at the time. This would be achieved by making education more accessible, useful, and even dynamic, while effectively masking the true intentions of educational reform. Between 1881 and 1886, under legislation instituted by Jules Ferry, free, compulsory, and lay elementary education was introduced in the French state, and yet immediate results were not forthcoming. As Weber argues, the continuing high rate of illiteracy in the late-nineteenth-century French state came, as much as anything else, from the fact that so many people still did not speak French.[117] Only by the turn of the century did the majority of the Third Republic's adult population know French, and the linguistic transformation was therefore slow until World War I.

Ferry's reforms, coupled with the separation of church and state in 1903, which led to a decree stipulating that French should be the only language allowed in the teaching of catechism (the penalty being the suspension

The new station at Donibane-Garazi, Nafarroa Beherea, 1898. Modern communications brought improved mobility and the idea of France to rural Iparralde. French therefore became the language of modernity and opportunity.
By permission of the "Les Amis de la Vieille Navarre" Association archives.

---

of government stipends), laid the basis for more lasting change, however. Inside the classroom, the use of French was enforced through carrot and stick.

FRENCH WAS presented as the language of modernity and civilization, as opposed to barbarous and tribal regional languages like Basque and Breton. Any child caught speaking an uncivilized language was punished by having to display tokens of shame,[118] a tactic also employed by the Spanish state both at the time and through the twentieth century. Importantly also, again as Weber notes, girls were encouraged to go through the educational process. Thus as mothers—the primary transmitters of language to children—they would increasingly adopt French as opposed to their own language of origin. State education was also made increasingly useful, particularly as the first step on the ladder to a safe and remunerative career in the growing civil service of the Third Republic. Through a combination of means, then, the educational system acculturated its pupils with republican and French values. In Weber's opinion, "the greatest function of the modern school" was "to teach not so much useful skills as a patriotism beyond the limits naturally acknowledged by its charges"[119]—so much so, in fact, that "a vast program of indoctrination was plainly called for to persuade people that the fatherland extended beyond its evident limits to something vast and intangible called France."[120]

By 1914, THE Third Republic had, in many ways against all odds, survived and even thrived. A strong and effective framework for creating a sense of French national identity had been established, and it was beginning to show clear and positive results for its makers. However, the final assault on the *other* identities of modern France would come, ultimately, from an unexpected source: total war. With the coming of World War I, modern France would, like other countries in Europe, change forever. Thereafter, the French state began to see the concrete effects of the policies introduced during the republic's early years. After 1918, and for the first time in its history, the majority of the inhabitants of the French state began to think of themselves as French. Before looking at more specific events in Iparralde, however, let us first consider how the idea of

French national identity was defined during the early years of the Third Republic.

FRENCH NATIONALISM

One of the earliest thinkers to form a theory about nationalism was a distinguished nineteenth-century Hebrew scholar from Brittany, Ernest Renan. It is surely no coincidence that he was moved to comment on the meaning of nationhood during the early years of the Third Republic. As a Breton turned Frenchman, Renan wrote at the beginning of a time of intense debate about what it meant to be French. France had recently been defeated in humiliating fashion by a resurgent German nation (and newly proclaimed state), and needed first to define itself before attempting to convert its citizenry to allegiance to the nation. As such, Renan's views tell us much about French nationalism at the end of the nineteenth century.

IN THE LECTURE "Qu'est-ce qu'une nation?" ("What is a Nation?"), delivered at the prestigious Sorbonne university in Paris in 1882, Renan observed that "the wish of nations" was "the sole legitimate criteria" for establishing nationhood.[121] Renan therefore established *collective will* as the basic criterion for a sense of national identity, not race or language, for example. This was tremendously important in a French state effectively inventing itself along the same principle. Renan urged France to make itself by fostering a notion of collective will through integrating policies such as conscription and education. However, as Homi K. Bhabha observes, "Renan's will is itself the site of a strange forgetting of the history of the nation's past: the violence involved in establishing the nation's writ. It is this forgetting—a minus in the origin—that constitutes the *beginning* of the nation's narrative."[122] In the

"To our sons that died in the war. The village of Biriatu." Plaque dedicated to the fallen soldiers in both World Wars of a small town in Lapurdi. The loss of life was greater in World War I, and therefore more dramatic for the village, because local men were mostly posted to the same battalion. Recognizing the social and demographic devastation this caused, the policy was reversed in World War II. The tremendous casualties suffered in the war were given "meaning" by dedicating the loss to the defence and building of the French nation.
Photo by the author.

narrative of French national identity, born in modern times during the Third Republic, France was effectively created through a conscious forgetting, or selective remembering, of its past.

A more extreme variant of French nationalism emerged during the Third Republic in the guise of a movement known as Action Française (French Action), created in 1898 and led by Charles Maurras. Maurras blended anti-Semitism with romanticist ruralism, religious mysticism, and monarchist sympathies to promote a vision of Frenchness based on authoritarian and racist values. That Maurras developed a racial dimension to French nationalism reveals the problematic issue of identity in the Third Republic. After 1870, for example, the French state assimilated over 100,000 Algerian Jews and thereafter received growing numbers of immigrants, most of them from within Europe. The Dreyfus case of 1894 to 1900 (during which an Alsatian Jewish officer in the French army was wrongly accused of spying for Germany) split the country and provided the Third Republic with its own fin-de-siècle malaise. Attracting the support of a considerable sector of the conservative middle classes, Maurras fostered a sense of nationalism against *bad* Frenchmen and against the parliamentary values of the Third Republic. This was an antiliberal *integral* nationalism rallying supporters to the call of establishing a strong and authoritarian French state (similar, in many ways, to the Castilian romanticism of the most authoritarian variants of Spanish nationalism during the same period).

ACCORDING to Lebovics, Maurras's "imagined France was unchanging. Regimes might come and go, but the essential *pays* would persist—even under political systems that for the moment falsified the true nature of the historical destiny that was France."[123] The movement gathered a great deal of momentum prior to the outbreak of war, but thereafter most French citizens had an external enemy on whom to concentrate. However, the legacy of Action Française would be felt through the twentieth century in the most extreme variants of French nationalism.

IPARRALDE

Right-wing parties won thirty of the forty-three general elections held in Iparralde between 1877 and 1932. Like their French counterparts, conservatives in Iparralde gradually transformed from monarchists into moderate republicans during this time. As had been the case through most of the nineteenth century, the politics of Iparralde continued to be controlled by rural notables, including a number of returning emigrants of humble peasant origin who had made sufficient money to establish themselves economically and therefore politically. The religious affiliation of Basque society similarly continued to be a defining factor in the politics of Iparralde: Throughout the first half of the republic's life, it acted as a constant barrier to creating a sense of *Frenchness*, particularly among the rural peasantry. Between 1877 and 1914, Iparralde remained politically opposed to practically all central government policy, from its centralization and educational policies to the separation of church and state. It eventually took a conscious effort by French administrators to disassociate Basque culture from the protective harness of the Church, coupled with the unexpectedly devastating effects of war, to truly make the Basques of Iparralde Frenchmen.

AS PREVIOUSLY mentioned, the Third Republic was more interested in consolidating its central power base than in taking its ideology to the provinces (despite the modest though not inconsiderable efforts described by Sudhir Hazareesingh[124]) between the mid-1870s and the mid-1890s. By the turn of the century, however, and as part of the general effort to create France, the state saw its primary task as extinguishing what it considered regional dialects. In Iparralde, this implied some degree of confrontation with the Church, for it was through religious instruction that the Basque language was effectively transmitted in a public way (as opposed to private use in the family household).

THE TURNING point came in the form of a state decree of 1903, declaring that French would be the only language allowed in the teaching of catechism. It was an open attack on the power of the rural Basque clergy, a corpus that had more than once in its history responded to such decisions with force. Yet this was not the response in 1903: As would occur later in the century in Hegoalde, a division within the Church between hierarchical and grass-roots sectors prevented the latter from fighting the decree. Without effective political mobilization on the part of the clergy, there was little opposition to the state, as the peasantry had traditionally looked to their priests for leadership in such matters. Building on this initial success, Paris introduced legislation separating church and state in 1904. Religious schools were closed and some clerical orders forced into exile.

In a relatively short space of time, then, Basque political culture changed dramatically. In Jacob's words, "much of the rural Basque population descended into a resolutely apolitical Catholicism from which they were reluctant to stir."[125] While Basque nationalism was gathering momentum in Hegoalde during the first two decades of the twentieth century, it never gained a foothold in Iparralde. Despite some modest contacts between the two Basque regions, a nationalist infra-

structure was never formally created at the time. Ultimately, communications between Hegoalde and Iparralde remained minimal, as is suggested by the fact that
the nationalist journals *Bizkaitarra* and *Baserritarra*
(both of which were produced in Bilbo) had only two
and five subscribers respectively in the north.[126]

From relatively haphazard beginnings, the Third
Republic had by 1914 survived longer than any of its
post-Revolutionary predecessors. During this time, from
1877 to 1914, the modern French state began to assume
a recognizable shape. At the root of this development
was a French nationalism based on civic, secular, and
assimilationist ideals. In spite of the emergence of a
more extreme variant, French state nationalism essentially relied on a political and inclusive sense of the
nation, but at a price—namely, the relinquishing of all
former national identities. Without doubt, this was the
historical moment that witnessed the greatest spread of
the French language. The expansion of railroads
together with the vast improvement of roadways encouraged both human movement and the subsequent slow
but increasingly important dissemination of information through French-language newspapers (parallel to
rises in literacy rates in the "national" language). By
1914, these developments and the cultivation of an
external threat (Germany) on the part of successive
French administrations had created a previously absent
sense of unity among the inhabitants of the French
state.

It was during this early period from 1877 to 1914 that
the inhabitants of Iparralde first began to relinquish an
identity based on family, locale, church, and region for
one based on state. Jacob captures the process in his
description of an "apolitical" and "reluctant" Basque
populace[127]; in many ways, a specifically Basque

The Coq Gaulois (Gallic Rooster), symbol of France
since the 1830s and subsequently displayed on coins,
stamps and official seals. The play on words of this
symbol comes from the Latin term gallus, meaning both
"rooster" and "Gaul". Gaul was a geographic region
inhabited by Celtic tribes during Roman times and
encompassing present-day France, Belgium, Luxem-
bourg and Germany west of the Rhine. The symbolism
therefore relates to a non-French-speaking area greater
than that of the French state itself but reality is only
moderately important in the invention of tradition.
Illustration from Jim Harter (ed): Animals.

---

identity in Iparralde began to slip into hibernation in the decade before World War I. The full effects of war would soon speed up this decline. In the next chapter, we will see how this took place.

Lesson fourteen

Note: Chapters 14 and 15 should be considered jointly. The reading lists and learning objectives that appear below and the written assignment in Lesson 15 all refer to the material covered in both Chapters 14 and 15.

REQUIRED READING (FOR CHAPTERS 14 AND 15)
Eugen Weber, *Peasants into Frenchmen: The Modernization of Rural France, 1870–1914* (Palo Alto: Stanford University Press, 1976), pp. 303–38 and 471–96.
James E. Jacob, *Hills of Conflict: Basque Nationalism in France* (Reno, Las Vegas, and London: University of Nevada Press, 1994), pp. 39–128.
Herman Lebovics, "Creating the Authentic France: Struggles Over French Identity in the First Half of the Twentieth Century," in John R. Gillis, ed., *Commemorations: The Politics of National Identity* (Princeton: Princeton University Press, 1994), pp. 239–57.

SUGGESTED READING (FOR CHAPTERS 14 AND 15)
Sudhir Hazareesingh, "The Société d'Instruction Républicaine and the Propagation of Civic Republicanism in Provincial and Rural France, 1870–1877," *The Journal of Modern History* 71, no. 2 (June 1999), pp. 271–307.
Ernest Renan, "What is a Nation?" in Homi K. Bhabha, ed., *Nation and Narration* (London and New York: Routledge, 1990), pp. 8–22.

LEARNING OBJECTIVES (FOR CHAPTERS 14 AND 15)
1. To examine the political, social, and cultural changes that took place in the French state between 1870 and 1945.
2. To understand the nature of the Third Republic and its attempts to impose republican values in Iparralde.
3. To examine the extent to which Basques retained a separate sense of identity from that of the French state.
4. To examine the impact of Basque nationalism in Iparralde.

15 · Iparralde, 1914–45
The Third Republic and the Gallicization of France (II)

THE HISTORY of Iparralde between 1914 and 1945 is dominated, not surprisingly, by war. Warfare and occupation were not new to the region, but the events of the twentieth century—the "most terrible century in Western history," as Isaiah Berlin described it[128]—took human destructiveness to new depths.

Weber observes: "Like the Great Revolution in peasant parlance, the Great War became a symbolic dividing line between what once was and what is. ... [B]y 1919 the old customs were no longer part of people's lives. Some were restored to their prewar prominence, but many were quietly forgotten."[129]

During this same period, the Third Republic began its slow decline. Ravaged by the effects of World War I, the post-1914 French state displayed none of the consolidating momentum it had generated in the fin-de-siècle period as it drifted slowly but inexorably into decline. Ironically, at the very moment it had created a solid French national identity, the republic began to implode from social and political divisions within its society. These divisions would lead to a fragmentation that would mark the French state even during World War II, when the country was divided between a Nazi-occupied zone and the Vichy puppet regime.

For Iparralde, the interwar period was most noteworthy for the general economic stagnation of its rural interior, the beginnings of a dramatic demographic decline, the consolidation of a conservative political tradition led by an elite that was keen to promote a monocultural French national identity, and the first stirrings of a specifically politico-cultural Basque nationalist movement.

WORLD WAR I

The first remarkable feature of the Great War, as it was commonly referred to at the time, was the response of Europe's youth to the call-to-arms. For at least a generation, most of western Europe had been increasingly plagued by social and political divisions generated by the emergence of an industrial class-based society and the rise of socialism as a very real threat to the political establishment. Yet in 1914, this was forgotten almost overnight as Europe's masses enthusiastically (for the most part) went off to war for their respective nations. This marked a triumph for the state-sponsored nationalism of the nineteenth century and a disaster for those supporters of the international creed of socialism. According to Weber, "for national integration, the war was an immense step forward."[130] In France, socialists sang "La Marseillaise" as Jacobin patriotism was invoked to unite the French citizenry against their German enemies.

YET THE reality of war proved a harsh lesson. Very quickly, the conflict became a defensive war of attrition, with both sides digging in on the principle that whichever of them could successfully absorb the greater number of human losses would eventually win. By 1916, this was more than apparent to the majority of conscripts fighting the war. At the battle of Verdun, between February and April that year, neither Germany nor France could claim an outright victory, and yet 300,000 men had been killed. In one French regiment alone, 1,800 men died out of a total force of 2,000. That same year, the battle of the Somme counted over a million casualties among the British, French, and German troops. Even so, the competing forces continued to drag out the conflict a further two years, until Germany was compelled to sign an armistice in 1918.

Germany was typically portrayed as a threatening, militaristic presence always ready to strike at the heart of Europe in its quest to dominate the continent.
Illustration Carol Belanger Grafton (ed): Humorous Victorian Spot Illustrations.

The "victory" came at a tremendous human cost to the
Third Republic: one and a quarter million military casualties, together with half a million civilian dead or soon
to die, and three-quarters of a million people (both civilians and military personnel) permanently injured.
Indeed, the loss of life among all the combatants of
World War I assumed a scale previously thought impossible.

FRENCH NATIONAL pride was restored at the Paris
Peace Conference of 1918–20 when Alsace and Lorraine were "returned" to the French state, following the
"principle of nationality" put forward by United States
president Woodrow Wilson (see Chapter 13). (The
French refused to vote on the debate over how to apply
the "principle of nationality" to those areas where
"national" minorities existed within larger states, due to
the fact, their representative explained, that the French
state "had no minorities.") Yet the legacy of war would
prove fatal for the republic. Much of the fighting had
taken place on French soil, resulting in a devastated
infrastructure. French war debts, coupled with the costs
(and therefore further debts) of rebuilding the country,
left the Third Republic in dire financial straits.

THE SLOW DECLINE OF THE THIRD REPUBLIC, 1920–39

Throughout most of the 1920s, the French state had to
face the brutal fact that it could no longer take complete
control of its own destiny. In international political
terms, it was impotent to act without the consent of its
wartime ally, Great Britain. Economically, the country
was dominated by the question of where to raise money
to pay for the crippling expenses of the war. This was
addressed through the introduction of an income tax in
1917, together with an international loans system (principally from British and American sources) and wartime

reparations from a vanquished Germany. Bolstered by a devaluation of the French franc, the economy actually began a recovery through the 1920s, but, as elsewhere in Europe, the 1929 Wall Street crash ended the continent's postwar recovery.

THE ECONOMIC depression of the 1930s arrived later in the Third Republic than in other countries in Europe, for the French state, with a smaller industrial base than that of Great Britain or Germany, could fall back on its predominantly agricultural economy to sustain the country's needs. However, when the Depression did arrive, it actually lasted longer—through to the outbreak of war in 1939. This contributed to the failure on the part of the various political factions throughout the 1930s to reach a consensus over how to solve the republic's ills. Politically, postwar France alternated between the Left and the Right, in much the same way it had done before 1914. On the right, a multiplicity of political parties could find no common ground beyond their ambivalence toward social reform and fear of communism, whereas the Left, theoretically in a better electoral position to formulate a politics of consensus, never governed effectively enough to promote more widespread confidence.

By the 1930s, the state was bitterly divided along political lines between the two camps. According to Herman Lebovics, "at the heart of the struggles in France in the 1930s over power in the parliament and in the streets, the class struggles over the division of the national wealth, the demand of workers for dignity, and the failure of the cultured elite to comprehend this new mood in the population lay the intertwined question of who made up the nation and what was the French heritage (*patrimonie*). These struggles of the mid-1930s might usefully be understood as major battles in a cultural war fought over French identity."[131]

In 1936, the first ever socialist government took office in France, with a Popular Front coalition comprising leftist republicans and communists. However, amid increasing international tension caused by the specter of a resurgent, Nazi Germany, the government fell barely a year later, before it was able to carry out many of its planned reforms. The Popular Front managed to form two more governments between this time and 1938, when, on the eve of war, the Radicals (leftist republicans) took office.

THE GREATEST domestic political problem to plague the French state during the interwar period was the failure of successive governments to formulate long-term solutions to what was, in effect, a rapidly changing society. However, in 1939, with the declaration of war for a second time in the space of a generation, the domestic problems of the French state were pushed aside as the Third Republic came to an ignominious end.

IPARRALDE IN THE INTERWAR PERIOD

Although, as has been noted, World War I exacted a terrible human and material cost, it also imparted a sense of unity among its combatants. James E. Jacob observes, "World War I provoked profound and irreversible demographic and psychological changes in rural France, disrupting the harmony and continuity of life for a generation of young Basques, many of whom had never before left their village and the shadow of its steeple. Thrown into units with young Bretons, Auvergnats, and Corsicans, they turned to French out of necessity as a *lingua franca*."[132]

Similarly, Weber notes that during wartime, "ways of speaking, eating, and thinking, which had been

SAINT-JEAN-PIED-DE-PORT — Au cimetière allemand L'inhumation (1914).

German Prisoners of War bury their dead in Donibane-Garazi, Nafarroa Beherea, 1914, as a Basque peasant looks on. Captured German soldiers were shipped to Donibane-Garazi as it was located far from the front line. This brought World War I closer to the inhabitants of the remote Basque province.
By permission of the "Les Amis de la Vieille Navarre" Association archives.

changing rapidly in any event, were thrown together into a blender and made to change faster still."[133] The wartime spirit of unity was therefore consciously cultivated in the postwar era to advance French national identity. November 11, Armistice Day, for example, became a day of national remembrance, and most towns erected memorials to their dead.

The war undoubtedly fostered a sense of French national identity among Basques. It has been estimated that between 6,000 and 7,000 Basques were killed in World War I, or 5 percent of the population of Iparralde. (That said, desertion rates were also high among the Basques, according to Jean Louis Davant.[134]) In the aftermath of war, those soldiers lucky enough to be able to return to their homes and villages increasingly insisted on the need to speak French. Many had seen something of their nation—the industry of the North, for example—and urged the use of French as the key to upward social and economic mobility, especially given the limited financial opportunity offered by agriculture.

DEMOGRAPHICALLY, World War I began a long process of depopulation in Iparralde. "[F]or many rural Basque villages," states Jacob, "the war simply severely reduced two generations of males and, with them, the reproductive capacity of the village."[135] This was coupled with an already established pattern of emigration. It has been calculated that the population of Iparralde decreased by as many as 20,000 inhabitants (roughly 17 percent) between 1911 and 1931.[136] By the early 1930s, more or less one-third of the approximately 100,000 inhabitants of Iparralde lived in urban areas, reflecting one of the increasing trends—namely, the rural-urban shift.

"Continuity" and "cohesion" were the watchwords of postwar Basque society. Iparralde remained a geographically (and therefore socially, culturally, and economically) peripheral region of a centralized French state. As such, when French industrial development did finally pick up some time in the late 1930s, the region was overlooked. In fact, coastal tourism and fishing remained the only industrial activities of any note in Iparralde. (Between 1920 and 1945, the port zone of Donibane-Lohizune [St. Jean-de-Luz] / Ziburu [Ciboure] remained the principal focus of sardine fishing in the French state.) Interior agriculture remained locked into a nineteenth-century mindset—in other words, it was principally a self-sufficient economy with little interest in commercializing agricultural production. Weber concludes, regarding France as a whole, "traditional communities continued to operate in the traditional manner as long as conditions retained their traditional shape: low productivity, market fluctuations beyond the producer's control, a low rate of savings, little surplus."[137]

As WE HAVE seen, Basque political culture remained a combination of stagnation and conservatism. The neutralization of the clergy as local political leaders and defenders of a specifically Basque identity before the war had paralyzed any hope of creating a significant Basque nationalist movement in Iparralde. However, the region had scarcely embraced with wholehearted enthusiasm the model of French national identity offered by the Third Republic. As Jacob maintains, perhaps the best representative of Basque political culture during the interwar period is Jean Ybarnégaray, deputy of Nafarroa Beherea for twenty years and later a minister in the collaborationist Vichy government of Marshal PhilEngrâce) theippe Pétain.[138] Ybarnégaray appealed to the instinctively cautious nature of his predominantly rural constituency, warning repeatedly against the dangers of cultivating a specifically Basque political culture and asserting his belief in the French state as the ultimate focus of political loyalty.

That said, a small movement did emerge that would remain faithful to the notion of defending a distinctively Basque identity amid the tremendous social, political, and cultural pressures of the Third Republic to become French. In 1933, the priest Pierre Lafitte formed the Eskualerriste (Basquist) movement. It was, to that date, the most openly Basque politico-cultural organization in Iparralde, though it refrained from declaring itself a separatist political movement. Instead, Lafitte's vision implied a strong regionalist policy aimed at defending Euskara (indeed, promoting it as a second official language in Iparralde) and Basque culture in general. As such, the group pursued as its principal political goal the creation of a statute of autonomy within the French state of the 1930s.

As with its early counterparts in Hegoalde, however, there were divisions within the movement. In particular, younger elements such as Eugèn Goyheneche and Marc Légasse favored a separatist policy. In 1934, the Eskualerriste group created the bilingual newspaper *Aintzina* as an attempt to spread their ideas. The content of *Aintzina* tells us much about this proto–Basque nationalism in Iparralde.

ACCORDING to Jacob, "The three broad elements of the ideology of *Aintzina* were its Christian social and family policy, its political tradition and view of the French state, and its awareness of the activity of other regionalist movements in France. Curiously absent was any ongoing coverage of the emerging Spanish Civil War and the plight of the Spanish Basque people."[139]

It was this latter point, in fact, that would be the most problematic issue for the Eskualerriste group and their journal, for popular hostility within Iparralde toward the Basques of Hegoalde fighting in the Spanish Civil War (a theme discussed in more detail in Chapter 18) and Basque nationalism in general resulted in pressure to close *Aintzina* in 1937.

WORLD WAR II AND GERMAN OCCUPATION, 1939–45

At the outbreak of war in 1939, there was little of the enthusiasm of 1914 among the five million mobilized French troops. This quickly proved justified as German forces invaded the Low Countries in May 1940, moving swiftly and easily into the French state at the same time. A month later, Italian forces attacked the country from its southern flank, and by late June all was lost. France had capitulated within two months to the invading forces. An armistice was signed, and thereafter the French state remained, throughout the duration of the conflict, an occupied territory. The Third Republic thus came to an inglorious de facto end in the space of several weeks.

UNDER THE terms of the armistice, Germany ruled the northern portion of the state, including the coastline down to and including Lapurdi and Nafarroa Beherea, with a puppet regime (known as Vichy France) being established in the southern half of the country (including Zuberoa) under an ex–World War I military leader, Marshal Philippe Pétain. The fall of France and German occupation brought forth the bitter divisions that existed within the French state. During the wartime years, many French citizens enthusiastically supported the Nazi regime in its persecution of Jews, communists, and foreigners. Others resisted, though often they too were divided between communists, socialists, Catholics, and followers of the exiled military leader General Charles de Gaulle.

IPARRALDE UNDER OCCUPATION

"Under the Vichy of Marshal Pétain," remarks Lebovics, "and with the penchant of the traditional Right for the countryside and the peasant, local ethnographic studies flourished, or, it is more correct to say, continued to

"Victor Ithurria, 1914-1944. Pilota player and a good man. Hero of the Free French Forces." Plaque dedicated to an inhabitant of Sara, Lapurdi, who was killed in World War II. The dedication makes a connection between the man's sporting prowess (and to a certain extent "Basqueness") and his bravery (and to a certain extent his "Frenchness"). Note the transformation from pilota player with ball in hand to commando about to throw grenade.

Photo by the author.

---

flourish, if in a new key ... [Indeed] the use of dialect was encouraged along with a sense of pride in one's region."[140]

PERHAPS DUE to this climate of regional tolerance, the Basque journal *Aintzina* was re-established in 1942 by Father Pierre Larzabal and Marc Légasse. The new incarnation was, however, limited to purely cultural issues promoting a latent and safe form of regionalism that complied with the restraints of occupation.

Given Pétain's apparent sympathy toward regional cultures, a plan was formulated by members of the Eskualerriste movement to lobby for the adoption of Euskara as a second official language in Iparralde. There were high hopes that this would take place between 1942 and 1943, but Vichy France failed to implement the regionalist decrees it passed during the period. Thereafter, with the war turning in favor of the Allies, the puppet regime had more worrying tasks to attend to. Despite the seemingly close ties between Eskualerriste members and their occupiers, and indeed the sympathy or ambivalence toward Vichy and German occupation on the part of many, the majority of Basque militants during the war sided with the resistance movement.

THE MOST important resistance activity in Iparralde took place in Zuberoa, where the Basque version of the wider French Maquis (slang for "Resistance," from the Corsican word for the scrubby Mediterranean hillside brush in which bandits traditionally hid) eventually helped liberate both Maule (Mauléon) and Atharratze (Tardets). In the Zuberoan village of Santa-Grazi (Sainte-Engrâce), the war is remembered, notes Sandra Ott, as "the black period" when many men of the village were rounded up by the Germans and transported to prisoner-of-war camps: "The people were rarely permitted to travel to the lowlands, and were required, under penalty of death, to be inside their houses by eight o'clock every evening."[141] In Nazi-occupied Lapurdi and Nafarroa Beherea, the principal resistance activity took the form of helping Jews and Allied airmen cross the border into (theoretically) neutral Spain. Prominent in this activity were the Basque clergy (including Father Pierre Lafitte) and the *mugalariak* (border guides), who had become used to furtive crossings in their prewar activity of smuggling. Indeed, the Nazis executed two men from Santa-Grazi for this very activity.

Basques also took an active role in combat. The Gernikako Batalloa (Gernika Battalion), formed principally by exiled Basques from Hegoalde, played a key role in the Allied victory at the battle of Point-de-Grave (discussed in greater detail in Chapter 20), moving de Gaulle to observe, "France will never forget the sacrifice of the Basques for the liberation of their territory." The Nazi occupation of Iparralde eventually came to an end in September 1944 as German forces retreated in the wake of the successful Allied counteroffensive.

"Seen from the safety of today's vantage point," argues Jacob, "the [Basque nationalist] ideologies of the 1930s and 1940s have been stigmatized as timid, reactionary, and weak. ... [However] the generation of the interwar years produced important role models for later Basque nationalists."[142] Certainly, when considering the Eskualerriste movement in political terms, we should remember the conservative society in which it was born. If Basque nationalism in Hegoalde emerged in the 1890s amid a complex and changing society represented by the clash of modernity and tradition, in Iparralde during the 1930s it had to confront a demographically weakening and overwhelmingly rural society that, within a short space of time between 1905 and 1914, had replaced one conservative politico-cultural elite (the nominally pro–Basque culture clergy) with another (Ybarnégaray, for example) more hostile to specifically Basquist demands.

MOST WORRYING for the nascent Basque nationalist movement in Iparralde was the undeniable fact that, with rural depopulation gathering momentum, the repository of the Basque language (and therefore of traditional Basque culture) was slowly but surely

To the left, the chateau of the Ybarnégaray family, the principal political dynasty of Iparralde during the interwar years, Donibane-Garazi, Nafarroa Beherea. In rural Iparralde, political power went hand-in-hand with economic status. It was therefore important to be "seen" to be successful. A chateau in the provincial capital was thus as much a political as a social statement.
By permission of the "Les Amis de la Vieille Navarre" Association archives.

diminishing. It was, in fact, a trend that would mark the social, cultural, and political life of Iparralde through the twentieth century.

ALL THE WHILE, of course, the Basques of Iparralde were becoming French. Weber notes that as "practices changed, traditions changed with them. National ceremonies appeared whose recurrence made them traditional," so that gradually they appeared to be normal and natural. "The 'traditions' of the twentieth century," concludes Weber (like speaking French), "are newer than most people think."[143] As late as the 1920s, according to Ott, the primary "outside" contact of villages in a remote community of Zuberoa (Santa-Grazi) was as much with Basques from the Hegoalde village of Izaba (Isaba) in Nafarroa as with lowland Zuberoan Basques.[144]

HOWEVER, amid momentous international and domestic upheaval, and ironically parallel to the gradual decline of the Third Republic, we might conclude that modern France—the country we conjure up from stereotypical images such as the Eiffel Tower— came into existence some time after 1918. Only from this time on can we really talk of a French national consciousness and a French-speaking majority among the country's inhabitants. It took the bloody effects of the most destructive war in human history to finally *make* France.

Lesson fifteen

WRITTEN LESSON FOR SUBMISSION (FOR CHAPTERS 14 AND 15)

1. Compare and contrast early Basque nationalism in Hegoalde with that of Iparralde. What, in your opinion, are the most important similarities and differences between the two movements? How would you explain these similarities and differences?
2. By the early twentieth century, which of the two regions of Euskal Herria (Iparralde and Hegoalde) had preserved a stronger sense of Basque national identity? Explain your answer.

16 · Modern Basque culture and society (I)

WHAT WE MIGHT think of today as the timeless essence of European culture and society is in many ways a recent invention. Modern Europe emerged during the late nineteenth century, and even then, especially in the social and cultural sphere, it took several generations to mature. Basque society and culture were no different from their European counterparts. In this chapter, we will examine the nature of a specifically *modern* Basque culture from the late nineteenth century through the first three decades of the twentieth.

How do we measure culture? Modern cultural studies, an interdisciplinary endeavor linked to late-twentieth-century social, economic, and political changes in Western society, has increasingly proposed the notion that the domain of culture rests in the relationship between all the elements that go to make up a way of life. This is an "open" notion that rejects the fixed definitions associated with "great" unchanging cultural precepts. Has Shakespeare always been a "great" playwright of English literature? Not really. During his own lifetime, his work was probably closer to what we would nowadays classify as popular culture. For a time, he even fell out of favor in the English-speaking world, to be revived during the late Victorian era as a *great* writer. Culture changes over time and is as susceptible to invention and reinvention as is identity, the central focus of our investigation.

As we will see, a vibrant modern culture emerged just as much within the realm of Basque-language works concerned with predominantly Basque cultural themes (both traditional and modern), as in its Castilian- and French-language counterparts. No one cultural tradition was necessarily any *better* than any other, and often, as is the case with such endeavors, a great amount of cultural exchange took place among them. Nineteenth-century Basque society (particularly, though not exclusively, in Hegoalde) developed in line with that of modern Europe: Industry and urbanization created a dynamic and confident bourgeois-dominated populace that, following European models, fostered an environment of creativity. With the confidence brought about by industrial gain, the Basque middle class sponsored a healthy intellectual and artistic community that both took inspiration from, and reacted against, the social upheaval taking place. However, it should be made clear that "culture" is not just the preserve of the middle class: there were also working-class and rural peasant cultural forms.

WITHIN THIS survey of modern Basque culture, we will highlight three trends: (i) the emergence of a high culture driven by the *two* modern middle-class cultural communities coinciding with the socio-cultural division of Basque society into specifically Basque- and French- or Spanish-oriented elements, (ii) the *national* dimension of popular culture in the Basque Country, and (iii) briefly, *international* culture in Euskal Herria. Space precludes a more detailed discussion, but it is hoped that the following survey accurately captures the principal cultural trends of the time.

THE BEGINNINGS OF A MODERN BASQUE HIGH CULTURE

Modern Basque society expressed itself in science, the humanities, and the arts. Dating from the late nineteenth century, several exponents of modern culture emerged, from the anthropologist Telesforo de Aranzadi y Unamuno to the philosopher Miguel de Unamuno y Jugo, from the writer Pío Baroja to the ethnologist José

Miguel de Barandiarán, and from the painter Ignacio Zuloaga to the composer Maurice Ravel. All, in their own ways, came to define and promote their Basque identities, and thus, as with every other dimension of Basque life, identity became a key theme for their cultural expression. We will therefore lace our examination of the modern Basque intellectual milieu with the central question of this study: To what extent do these developments represent a specifically Basque identity?

BASQUES AS EXPONENTS OF A SPECIFICALLY MODERN BASQUE CULTURE

An early exponent of modern cultural preoccupations in Basque life was the anthropologist Aranzadi. Born in Bergara (Vergara), Gipuzkoa, Aranzadi studied pharmacology and natural sciences in Madrid, arriving at an interest in the nascent discipline of anthropology during the mid-1880s. In his 1889 doctoral thesis, "El pueblo euskalduna" ("The Basque People"), he sought to survey positivist scientific attempts (that is, the search for universal truths through the application of reason) to explain Basque origins. He thus began a modern scientific quest—through the separation of fact and value—in a field limited until that time by "parochial" and "archaic" interests.[145]

ARANZADI continued his investigation of Basque origins for the rest of his life, arriving at several key conclusions: that there was evidence of continuous Basque settlement in the region dating back to prehistoric times; that Basques displayed no special racial peculiarity distinguishing them from the rest of Europe's peoples; and that present-day Basques represented the remaining example of a European people whose population had been more extensive during prehistoric times. Furthermore, he reasoned, there had to

Logging mill in Mendibe (Mendive), Nafarroa Beherea. After World War I an attempt was made to rebuild the shattered economy through a number of intitiatives such as government-sponsored construction. The forest of Irati in Iparralde was an ideal source of timber for this industry.
By permission of the "Les Amis de la Vieille Navarre" Association archives.

be a close connection between the distinctiveness of the people and the Basque language. He concluded that Basques did indeed represent a distinct people, but he did not, personally, support the nationalist creed of Sabino de Arana y Goiri.

ARANZADI'S corpus complies with the standards of modern scientific inquiry in place toward the end of the nineteenth century. Although he concerned himself with the core themes of early Basque nationalist (and therefore *antimodern*) ideology—race and culture—there is an obvious difference in his conclusions from those of Arana.

H E STATES, for example: "modern archaeological, prehistoric, anthropological and ethnographic studies tend to demonstrate that all civilizations contain a hybrid combination of cultural elements of diverse origin and have been preceded in greater or lesser proportion by miscegenation of blood types."[146]

This is hardly the language of the nineteenth-century romanticist apologists of Basque specificity. Nor, indeed, is it the rhetoric of the political ideologues bent on inventing nations. While Aranzadi pursued a quest in search of elements of Basque specificity, it would seem a harsh claim to brand him as ethnocentric. Instead, he represented a modern attempt to explain Basque origins and, by definition, the distinctive quality of Basque culture.

Barandiarán, a priest and Aranzadi's most distinguished disciple, led a long and extraordinary life in ethnographic pursuit of Basqueness. Born in Ataun, Gipuzkoa, he went at an early age to a seminary in Gasteiz (Vitoria), where his first object of study was the Castilian language, previously unknown to him. In the 1920s, from his Gasteiz base, he began a series of ethnological investigations initiating the modern (that is to say, "scientific") study of Basque folklore. In 1921, he founded the Sociedad de Eusko Folklore (Basque Folklore Society), followed by the publication *Anuario de Eusko-Folklore* (Basque Folklore Yearbook). He later discovered, with Aranzadi, four prehistoric skulls from the Upper Paleolithic to the Bronze periods in the cave of Urtiaga, Gipuzkoa, and thereafter, between 1928 and 1936, pursued an archaeological investigation of Basque origins, from which he concluded that Basques must have developed in situ, a contentious idea for many. During the Civil War, from 1936 to 1939, he fled the Spanish state to Iparralde, where, for seventeen years, in Sara (Sare), Lapurdi, he continued his research.

Barandiarán's ethnography did not follow the style of more rigorous anthropological studies based on specific fieldwork. Rather, he sought to list and record the persistence of past cultural forms in the present—that is, his ethnographic investigation of Basque culture was based on both archaeological evidence and observation. As such, while adopting some of the tools of modern intellectual inquiry, he was also *using* folklore to fit a prescribed theory: the existence of a separate Basque identity. Despite his exile, and like Aranzadi, Barandiarán considered himself a *Basquist* rather than a Basque nationalist, refusing outright to involve himself in the nationalist debate of the 1930s. Barandiarán may not have the unquestionably modern credentials of Aranzadi or Unamuno, but he is an important symbol of a tendency among both Basque and non-Basque intellectuals of the early twentieth century to move away from generalized observations about the Basque *race* to more specific investigations of cultural phenomena based on scientific and social-scientific criteria.

WHILE ARANZADI and Barandiarán stand out as the two most prominent individuals of an emergent modern Basque intellectual culture, the key development for this culture took place in 1918 with the creation of the Euskaltzaindia (Academy of the Basque Language) and Eusko-Ikaskuntza (Society of Basque Studies). A forerunner of these major 1918 initiatives was the Eskualzaleen Biltzarra (Association of Basque Studies), founded by a small group of people from Iparralde in 1902. This was little more than an enthusiastic

Donibane-Garazi, Nafarroa Beherea. Between the two world wars motorized public transport came to the interior areas of Iparralde, bringing with it greater mobility and access to the more modern coastal zone.
By permission of the "Les Amis de la Vieille Navarre" Association archives.

---

literary society, but it did serve as a point of contact between Basques of both Iparralde and Hegoalde.

THE EUSKALTZAINDIA and Eusko-Ikaskuntza represent, as Jacqueline Urla argues, a "quest for modernity": "[T]he Basque Studies Society sought to rationalize Basque studies and society, bringing them out of an era of 'obscure provincialisms', applying them to the latest theories of the modern world."[147] The members of these two groups fall within what Juan Pablo Fusi terms an "ethno-Basque culture,"[148] due to their sympathy for the claims of a distinct Basque identity (however far removed from Arana's vision). Francisco Letamendia Belzunce disagrees with this ethno-cultural definition, however, classifying the groups' members as a modernizing social and political Basque nationalist community.[149]

THROUGH Euskaltzaindia and Eusko-Ikaskuntza, then, as in the research of Aranzadi and Barandiarán, Basques became for the first time the object of scientific inquiry *by Basques themselves*. Coupled with the founding of the academic *Revista Internacional de Estudios Vascos* (International Review of Basque Studies) by Julio de Urquijo in 1907, the creation of the Museo Etnográfico (Ethnographic Museum) in Donostia by Aranzadi in 1919, and the beginning of the popular literary review *Gure Herria* (Our Land) in Iparralde in 1921, these efforts came to signal the presence of a modern Basque cultural community interested in specifically Basque topics. This community tended toward an open acknowledgment of the need to consciously know or even to create Basque identity (rather than to rely on Aranist predestination). At the same time as they looked favorably on the idea of Basque distinctiveness, however, they disseminated the majority of their findings in Spanish and French, thus reflecting their own hybrid cultural formation. The use of Basque was increasingly encouraged as a medium of cultural expression, but it remained a minority language of literary communication.

BASQUES IN MODERN SPANISH AND FRENCH CULTURE
Without question, the vast majority of Basques engaged in modern cultural endeavors at the turn of the century

reflected a more regional, rather than national, conception of Basque identity—if they represented a Basque
identity at all, that is. Chief among the painters associated with the post-1898 crisis of modern Spain was
Zuloaga. His work, drawing inspiration from French
Impressionism, tended to celebrate an "uncorrupted"
(and principally Spanish) peasantry in contrast to the
cacique-ridden political establishment. In 1922, Zuloaga
organized—together with the poet Federico García
Lorca—a *cante jondo* or *flamenco* competition in
Granada to revitalize traditional Andalusian folk music.
This and other initiatives by Zuloaga confirmed his
ambivalence toward specifically Basque cultural production.

The principal Basque literary figures of fin-de-siècle
Spain were Unamuno, Baroja, and Ramiro de Maeztu, all
of whom rejected Basque as a medium of modern
expression. Baroja, a Nafarroan writer, was, in the words
of Raymond Carr, "a natural intellectual anarchist who
rejected all superiorities."[150] Breaking free of nineteenth-century norms, he likewise challenged the post-
1898 political establishment, developing a modern, progressive style. Baroja tended to celebrate ordinary
people in his novels, as Zuloaga did in his paintings. He
set much of his work in his native Nafarroa—as in his
Carlist novel *Zacalaín el Aventurero* (*Zacalaín the
Adventurer*, 1909), for example—and displayed an aesthetic sensibility to Basque culture (unlike Unamuno in
his later writings).

MAEZTU, born in Gasteiz, began his career as a progressive and an internationalist, but evolved, in
an even more extreme change of heart than that of Unamuno, toward what Letamendia terms "proto Spanish
fascism." He became an apologist for General Miguel
Primo de Rivera (who named him Spanish ambassador

to Argentina) and the most authoritarian version of Spanish nationalism in the 1930s. "Majorities," wrote Maeztu, "are at the mercy of minorities and as majority rule is the kernel of parliamentary government this means we do not understand parliamentary government."[151]

Unamuno, who was Aranzadi's cousin, was born in Bilbo (Bilbao) on the eve of its spectacular transformation at the close of the nineteenth century, later becoming fin-de-siècle Spain's premier philosopher as well as the most distinguished modern critic of Basque distinctiveness. As the leading figure of the so-called "Generation of '98," a group of literary figures dedicated to examining the soul of Spanish society in the wake of the national identity crisis engendered by the loss of the empire in 1898, Unamuno came to represent the paradoxes and tensions of Restoration Spain.

AFTER ARRIVING in Madrid in 1880 to study philosophy and share student lodgings with Aranzadi, Unamuno's academic investigation began, like his cousin's, with the question of Basque origins. In his doctoral thesis, titled "Crítica del problema sobre el origen y prehistoria de la raza vasca" ("A Critique of the Problem Concerning the Origin and Prehistory of the Basque Race") and defended in 1884, Unamuno criticized the lack of intellectual and scientific rigor in the study of Basque origins. That same year, he returned to his native city to take up part-time tutoring while preparing for teaching examinations, and in 1888 applied for the position of first chair of Basque at the Instituto Vizcaíno (Bizkaian Institute), the secondary institute of Bilbo. (Interestingly, Arana also applied for the position, although it eventually went to the *euskalerriaco* ideologue Father Resurreción María de Azkue.) Thereafter, Unamuno, a keen follower of the romanticist tradition of Basque cultural production in his youth, gradually relinquished all notions of particularism in favor of a universalist creed that masked a growing Spanish national preoccupation in the young Bizkaian. Appointed professor of Greek at the Universidad de Salamanca (University of Salamanca) in 1891, and later rector (in 1900), Unamuno settled into an academic career.

During the 1890s, Unamuno flirted with socialism, contributing regular articles (principally directed against Basque nationalism) to the Bilbo-based socialist newspaper *La Lucha de Clases*. By 1895, he was already gravitating toward an intrinsically Spanish preoccupation. In a book of essays published that year, *En torno al casticismo* (About Spanishness), Unamuno sited the "nucleus" of an "eternal Spain" (in the words of Michael Richards[152]) in the peasantry of Castile: "There in the interior lives a race of dry complexion, hard and wiry, toasted by the sun and cut down by the cold, a race of sober men, the product of a long selection by the frosts of the cruelest winters and a series of periodic penuries, suited to the inclemencies of the climate and the poverty of life."[153]

THIS SOCIAL Darwinian language would seem to bear out Letamendia's view that Unamuno cannot be described as a *universal* modernist since he employed such essentialist rhetoric.[154] According to Raymond Carr, he was a Spanish patriot who could scarcely be considered liberal in the most general meaning of the term since his hostility to foreign influence (which he termed "Japanization") was intrinsically rooted in a timeless vision of Spanishness.[155] This was increasingly apparent after 1898, when Unamuno's thoughts about national identity intensified. Debating the worth of internationalizing Spain, he arrived at the conclusion

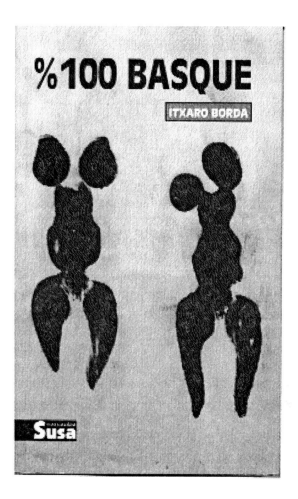

%100 BASQUE

ITXARO BORDA

Susa

In %100 Basque Itxaro Borda, from Iparralde, takes a wry look at different meanings of Basque identity. Gone are the days when the Basque language routinely served to define Basquness in one particular way.

that it was more important to cultivate an intrinsically Spanish national identity. This then provoked a religious crisis in the previously lay thinker, given the role of religion in Castilian identity.[156]

WHAT, THEN, of Unamuno's Basque identity? He viewed Euskara as a language unfit for the needs of modern society. As Urla points out, for Unamuno the *new* man could not be a *Basque* man.[157] In 1901, he remarked before a crowd gathered to celebrate traditional Basque culture: "[T]hat language you speak, Basque people, that Euskara, will disappear with you, and this is of no importance as you too must disappear. Hurry up and kill it, bury it with honor, and speak Spanish."[158] Indeed, it was Unamuno who, as a member of the Constituent Spanish Assembly of 1931–33, presented an amendment to the draft constitution in the following terms:

"The Spanish language is the official language of the Republic. All Spanish citizens have the duty to know it and the right to speak it. In each region the language of the majority of its inhabitants may be declared co-official. No one will be bound to use any regional language."

Maurice Ravel Delouart was born in Ziburu (Ciboure), Lapurdi, to a Swiss father and Basque mother ("Delouart" is the Gallicized version of the Basque "Eluarte" or "Deluarte"), and went on to become one of the twentieth century's most famous composers and the clearest exponent of Impressionist music. Classically trained in Paris, he blended classical forms with both Basque and Spanish folk elements—the Basque *zortziko* rhythm, in particular—to produce some of his most memorable work. (Perhaps the most recognizable of his compositions, by the end of the twentieth century, was

---

Bolero.) He was not a folklorist in the proper sense, however.

While Ravel unquestionably represents modern French culture, he never forgot his Basque identity. This was increasingly the case after the death of his mother in 1917. H. H. Stuckenschmidt observes: "of the two heritages given to Maurice Ravel, the Swiss-Savoyard of his father, the Basque of his mother, the latter prevailed throughout his life. ... Ravel was a Basque in all that directly affected his work and his person. He consciously cultivated his Basque reactions."[159]

Yet Ravel also praised what he saw as the *civilizing* influence of French culture. Ravel's recognition of an identity comprised of multiple cultural influences and the translation of this to his work is echoed in the compositions of the classical Basque composer Jesús Guridi and the conductor and composer Pablo Sorozábal. In 1928, Sorozábal organized an evening of Basque-inspired music in Madrid, at which Guridi's "El Caserío" ("The Farmhouse") and "Espata-dantza" (the name of a traditional Basque dance) were performed, together with José María Usandizaga's "Las Golondrinas" ("The Swallows") and his own compositions "Mendian" ("On the Mountain") and "Txistulariak" ("The *Txistu* or Basque Flute Players").

Figures like Unamuno and Baroja never really found the Spain they were looking for. Unamuno hailed Francisco Franco's uprising, but ultimately fell victim to the regime. Baroja fled Francoist Spain, but was no supporter of the Spanish Second Republic. He retained more of a sympathetic connection to his Basque identity than did either Unamuno or Maeztu, but never quite resorted to the romanticist tendencies of Zuloaga. Indeed, although a member of the modern "Generation of '98" and thus drawn into the intellectual debate surrounding the nature of Spanish national identity, Baroja remains the most enigmatic figure of the three principal Basque writers of the era, due in the main to his undeniable sense of (and literary reliance on) a Basque quality to his work. Similarly, Ravel and the composers of Hegoalde, such as Guridi, Sorozábal, and Usandizaga, echoed this dual sense of identity.

Lesson sixteen

Note: Chapters 16 and 17 should be considered jointly. The learning objectives that appear below and the written assignment in Lesson 17 all refer to the material covered in both Chapters 16 and 17.

REQUIRED READING

Jacqueline Urla, "Reinventing Basque Society: Cultural Difference and the Quest for Modernity, 1918–1936," in William A. Douglass, ed., *Essays in Basque Social Anthropology and History* (Reno: Basque Studies Program, 1989), pp. 149–76.

Joseba Agirreazkuenga, "Past and Present of Eusko Ikaskuntza, The Society of Basque Studies: An Expression of the Basque Scientific Community (1918–1998)," in William A. Douglass, Carmelo Urza, Linda White, and Joseba Zulaika, eds., *Basque Cultural Studies* (Reno: Basque Studies Program, 1998), pp. 275–94.

SUGGESTED READING

Shlomo Ben-Ami, "Basque Nationalism between Archaism and Modernity," *Journal of Contemporary History* 26, no. 3–4 (September 1991), pp. 493–521.

LEARNING OBJECTIVES (FOR CHAPTERS 16 AND 17)

1. To critically analyze the meaning of *culture* in modern Basque society.
2. To explore variants of both high and low culture in modern Basque society.
3. To examine the relationship between culture and identity.

17 · Modern Basque culture and society (II)

FIN-DE-SIÈCLE BASQUE POPULAR CULTURE

"Popular culture" refers to the cultural forms of ordinary people ("the people" or "folk," in a romanticist sense). In Euskal Herria, it took two forms in the modern period, one urban and the other rural. Modern popular culture is generally associated with the industrial masses, and this was the case in Euskal Herria going into the twentieth century; however, we might add to this a re-creation or persistence of traditional Basque culture as a popular cultural expression that differed from its urban counterpart in both its "traditional" origins and distance from industrial society. Around the 1920s, the Basque urban masses began to develop their own particular nonrural cultural forms, in the process displacing many of the traditional rural pastimes. Juan Pablo Fusi characterizes modern Basque popular culture as "a subculture of evasion" that manifested itself in the rise of professional sport as well as in cinema and radio.[160]

AS JOHN K. WALTON points out, the Basque Country—in particular, Bilbo (Bilbao)—was especially susceptible to British cultural influences due to trading links with Great Britain, which proved to be "one of the earliest and most effective vectors for the introduction of football [soccer] into Spain."[161] In 1909, the Club Ciclista de San Sebastián (Donostia Cycling Club—in effect, the soccer team Real Sociedad) won the embryonic Spanish championship, and in 1914–15 a Basque championship was inaugurated. The period between 1920 and 1936 marked the "golden age" of Basque teams (as Fusi puts it), with Athletic de Bilbao and Real Unión de Irun proving victorious in the Spanish

national competition—the Copa del Rey (King's Cup)—
in 1923 and 1930, and 1924 and 1927, respectively, and
Athletic de Bilbao also winning the newly constituted
Spanish league championship during the 1929–30
season.

The popularity of soccer as a spectator sport was
rivaled only by that of cycling, which was actively sponsored by the Gipuzkoan industrial town of Eibar, where
bicycles were manufactured. The first Vuelta al País
Vasco (Tour of the Basque Country) took place in 1924,
with the participation of notable Basque cyclists
including Federico Ezquerra and the brothers Ricardo
and Luciano Montero.

The first decades of the twentieth century saw other
sports gaining popularity as well, and the rise of other
sports stars. The boxer Paulino Uzcudun, "one of the
first modern mass idols," according to Fusi,[162] was the
most famous Basque sportsman of the early twentieth
century. A champion *aizkolari* (woodchopper), he took
up boxing and toured the United States on several occasions, even managing a heavyweight world title challenge with Joe Louis. Jean Borotra, known as "the
bounding Basque," was a famous tennis player during
the 1920s, a decade that also saw a rise in the popularity
of track and field athletics, in particular cross-country
running. Mass-cultural forms, such as sports, were consciously promoted by the modern Spanish state.
Graham and Labanyi observe: "'[T]he popular' is a construction of the modern state, which turned peasants
into 'the people.'"[163]

TRADITIONAL Basque cultural pastimes are characterized by the concept of *indarra*, which implies a
variety of qualities, including physical strength, force,
power, authority, influence, abundance, energy, efficacy,
and life force,[164] and which ran through many of the

Violent conflict and warfare have been everpresent
themes of modern Basque history.
Illustration from Richard Sutphen (ed): Old Engravings
and Illustrations II.

---

resurgent traditional Basque pastimes during the
modern period. In the late 1920s, the priest José de Ariz-
timuño organized a series of traditional Basque cultural
festivals, known as Días de Euskara (Basque-Language
Days), in several towns and cities, including Donostia
(San Sebastián), Arrasate (Mondragón), and Zumarraga.
As part of these cultural celebrations, competitions were
held in traditional sports (all of which were enthusiasti-

cally gambled on, as happened also with the more *modern* sports, from cycling to cross-country running). These traditional sports included *pilota* (handball), *traineru* (fourteen-man rowboat) racing, as well as *aizko-lari* (woodchopping) and *irrintzi* (literally, a loud shrill yell) contests. Most popular of all, however, were the *bertsolariak* (improvisational versifiers), whose trouba-dorial competitions (predominantly in Hegoalde) drew large crowds. Gorka Aulestia points out that the new form taken by Basque society during the modern period offered *bertsolaritza* an expanded framework in which to flourish.[165]

OTHER TRADITIONAL pastimes were likewise enjoyed during this period. Sandra Ott observes that in Iparralde a form of popular versifying, *xikito*, in which opponents shouted insults at each other through the controlled use of *indarra*, found renewed popularity.[166] Popular theatrical and musical troupes, such as Oldargi (Bright Energy) and Saski Naski (Mish-Mash), toured Hegoalde staging pantomimes and dance evenings in the 1920s. Also prominent were the *mendigoizaleak* (mountaineering or hiking fraternities). In Iparralde, the traditional *pastoral* of Zuberoa, known as *maskaradak*, in which entire communities participated in enacting tales sung to set rhythms, continued to serve as a means of popular theater well into the twentieth century. These were accompanied by more comedic forms—such as the *mustrak* (general comedic perform-ances), *galarrotsak* (involving a wedding or courtship theme), and *kabalkadak* (involving horses)—where whole villages used the theme of a world turned upside down to celebrate, lament, and complain about their daily lives. Thus through ridicule and boisterous, even (symbolically) violent performances did these villages alleviate their social grievances.

Popular culture, like many other dimensions of Basque life, revealed the tensions inherent in a society defined by multiple identities, not the least of which were the competing national identities of Basqueness and Spanishness or Frenchness. Walton's summary of the sporting options available to the inhabitants of Donostia during the early twentieth century evokes this complexity: "Football, bullfighting and pelota occupied differing niches in the sporting life of the town ... bullfighting as an occasional and expensive luxury item, pelota as a bread-and-butter event (though with regular special treats when important matches on Sundays featured star players), and football as occupying a middle ground."[167]

Whereas bullfighting symbolically represented both "wealth" and, for some, a Spanish cultural form, *pilota* remained a humble Basque endeavor and soccer fell somewhere between the two—which perhaps explains its rising popularity during the modern period. It is thus difficult to completely disassociate modern mass-cultural forms from the persistence of a distinctively Basque national identity. As Walton remarks, "football was seen as promoting Basque virtues of strength, virility, fairness, honesty and a vigorously healthy open-air life, and its Basque proponents laid claim to a distinctive footballing style which emphasized these qualities."[168]

IF ONE FIGURE of the period transcended these two worlds of popular cultural expression—traditional and modern—it was the woodchopper Uzcudun, who not only gained renown through his success in the sport of *aizkolari*, but who also became a popular idol among the urban population of Euskal Herria when he took up boxing on an international stage. The distinction between the traditional and the modern was likewise blurred as many traditional cultural forms—*bertsolaritza*, for example—were modernized through increased competition and their extension (and therefore movement of *bertsolariak*) throughout the Basque Country. Previously, *bertsolaritza* had taken the form of informal, localized contests between groups of friends, usually in social settings such as taverns, village festivals, weddings, and so on. Any sense of a reward-based competition, beyond paying for a round of drinks or perhaps a meal, had been minimal.

THE INTERNATIONAL DIMENSION OF MODERN CULTURE IN EUSKAL HERRIA

"WE PASSED some lovely gardens and had a good look back at the town, and then we were out in the country, green and rolling, and the road climbing up all the time. In the Basque Country the land looks very rich and green and the houses and villages look well-off and clean. Every village has a pelota court and in some of them the kids were playing in the hot sun. There were signs on the walls of the churches saying it was forbidden to play pelota against them, and the houses in the villages had red tiled roofs, and then the road turned off and commenced to climb and we were going up close along a hillside, with a valley below and hills stretched off back toward the sea. You couldn't see the sea. It was too far away. You could see only hills and more hills, and you knew where the sea was."
—Ernest Hemingway, *The Sun Also Rises* (1926)

Hemingway's fictional account of a journey from Iparralde to Hegoalde in *The Sun Also Rises* was based on a real-life experience. Foreign visitors to Euskal Herria were nothing new at this time—Victor Hugo had been an enthusiastic visitor, and the English Romantic poet

William Wordsworth had eulogized Basque traditions
and culture—but a new breed of foreigner began to take
an interest in Basque culture in the early twentieth century: namely, modern writers. To Hemingway, we might
add the names of two British literary figures: writer
Rodney Gallop and poet C. Day Lewis.

H EMINGWAY was, of course, the most famous of
modern writers to evoke the Basque Country and
its traditions. A great admirer of Pío Baroja, Hemingway
was introduced to Euskal Herria in 1923 after his experiences in Europe during World War I. In the summer of
1923, he traveled to the Nafarroan capital of Iruñea
(Pamplona), where he experienced for the first time
what would become, not in the least due to his own
descriptions, the world-renowned festival of San Fermín
and the running of the bulls. Thereafter, up until the
1950s, the American writer regularly visited the Basque
Country.[169]

Iruñea, and Nafarroa in general, remained the principal focus of Hemingway's affection. He would often
escape from the heady activity of Iruñea to fish the Irati
river, an experience meticulously re-created in his literary work. In the Basque Country, Hemingway found
the link to nature that had been missing during his time
in Paris. "The young writer," contends Angel Capellán,
"found the Basque landscape more appealing and
soothing than any other—excluding, perhaps, his childhood's Upper Michigan—and its people the most cordial in the world."[170] He also discovered models of
bravery and courage in the mythical tales of invincible,
heroic Basques in "Chanson du Roland" (the most
famous medieval European epic poem, recalling the
Basque ambush of the emperor Charlemagne's army)
and in acounts of the Carlist wars. Although he was far
from taking any interest in Basque politics, Hemingway

A priest enjoys a game of pilota with vilage men. Arnegi,
Nafarroa Beherea, mid 20th century. The relationship
between the Church and traditional culture has been
important in maintaining a specifically Basque identity
in Iparralde.
*By permission of the "Les Amis de la Vieille Navarre"
Association archives.*

---

undeniably viewed a distinct quality to Basque identity
that distinguished it from the other regions of the
Spanish state he had visited (Andalusia, for example).

G ALLOP WAS a noted folklorist who left his native
England to live in Iparralde for some time during
the early years of the twentieth century. The product of
his many years spent in the Basque Country was *A Book*

of the Basques (1930), probably the first modern intellectual treatment of Basque folklore by a foreign observer. Distancing himself from some of the more romantic theories of the nineteenth century, Gallop explored Basque origins in a manner that was not too dissimilar from that of Barandiarán, arriving at the conclusion that much of the supposed mysteriousness of Basques was pure artifice. He believed that Basque culture possessed an intrinsic survival instinct that encouraged the persistence of cultural forms through generational change. In a passage that still seems pertinent today, he wrote: "There can be few parts of the world about which so many wild and inaccurate statements have been made and so much irresponsible and unauthoritative literature has been written, as that of the South-west of France and the North-west of Spain which is inhabited by Basques."[171]

DAY LEWIS never visited the Basque Country, but saw the struggle of many Basques against the military uprising of Francisco Franco as a universal theme. His epic prose poem "The Nabara," published in 1938, pays homage to what he considered to be the indomitable spirit of the Basque people, suggested by an event that took place in 1937 during the Civil War, when five modestly armed Basque trawlers engaged in a hopeless naval battle with a Spanish rebel cruiser in the waters of Bilbo, in a bold attempt to break a Spanish blockade of the Basque city that was starving Bilbo's inhabitants. The struggle of the ill-equipped fishing boats lasted longer than might have been expected, ending only when the last of their number, the _Nabarra_ (Nafarroan), was finally sunk by superior forces, losing thirty-eight members of its original fifty-two-man crew. Day Lewis wrote: "Freedom is more than just a word, more than the base coinage of Statesmen, the tyrant's dishonoured cheque,

---

or the dreamer's inflated currency. She is mortal, we know, and made in the image of simple men who have no taste for carnage but sooner kill and are killed than see that image betrayed ... a pacific people, slow to feel ambition, loving their laws and their independence— men of the Basque Country."[172]

ACCORDING TO Fusi, "modern culture" was a general phenomenon without national identity. There are two arguments against this view: First, by viewing modernity simply as an expression of universalism, Fusi overlooks the role of the state in promoting its own agenda through the agency of culture. Indeed, a general critique of modern culture is that, while it supposedly promoted open, universal investigation and reflection, this could only occur within prescribed boundaries, most obviously those that posed no challenge to the state and its power. Miguel de Unamuno y Jugo, for example, who without doubt served as an intellectual critic of various political incarnations within the Spanish state, never went as far as to question the state itself. Second, in his separation of modern (generally liberal) culture and ethnocentric Basque culture, Fusi implies that the latter could not in effect be *modern*. After all, its particularist focus went against the values of modernity. As we have seen in the work of Telesforo de Aranzadi y Unamuno, this was not necessarily the case. Indeed, as Urla's detailed work demonstrates, there arose during the first three decades of the twentieth cen- tury a wave of cultural works that were both modern and Basque-focused. Similarly, the works of modern foreign writers of the time suggest that there were sufficient grounds for establishing a separate or distinct Basque identity.

Fusi is quite dismissive of Basque culture prior to the advent of modernity. He claims that during the first

three decades of the twentieth century, "the culture of
the Basque Country abandoned those provincial, elementary and coarse levels that had characterized Basque
culture in previous centuries and that still characterized,
to give one example, the idealist and simple literature of
a Trueba or a Navarro Villoslada [traditionalist authors
of the foralist school], still during the second half of the
19th century, and in general, the literature of religious
works in Basque."[173]

Similarly, Ben-Ami states that in the late nineteenth
and early twentieth centuries, "Basque literature
remained the archaic, 'savage' and primitive concern of
dedicated, narrow parochial minds," whereas Unamuno
"preferred [the language] of Cervantes,"[174] thereby
suggesting that this preference for Spanish was
somehow "better" than a preference for "Basque." What
seems to emerge from the conclusions of these scholars
is that modernity is something other, culturally and aes-
thetically, than the work they critique. As a consequence, all cultural forms that fail to follow this ill-
defined norm representing modernity—in this case,
those representing a specifically Basque as opposed to
Spanish or French identity—become stigmatized. Thus,
to be a romantic or traditionalist is to be "provincial,
elementary and coarse," and to write in Basque is to be
"archaic," "savage," "primitive," and "parochial"—
highly charged words that unquestionably invoke a
sense of cultural hierarchy.

FOR JOSEBA ZULAIKA, Unamuno's universalism
worked, as much as Arana's racial theories, in
nativizing Basque culture into Fusi's ethnocentric
ghetto, for it was Unamuno who employed Social Darwinian rhetoric to call for the annihilation of the primitive and barbaric Basque language—this, it should be
remembered, in the name of the *civilizing* mission of

universalism (as represented by Spain and the Spanish language).[175] Like Arana, Unamuno saw the existence of Castilian and Basque as incompatible; it was an either / or situation, the classic frame of definition by which universal modernity had emerged. True universalism had to be imposed from above, as in Unamuno's amendment to the draft constitution.

THERE WAS little place, then, for multiculturalism in this totalizing discourse. "Universalist philosophy," observes Zulaika, "is bound to the existence of the native, who it needs as a victim of its superior philosophical horizon. ... [T]he modern project is finished by the 'killing' off of what remains of his [the native's] autochthonous language and culture."[176] Unfortunately for the universal project, Basque culture responded to the changes imposed by modernity (industrialization and a rapidly changing society) by framing a new culture, from anthropologists to *bertsolariak*, seemingly well equipped to deal with the transformation.

Lesson seventeen

REQUIRED READING

John K. Walton, "Reconstructing Crowds: The Rise of Association Football as a Spectator Sport in San Sebastián, 1915–32," *The International Journal of the History of Sport* 15, no. 1 (April 1998), pp. 27–53.

Gorka Aulestia, *Improvisational Poetry from the Basque Country* (Reno: University of Nevada Press, 1995), pp. 16–21 and 85–99.

SUGGESTED READING

Sandra Ott, "*Indarra*: Some Reflections on a Basque Concept," in J. G. Peristiany and Julian Pitt-Rivers, eds., *Honor and Grace in Anthropology* (Cambridge: Cambridge University Press, 1992), pp. 193–214.

WRITTEN LESSON FOR SUBMISSION (FOR CHAPTERS 16 AND 17)
Consider Juan Pablo Fusi's implication that modern culture must, by its very definition, be universal, and that ethnic or national cultural endeavor goes against the very concept of modernity. Citing specific examples you have come across so far, to what extent do you believe this is a valid argument? In your response, think as much about state as national cultural endeavors.

18 · The Spanish Second Republic

As JUAN PABLO FUSI notes, "the coming of the Second Republic with its promise of autonomy for the regions [of Spain] led to a marked strengthening of the Basque sentiment of a separate identity."[177] Indeed, during the crucial watershed period of the republic, from 1931 to 1936, the political dimension of Basque nationalism grew into a major force. Yet while the republic promised Basque nationalists an opportunity to advance their claims, many among them remained skeptical. After all, Basque nationalism was still dominated by a conservative, confessional element that had little in common with the new regime's keenest defenders: a liberal, republican, Madrid-based elite supported by the Partido Socialista Obrero Español (PSOE; Spanish Socialist Workers Party). Ultimately, however, the liberal (rather than conservative) path would be the direction that Basque nationalism followed, proving the strength of national sentiment over other personal or group allegiances.

In this chapter, we will concentrate on the fortunes of Basque nationalism, both at the regional and the state level, in an attempt to understand why the call of nationalism proved so attractive in the 1930s. This is also a starting point for understanding the extreme Spanish nationalist backlash that eventually led to the downfall of the republic and the coming of civil war in 1936.

AZAÑA'S FIRST MINISTRY, 1931–33

With conservative attempts at resolving the institutional weaknesses of the Restoration system failing under the ineffective dictatorship of General Miguel Primo de Rivera, the task fell to the Spanish Second Republic, proclaimed in the constitution of 1931. This task had three

Basque dancers in Iparralde, early twentieth century. Popular festivals where whole villages took part in the proceedings served as a means of preserving specifically Basque customs during the extension of the French state in other areas such as education, work and so on. *By permission of the "Les Amis de la Vieille Navarre" Association archives.*

main aims: instituting a progressive and democratic state; limiting the traditional power and influence of the Church, armed forces, and landed elite; and accommodating growing Catalan and Basque nationalist aspirations. While the aims were clear, their implementation would be more complex.

THE FIRST ministry of the republic (1931–33), under Manuel Azaña, had at its disposal a beneficial instrument of radical reform—a single parliamentary chamber—and the Spanish premier invoked this power

in a bold attempt to create a new society. His government introduced a program of regional reform in
Catalunya, together with social legislation aimed at
reforming religious matters, labor relations, and the
principal agrarian question, the issue of land redistribu-
tion for the rural poor of Spain. The new republican government thus gradually withdrew state support of the
Church and drew up plans for an autonomy statute for
Catalunya that came into effect in 1932. At the same
time, the new regime, recognizing the value of education
in promoting state values, introduced an ambitious plan
of educational reform, including the Misiones Pedagóg-
icas (Pedagogical Missions), a form of free civic education for the illiterate rural masses of the state. Under the
plan, moreover, Castilian was also aggressively promoted as the language of modern life.

HEGOALDE DURING THE EARLY YEARS OF THE
REPUBLIC, 1931–33
Economy: During the 1920s, the Basque economy had
enjoyed a period of consolidated growth, although the
mining industry had been in steady decline since the
turn of the century.

WITH THE upheaval of Primo de Rivera's abdication,
a small but noteworthy depression set in. For
example, by 1934 Bizkaian production of iron rails for
use in the railroad industry had fallen to 12 percent of
1929 levels, and in 1933 the Basque cement industry was
working at only 42 percent of its productive capacity. As
a result, by 1935 one-quarter of Bizkaia's labor force was
out of work. The Basque agricultural sector had cautiously modernized through the first three decades of
the twentieth century, though with this modest economic growth came a greater freedom and mobility,

which in turn increased the appeal of urban centers for younger generations of Basques engaged in agriculture.

Politics: The Basque nationalist response to Azaña's first ministry was muted. The immediate concern of Basque nationalism in the aftermath of Primo de Rivera's dictatorship was the resolution of party differences that had split the movement between 1916 and 1922. Ironically, despite its (forced) removal from public politics by the dictatorship, Basque nationalism had gained much support through the 1920s as a result of the cultural activity sponsored by the movement. Sensing the opportunity, in November 1930 representatives of the two Basque nationalist factions met in Bergara (Vergara), Gipuzkoa, to reform the party under its original acronym, EAJ-PNV. Chief among the architects of the reconciliation was a young lawyer from Bilbo (Bilbao) named José Antonio Aguirre y Lecube, who would thereafter have the greatest influence on the party, eventually rising to become its leader as well as the first president of the Basque Autonomous Government in 1936.

DESPITE THE reformation of the EAJ-PNV, Basque nationalism remained ideologically divided. The 1930 agreement had been a pragmatic compromise in response to the possibilities offered by promoting a solid front in the republic, yet many sympathizers held onto their own distinct beliefs. Within the party itself, there remained two factions, moderates and radicals, while a breakaway group, unable to accept the terms of the 1930 agreement, created a new party, Acción Nacionalista Vasca (ANV; Basque Nationalist Action), that same year. ANV declared a liberal republican platform rejecting all forms of traditionalist ideology. Four years later, another group of discontented Basque nationalists, led by Elías de Gallastegui and comprising many former members of the 1922 splinter faction that had disagreed with the conservative outlook of the party at that time, broke away from the EAJ-PNV to form Jagi-Jagi (Arise, Arise) for the same general reasons. Furthermore, the Jagi-Jagi faction believed in outright independence for the Basque Country as opposed to the autonomous line followed by the EAJ-PNV.

The early signs were favorable for the EAJ-PNV. In the 1931 parliamentary elections, the party, together with their traditionalist and right-wing political allies, Catholic Independents (in Bizkaia) and Carlists (in Nafarroa), gained over 60 percent of the vote in Bizkaia and seven of the twenty-four Basque seats available in the chamber (the Independents taking three and the Carlists five). The immediate aim of the EAJ-PNV was the acquisition of an autonomy statute similar to that about to be ceded to Catalunya.

On the left, both socialism and communism grew at an important rate in Hegoalde, counting 30,000 and 9,000 militant activists, respectively, during the early 1930s. The dominant figure of the Basque socialists, and representative of conciliatory evolutionary socialism at state level, was Indalecio Prieto. He faced a double battle throughout the 1930s, both with Basque nationalists in his own region, and with the more revolutionary wing of the socialist movement at the state level.

THE EARLY years of the republic were marked by rising social tension in Hegoalde, exploding on several occasions in bloody street confrontations between Basque nationalists (of all persuasions) and socialists, communists, and state authorities, as well as between the two leftist factions themselves. The street confrontations increased between the fall of 1932 and summer of 1933, the period of the demise of the first republican government.

THE SPANISH RIGHT-WING REACTION, 1933–35
Azaña's first reforming ministry had progressively
incurred the wrath of the traditionalist Right in the
Spanish state and, as a result, in 1933 lost the general
election to a coalition of rightist Spanish Catholic parties known as the Confederación Española de Derechas
Autónomas (CEDA; Spanish Confederation of Right-
Wing Groups), under the leadership of José María Gil
Robles. While hostile to the secular tendencies of the
1931–33 administration, the new government pledged a
commitment to social activism based on conservative
Catholic principles, through which it had engaged the
support of the moderate republican parties. There was
little chance that the new administration would be sympathetic to the autonomous demands of the Basque
nationalists, however. Indeed, this was the moment
when, as Fusi comments, José Calvo Sotelo, leader of the
extreme Right, coined the famous phrase that Spain was
"better red than broken."[178]

WITH POLITICAL commentary of this kind, it was
clear that Spanish political culture was not ready
for centrist accommodation. Government reshuffles
resulted in a significant shift to the right, and the
response of the more radical sectors of the Spanish Left
was confrontation. In October 1934, Asturian coal
miners rose up in protest against the government in the
hope of provoking a more widespread, statewide revolution. This was, however, not forthcoming, and while the
rebels held out for two weeks, the uprising was viciously
put down.

Spanish Nationalism: The electoral triumph and consolidation of the CEDA reflected a crucial step in the
modern definition of Spanish nationalism in the 1930s.
Drawing obvious inspiration from those forces of the

A memorial to the versifier Joxe Manuel Lujanbio, better known as "Txirrita." Bertsolariak are held in great esteem as guardians of the Basque oral tradition.
Photo by the author.

Spanish Right—the Church, the armed forces, and the great landowning interests of the aristocracy—Spanish nationalism also borrowed heavily from the short but important liberal tradition in the country, particularly in regard to state-building policies that blended legal and cultural integration. Even José Ortega y Gasset, the premier liberal philosopher of the time (having inherited the mantle from Miguel de Unamuno y Jugo), centered his social vision on the absolute historical and cultural unity of the Spanish nation, and, as Fusi points out, many members of the republican Left such as Azaña and Prieto, "though sympathetic towards the cultural and political demands of both Basques and Catalans, saw Spain as a unitarian state, as a historical and cultural unity."[179] The *national* question was thus central to the fortunes of the Second Republic, and, despite the granting of autonomy statutes to both Catalunya and (eventually, in 1936) the Basque Country, the territorial integrity of the state remained a paramount concern for both left- and right-wing variants of Spanish nationalism.

IN 1933, THE EAJ-PNV ratified its commitment to securing an autonomy statute by parliamentary means, but this led to a break in its alliance with the traditionalist Carlists, whose support for the unity of Spain rested on foral rather than autonomous or federal lines, over the inability of the party to gain significant support in Nafarroa.[180] The party's commitment to the autonomy statute, together with concerns expressed by many of its members about the escalating violent confrontations of the party's youth, also led to a split with the more radical elements within the party itself, who left to form Jagi-Jagi in 1934. Jagi-Jagi pursued the most radical Basque nationalist policy, advocating a complete break with all state institutions and unambiguously seeking full independence. Similarly, their tactics differed from those of the EAJ-PNV and ANV, in that they espoused a program of civil disobedience to draw attention to their cause. Following these splits, the EAJ-PNV gradually realized that the autonomous path it had chosen could only be pursued through a moderation of its more traditionalist rhetoric and an accommodation with both the Basque socialists and the Spanish republican parties (the plan proposed by ANV in 1930). This coincided with a decision among the socialists (who held a strong electoral base in Hegoalde) to support regional reform as a bulwark against right-wing CEDA power in Madrid.

W HILE THE EAJ-PNV officially remained neutral during the 1934 uprising by Asturian coal miners, both ANV and Jagi-Jagi supported the miners, and many Basque nationalists took to the streets to protest the government's response. Sporadic demonstrations took place in Bilbo (Bilbao) and the Gipuzkoan industrial towns of Eibar and Arrasate (Mondragón), bastions of Basque socialism and communism. That same year, Madrid increasingly stalled on the question of regional autonomy, pushing the EAJ-PNV away from its conservative right-wing tendency and more toward the political center than ever. In the wake of the events of 1934, the EAJ-PNV remained isolated between the forces of the reactionary Right and the radical Left with little hope, seemingly, of successfully pursuing the autonomy goal.

BASQUE NATIONALISM AND THE COMING OF THE SPANISH POPULAR FRONT, 1935–36
Toward the end of 1935, a politically rejuvenated Azaña, together with the Basque socialist leader Prieto, formed a new liberal-left coalition, the Frente Popular (based on the contemporaneous Popular Front in France) to

A post-Civil War photo of José Antonio de Aguirre y
Lecube (on the left) with the man who would succeed
him as Basque-president-in-exile, Jesús María de
Leizaola. Aguirre led Basque nationalism for over twenty
years and died in exile in 1960. He was buried in Ipar-
ralde.
*By permission of Abertzaletasunaren Agiritegia. Sabino
Arana Kultur Elkargoa archives.*

counteract the CEDA alliance. As the Left began to unite, the Right gradually fragmented. Gil Robles had by this time come under internal power to implement more radical right-wing policies, provoking a split within the CEDA between moderate and extreme factions. Elections were called for February 1936, and in the resultant poll the Popular Front recorded a slender victory to herald a new left-of-center republican administration, with Azaña leading the government once more. In May, Azaña would become president of the republic, being replaced in his former role by Casares Quiroga.

THROUGH 1935, the EAJ-PNV, nervous at formulating an electoral alliance with political parties with which it had little in common, hesitated at making a full commitment to the Popular Front. What finally convinced the party to at least remain neutral was the guarantee of an autonomy statute. Prieto had suggested this to the other members of the Popular Front as the only means of potentially integrating Basque nationalism once and for all into the structure of the republic. At the same time, it made sound electoral sense, as clearly a majority of people in the Basque Country approved of the measure. As a consequence, the EAJ-PNV remained officially neutral during the 1936 election, gaining a disappointing (given its earlier successes) 35 percent of the vote in Bizkaia, Gipuzkoa, and Araba, a decline of 10 percent from the 1933 result. However, the party had gained 130,000 independent votes, thus considerably aiding the Popular Front (whose statewide majority was a modest 700,000), and remained the strongest single party in Hegoalde.

The task of maintaining the broad electoral alliance through 1936 was especially troublesome, as the Popular Front was beset by a host of internal difficulties, resulting, in the main, from the contradictory ideologies

of its constituent parties. Furthermore, the Spanish
Right found the presence of socialists and communists
in the institutional framework of the state unacceptable.
From February 1936 on, the country rapidly descended
into violent political confrontation as competing party
militias fought openly in the streets.

Basque participation in the political violence of the
spring of 1936 was most evident in the actions of Nafarroan Carlists. In the early 1930s, a militia—known as the
requetés—had been formed to safeguard and defend
Carlist political goals. It counted a membership of 6,000
and was well organized through a network of towns and
villages, with the local clergy often taking a leading role.
After the attempted revolution of 1934, the *requetés* took
their role more seriously still by establishing a military
committee to coordinate the transportation of arms
between the various groups, including branches outside
Nafarroa.

DURING THE same time, the EAJ-PNV hesitated to formally declare itself in favor of one side or the
other. Naturally sympathetic to the Right, it was the Left
that promised the cherished goal of autonomy. That
said, the party (like all other political groups in the
state) prepared for military confrontation through the
spring of 1936, though at the outbreak of hostilities that
summer, when elements of the Spanish military rose up
against the newly elected coalition, it found itself
lacking in materials and organization, compared to, say,
the Carlists. Officially, however, the principal concern of
the EAJ-PNV remained the autonomy statute. The plans
for the statute were drafted and ready for implementation before July, but the summer recess of the Spanish
congress delayed its final approval and events soon over-
took the democratic process. On July 18, a military
revolt took place that launched the Spanish state into

_____

civil war. The government of Quiroga resigned as the country geared itself for the not wholly unexpected war. Between July 19 and 24, the military demarcation of the future conflict was effectively established.

The Spanish Second Republic marks a key moment in the political fortunes of Basque nationalism. While the political expression of Basque national identity was only hesitantly received in Nafarroa, a significant majority of people in Araba, Bizkaia, and Gipuzkoa—despite politically plural electoral results (not the least of which remained a strong showing for the parties of the Spanish Left)—seemingly favored some degree of autonomy. What might we conclude from this? That a sense of Basque national identity prevailed in these three provinces over and above that of ideological affiliation, but that this sense of identity did not extend, in the majority at least, to Nafarroa.

AT THE STATE level, the Spanish Second Republic, like its French counterpart, continued the work of state building. Indeed, the ceding of autonomy statutes to Catalunya and, later, the Basque Country reflected an alternate, "looser," but still unitary vision of the Spanish nation. We need only remember Unamuno's clause to the draft constitution (see Chapter 16) to see what was implied by the emergence of a modern liberal Spanish nationalism during the 1930s. Ultimately, this nationalism was too liberal for the forces of tradition in the Spanish state, and this was reflected in the military uprising of July 1936.

Lesson eighteen

REQUIRED READING

Stanley G. Payne, *Basque Nationalism* (Reno: University of Nevada Press, 1975), pp. 117–56.

Juan Pablo Fusi, "The Basque Question 1931–7," in Paul Preston, ed., *Revolution and War in Spain* (London and New York: Methuen, 1984), pp. 182–201.

SUGGESTED READING

Martin Blinkhorn, "'The Basque Ulster': Navarre and the Basque Autonomy Question Under the Spanish Second Republic," *Historical Journal* 17, no. 3 (September 1974), pp. 595–613.

Helen Graham, "Community, Nation and State in Republican Spain, 1931–1938," in Clare Mar-Molinero and Angel Smith, eds., *Nationalism and the Nation in the Iberian Peninsula: Competing and Conflicting Identities* (Oxford and Washington, D.C.: Berg, 1996), pp. 133–47.

LEARNING OBJECTIVES

1. To examine the impact of the Spanish Second Republic in Hegoalde.
2. To examine the course of Basque nationalism during the Second Republic.
3. To highlight the national tensions behind the eventual fall of the Second Republic.

WRITTEN LESSON FOR SUBMISSION

1. Compare and contrast the state-building efforts of the French Third Republic and the Spanish Second Republic. What similarities and differences do you see between the two? Which of the two was more successful, and why?

2. How do you account for the apparently paradoxical (autonomist / separatist) composition of the Basque Nationalist Party (EAJ-PNV) in the 1930s? Could it ever have hoped to maintain its separate factions? If so, how? If not, why not?

19 · "Death to intelligence!"
The Spanish Civil War, Franco, and the Basques

SOON AFTER the outbreak of the Spanish Civil War, an insurgent Press and Propaganda Office was established at Francisco Franco's wartime headquarters in Salamanca. The head of the office, General Millán Astray, quickly earned notoriety for his "patriotic" slogans, among the most memorable of which were "Death to intelligence!" and "Long live death!" The slogans seem, with the benefit of hindsight, sadly prophetic for a period of history that would indelibly alter the fortunes of Hegoalde.

The Spanish Civil War was a complex struggle that involved the entire state across class, gender, national, social, and political divides. In the short space of a chapter, we can only hope to scratch the surface of this complexity. We will focus here on the basic events of the period and the interplay of cultural identities during the conflict. What did the Spanish Civil War and the eventual triumph of Franco mean for Basque identity?

GENERAL FRANCISCO FRANCO

At first, Franco took only a tentative role in the military uprising and was not considered one of the main leaders of the conspiracy. He was a prominent officer in the Spanish army—for a time even the youngest general in Europe—and had distinguished himself in action in several colonial campaigns in North Africa, where he had earned the respect (if not the liking) of his peers and the fear of his enemies for the sanguinary efficiency of his leadership. He was an unobtrusive though cunning and ambitious individual, prone to caution and blessed with a great deal of fortune throughout his life.

With a firm commitment to the uprising, Franco quickly assumed a central leading role in the strategy of the insurgent officers due to his greater experience in battle. From his initial command base in North Africa, he flew to the south of the Spanish mainland at the end of July 1936, from where, with relative ease, he swept north with his African troops (said to be the best organized units in the Spanish army), quickly uniting the rebel gains in the southern region of Andalusia with those of Extremadura in the southwest. By early fall, he was pushing toward Madrid, and at a September meeting of the various conspirators, he took control of the overall military operation as commander-in-chief of the uprising. Thereafter, he would control the state for close to fifty years.

THE IMMEDIATE RESPONSE IN HEGOALDE

Hegoalde was split along party lines in response to the military uprising. In Araba and Nafarroa, the military insurrection enjoyed sufficient popular support or acquiescence, together with a good infrastructure, to take control of the two provinces almost immediately. Indeed, Nafarroa quickly proved to be a bastion of the insurgent cause, while Araba's response was one of gradual but widespread support.

IN IRUÑEA (Pamplona), General Emilio Mola Vidal led the insurrection, harnessing and galvanizing the zealous support of the predominantly Carlist population into a crusade against the godless republicans. Together with that of Franco, the role of Mola was central to the overall strategy of the military conspirators. From Nafarroa, he launched the northern offensive by striking immediately westward into Gipuzkoa.

In Gasteiz (Vitoria), Araba, the situation was less straightforward than in the Nafarroan capital. There, the local army garrison, with the aid of the Civil Guard, the Assault Guards (a police force set up by republican Spain), and Carlist *requeté* militias, seized control of the city, but found a less compliant local population. A policy of terror was implemented by the insurgents to cajole people into submission, with the republican mayor of the city, Teodoro González de Zárate, socialists, and other republicans being quickly executed.

During the initial months of the conflict, sympathizers of the Euzko Alderdi Jeltzalea-Partido Nacionalista Vasco (EAJ-PNV; Basque Nationalist Party) in Araba were not targeted, as the traditionalist insurgents believed that most Basque nationalists would, for their religious convictions and social conservatism, join the uprising. Yet from September 1936 on, with no statement of solidarity from the Basque nationalists, they too were subject to arrest, imprisonment, torture, and execution. The Spanish military governor of Araba, General Gil Yuste, would comment: "These abominable separatists do not deserve to have a homeland. Basque nationalism must be ruined, trampled underfoot, ripped out by its roots."[181]

BIZKAIA AND Gipuzkoa, marked by an efficient grass-roots militia organization (principally of socialist, anarchist, and communist industrial workers, but including Basque nationalist sympathizers too) remained loyal to the republic. In Bizkaia, the military commander of the Bilbo (Bilbao) garrison refused to support Mola's northern uprising and instead elected to defend the republic. The Bilbo-based leadership of the EAJ-PNV considered granting support to the insurgents, but ultimately found that the promise of an even more extensive autonomy statute, ceding virtual self-rule, was too much to refuse. By the late summer of 1936, the

"Stamps of Euskal Herria, Stamps to Help, No Commercial Value, Collection 2: Independence" Faced with the difficult legal task of creating their own nation-state in a Europe dominated by larger powers, some Basques have taken to imagining the day-to-day symbols of an independent Euskal Herria.

party, and with it the majority of Basque nationalists, declared for the republic.

IN THE GIPUZKOAN capital, Donostia (San Sebastián), an attempted uprising by the military garrison was successfully thwarted by an amalgam of party militias, together with the Civil Guard and the Assault Guards. However, Gipuzkoa found itself in a strategically weaker position than that of Bizkaia, as Mola swiftly advanced into the easternmost part of the province from his Nafarroan base. Though countered by an embryonic, ill-organized Basque army, Euzko Gudarostea, the insurgents took Irun on September 2, thereby sealing off the border (and with it an escape route for pro-republic sympathizers), and Donostia on September 13. By September 22, the insurgent forces had charged across Gipuzkoa to the Deba river, an industrial artery of the province along which were located several important towns, but were halted in their progress by a successful counteroffensive by the rapidly improving Euzko Gudarostea. Thereafter, Franco called for a concentration of rebel efforts on the capture of Madrid, and the northern rebel campaign was temporarily suspended.

In an effort to alleviate pressure on their beleaguered republican allies in Madrid, Euzko Gudarostea launched an offensive from its Bizkaian power base into northern Araba in the early winter of 1936. The Villareal Offensive, as the attack was known (after the town it sought to capture), was a disaster. During the first two weeks of November, a series of uncoordinated assaults on rebel positions failed to capture the town, and, amid deteriorating winter conditions, the offensive was suspended on December 12.

The second phase of the war in Hegoalde, the winter of 1936–37, was largely one of consolidation among the insurgent forces. A Basque front existed in a line paralleling the southern extent of Bizkaia through to the Deba river in the westernmost part of Gipuzkoa. During this period, two important developments took place: The Basque Statute of Autonomy was ratified and Euzko Gudarostea was finally mobilized into an effective fighting force.

THE STATUTE OF AUTONOMY AND THE CREATION OF A BASQUE ARMY

In Madrid, on September 4, 1936, a new Popular Front government was established under the leadership of the revolutionary socialist Largo Caballero. The new government, realizing the importance of gaining Basque nationalist support to defend the republic, decided to offer an improved autonomy statute as quickly as possible. Therefore, on October 1, the statute was granted. With it, an autonomous (and virtually independent) Basque government, controlled by the EAJ-PNV, officially dictated wartime policy in what remained of non-rebel-controlled Hegoalde. On October 7, José Antonio Aguirre y Lecube, the EAJ-PNV leader, went to Gernika (Guernica) to swear the traditional oath of loyalty before the town's oak tree, the symbol of Basque foral rights.

AT THE OUTBREAK of war (July to September 1936), there had been limited formal military resources in Bizkaia and Gipuzkoa beyond the small Spanish army garrisons regularly stationed in the provincial capitals and the hastily formed, badly organized Euzko Gudarostea. As such, the newly installed Basque government introduced conscription in October 1936 to properly organize its army. By the beginning of November, a general staff had been established, overseeing an army comprising twenty-seven infantry battalions of approximately 750 men each. In total, Euzko Gudarostea counted 25,000 *gudariak* (soldiers), together with

Euzkalerria, Doiŝlar (Alemanak)
egazkiñak erailduba
Gernika ziñopa. *1937'ko jorrailak 26*

"The Basque Country, attacked by German planes.
Gernika the Martyr. April, 26, 1937." Postcard commem-
orating the bombardment. Hitler's Condor Legion left
no doubt as to the Nazi capacity to destroy lives by
razing the small Bizkaian town in arehearsal for World
War II. The terrorism of the brief attack scarred many
Basques for generations to come.
*By permission of Abertzaletasunaren Agiritegia. Sabino
Arana Kultur Elkargoa archives.*

12,000 to 15,000 volunteers organized in militias,
defending the temporarily inactive front. Finally, these
battalions were organized along political party lines: that
is, each battalion corresponded to a political party loyal
to the republic and the democratically elected Popular
Front government.

THE BASQUE CIVIL WAR, 1937

In the early spring of 1937, the rebel forces, unable to take Madrid in the winter offensive, redoubled their efforts in Hegoalde. Mola, together with four newly formed Nafarroan brigades (totaling 28,000 men) and ten battalions of recruits (compliant or otherwise) from Araba and Gipuzkoa, began a renewed offensive to take Bizkaia and, above all, industrially and strategically important Bilbo. From this moment on, the conflict truly became a Basque civil war. On March 31, Mola issued a proclamation to the pro-republic Basques in Bizkaia (which was also at the time a temporary home to many refugees from the other provinces of Hegoalde): "I have decided to end the war rapidly in the north. The lives and property of those who surrender with their arms and who are not guilty of murder will be respected. But if the surrender is not immediate, I shall raze Bizkaia to its very foundations, beginning with the war industry. I have the means to do so."[182]

MOLA SUBSEQUENTLY carried out his chilling warning through a campaign of heavy aerial bombardment, followed by the swift ground action of troops who had experienced eight months of intensive military action. Euzko Gudarostea could not respond with anything like the air power of the Nazi Condor Legion, Hitler's principal aid to Franco during the war, placed at the service of Mola for the duration of the Basque offensive. The pro-republic Basque army was, furthermore, hampered by poor coordination and communication between the politically different battalions. Its only two advantages were the heavy rainfall of a Basque spring (unfavorable to air attacks) and the mountainous terrain separating Bizkaia from Gipuzkoa (which slowed down offensive infantry action).

Ultimately, however, these were only temporary barriers to the insurgent offensive. On March 31, 1937, Durango, a Bizkaian town of 12,000 inhabitants well behind the front, was the first target of Mola and the Condor Legion's strategic bombing campaign. One hundred and twenty civilians were killed during the attack. In the second part of a twin offensive aimed at taking Bilbo, insurgent forces broke through the defenses of the southern Basque front to take the Bizkaian town of Otxandio (Ochandio) by early April. Bad weather delayed any more advances for the time being, and Euzko Gudarostea took the opportunity to regroup its forces. However, Mola initiated a renewed offensive on April 20, when the Basque insurgent troops took the final piece of Gipuzkoan territory, in the mountainous terrain around the hilltop town of Elgeta (Elgueta). This victory gave Mola a strategic point atop a mountain from which to plan his advance downward into Bizkaia, and soon afterward his troops took the Bizkaian town of Elorrio.

THE CONDOR Legion then once again took a leading role in the offensive. On April 26, 1937, it bombed the symbolically important town of Gernika. Ten miles within the front, twenty-six miles to the northeast of Bilbo, and with a peacetime population of 7,000 people, Gernika was a market town of little obvious strategic significance compared to, for example, the more important port of Bermeo, which lay just to its north. April 26 was a Monday, which was market day in Gernika, bringing additional people to the town; this, along with the refugees who had temporarily set up home there, brought the town's population to well above the usual peacetime number. At 4:40 in the afternoon, a bombing raid began that continued until 7:45 that evening. In three hours, several waves of Nazi planes dropped a combination of incendiary, high-explosive, and shrapnel bombs, weighing a total of 100,000 pounds. Many of those who managed to survive the carnage were gunned down as they attempted to flee the burning center. The final casualty count, still disputed by many, may have reached as many as 1,650 killed and nine hundred wounded, all civilians.

THE GERMAN Luftwaffe used Gernika to test new incendiary bombs (which they would soon unleash on Europe during World War II). According to the historian Paul Preston, however, the attack was ordered from Salamanca, Franco's wartime center of operations, rather than from Berlin,[183] and thus it might be argued that the destruction of Gernika was not just a test of German weaponry, but also a specifically orchestrated attack of a symbolically important Basque town—that Franco had ordered the destruction of this symbol of Basqueness. A day after the assault, the advancing insurgent forces took the still smoldering town.

Mola's forces then began their final push toward Bilbo. By early May, the *gudariak* had withdrawn to the defensive position around the city known as the "ring of iron," and for seven more weeks, five divisions of Euzko Gudarostea defended the remaining twenty miles between Bilbo and Mola's troops. Bad weather continued to slow the insurgent advance, but it was increasingly clear that the war was lost for the pro-republic Basques. In these remaining weeks, Bilbo was a city under siege, suffering the twin effects of a naval blockade and heavy aerial bombardment. By early June, the "ring of iron" had been pierced, and the city lay just six miles away from the advancing insurgents. On June 3, Mola died in an air crash. "There is nothing to prove foul play," observes Hugh Thomas, but Franco was not a little relieved by the removal of a more than capable adversary to his own leadership.[184] It made little difference to the Basque campaign, however. Most of the *gudariak* now fled westward into the Spanish province of Santander as the civilian population braced itself for the arrival of the rebel troops. On June 17, 20,000 shells were dropped on the city, and the following day the remaining military units of Euzko Gudarostea were ordered to evacuate. Finally, at noon on June 19, rebel tanks entered Bilbo. That same afternoon, the 5th Nafarroan Brigade raised the monarchist flag over city hall.

Approximately 30,000 soldiers of Euzko Gudarostea had retreated into Santander from Bilbo, and there they would engage once more with the advancing insurgent forces (which still had a strong Nafarroan presence) on August 14, 1937. However, the fighting spirit had been drained from the Euzko Gudarostea soldiers. The Santander campaign lasted less than ten days, and between August 18 and 22 members of the Basque government were evacuated by sea to the French state. Basque troops thereafter refused orders from Madrid to retreat further west into Asturias, preferring to surrender to advancing Italian troops (Fascist Italy's contribution to Franco's war effort) and evacuating as many of their number as possible from the port of Santoña. On August 24, Basque representatives began negotiating with the Italians over the surrender of the *gudariak*. By the terms of the surrender, 60,000 Basque and non-Basque prisoners were handed over to the rebels. At the same time, Basque forces released insurgent prisoners in return for Italian guarantees that the lives of the *gudariak* would be spared. However, in early September insurgent Spanish forces took over control from the Italians, and the remaining Basque nationalist leaders still in Santoña were rounded up and, together with the captured troops,

Membership card of the EAJ-PNV from the 1930s.
Basque nationalists were more than just a political
party. They encouraged their members to consider their
cause as a family one and transmit a series of values
accordingly.
*Photo by permission of Abertzaletasunaren Agiritegia.
Sabino Arana Kultur Elkargoa archives.*

subject to harsh reprisals. After several show trials,
political militants (including Basque nationalists, socialists, communists, and anarchists) were executed. "It
would be impossible to exaggerate the importance of the
Spanish Civil War for Basque national identity," argues
Robert P. Clark in his thoughts about the effects on
Hegoalde of the tumultuous events of 1936–37.[185] To be

sure, war is a great leveler of humanity, an experience that ironically does much to bind people together at the very time it is tearing others apart. This aspect of war was recognized by the nineteenth-century French scholar Ernest Renan and proven by the experience of World War I, which did much to build a sense of French nationhood, as we have seen.

UNDOUBTEDLY, then, the experience of civil war did much to consolidate a sense of Basque national feeling among, it should be remembered, an already established nationalist community. However, we should add that at the same time, the experience of war also divided Basques. For many in Araba and, more especially, Nafarroa, Basque identity came to signify something other than the Basque nationalism of Bizkaians and Gipuzkoans. Perhaps the most important dimension of the Spanish Civil War for Hegoalde was the fact that it was also a *Basque* civil war, and, as such, the wounds within Hegoalde would take a long time to heal. The ferocity of the conflict, in particular (though not exclusively) the bombing of Gernika, would leave a scar on Basque society that would remain through to the late twentieth century.

Lesson nineteen

REQUIRED READING

Robert P. Clark, *The Basques: The Franco Years and Beyond* (Reno: University of Nevada Press, 1979), pp. 57–76.

Stanley G. Payne, *Basque Nationalism* (Reno: University of Nevada Press, 1975), pp. 177–225.

SUGGESTED READING

Michael Alpert, "Great Britain and the Blockade of
    Bilbao, April 1937," in William A. Douglass,
    Richard W. Etulain, and William H. Jacobs, eds.,
    *Anglo-American Contributions to Basque Studies:
    Essays in Honor of Jon Bilbao* (Reno: Desert Research
    Institute Publications on the Social Sciences, no. 13,
    1977), pp. 127–33.

LEARNING OBJECTIVES
1. To examine the nature of General Francisco Franco's
    uprising.
2. To examine the social, political, and cultural effects of
    civil war in Hegoalde.

WRITTEN LESSON FOR SUBMISSION
Document Question 4
Carefully study the following primary texts and write a
brief report about the bombing of Gernika in 1937 from
the information provided. Feel free to incorporate contextual information from other sources (including lecture notes), but try as much as possible to *construct* a
piece of historical writing from the primary texts themselves.

Father José Axunguiz, witness to the bombardment,
parish priest of Markina (a neighboring town of
Gernika) in 1937:

*It was an outing for the youth [Gernika's market day];
buses brought people from as far away as Lekeitio on
the coast. The people lacked war training. I blame the
Basque authorities. They shouldn't have allowed the
practice to continue, they were responsible for a great
number of deaths. Those of us who lived virtually on the
front, as in Markina, had learnt the importance of*

Basque soldiers pose for a photo during the Spanish
Civil War. The conflict, fought as a cause to be defended
to the death, later led to widespread poverty and suf-
fering in Euskal Herria.
*By permission of Abertzaletasunaren Agiritegia. Sabino
Arana Kultur Elkargoa archives.*

---

*building good shelters. But in Gernika they hadn't taken
adequate precautions; the shelters were rudimentary. I
kept telling my mother: "Build a good one." "Poor child,
poor child ... " was all she could say.*[186]

Hans Hemming von Boist, witness to the bombardment,
Squadron Commander of the Condor Legion in 1937:

I will try to recall the situation of the 26th of April, 1937, as far as it is possible after such a long time. ... [T]he order was to destroy a small bridge situated close to, but not in Gernika, and to attack troops and convoys on the roads from Gernika to the front. That was a normal ground-support mission. Weather and other conditions were normal. When the first flight had dropped his bombs, clouds of smoke and dust came up, so the visibility for the next pilots became very bad, and it was difficult to approach the targets and to hit them exactly ... maybe a few bombs hit Gernika instead. [187]

Father Dionisio Ajanguiz, witness to the bombardment, parish priest of Aulestia (a neighboring town of Gernika) in 1937:
The fighters dived down and machine-gunned people trying to flee across the plain. The bombers were flying so low you could see the crewmen. ... [I]t was a magnificent clear April evening after a showery morning. [188]

Ignacia Ozamiz, witness to the bombardment, housewife and resident of Gernika in 1937:
"Ignacia, where have we come to die?" the church organist from my home village said. "Here," I replied. The shelter was packed: 150 people at least between neighbors and people who had come for the market. The bombs crashed on the nearby hospital, killing twenty-five children and two nuns. Debris fell on the shelter, and we thought it had been hit. It was little more than a roof of sandbags, narrow and short, in the patio next to our house. Soon it was filled with smoke and dust. "Amatxu, take me out," my son began to cry in Basque. "I can't breathe." ... [P]eople started to panic ... "The house is on fire, we're going to be burnt alive," they screamed. Gudaris guarding the shelter let no one leave.

*One man tried to force his way out with his young child.
"I don't care if they kill me, I can't stand it here." He
was pushed back. "Keep calm," the soldiers shouted.*[189]

Juan Manuel Epalza, witness to the bombardment,
industrial engineer and EAJ-PNV member, resident of
Gernika in 1937:

*"And to think that we shall be blamed for this," I said
to Dr. Junod, the Swiss Red Cross representative, as we
walked through the still burning ruins a few hours later.
"No," replied Dr. Junod, "that's impossible." "You don't
know the enemy we have in front of us," I replied.*[190]

Saturnino Calvo, communist miner stationed with a battalion near Gernika in 1937:

*The effect of Gernika on the soldiers of my JSU bat-
talion was much worse than if they had been in combat
and suffered casualties. ... [T]o know that women and
children were being killed in the rearguard—we saw the
ambulances on the road below our positions—demoral-
ized them. I won't say it lowered their combat spirit—
the battalion was almost entirely Basque-speaking—but
it affected them deeply.*[191]

Claude Bowers, United States Ambassador to Spain,
extract from a letter to the United States Secretary of
State (April 30, 1937):

*Guernica "holy city of the Basques" totally destroyed
though an open country town with unarmed population
by huge bombs dropped from insurgent planes of
German origin and pilotage. Population fleeing to the
country attacked with hand grenades and machine guns
in planes. ... [T]he extermination of the town in line
with Mola's threat to exterminate every town in province
unless Bilbao surrenders.*[192]

George Steer, witness to the aftermath of the bombardment, foreign correspondent to the London *Times* covering the Spanish Civil War in 1937:

*There were four dead near the church. Two cottages
sprawled in smoking pieces across the road, and we
climbed over them down the fields to see the biggest
bomb-holes we had ever seen, warm and stinking of
metal still. They were over twenty feet deep and forty feet
wide. They were moon craters. ... Then silence in the village; nothing to see but the smoking houses and walls
smirched grey with fire. ... On the shattered houses,
whose carpets and curtains, splintered beams and floors
and furniture were knocked into angles and ready for
burning, the planes threw silver flakes. Tubes of two
pounds, long as your forearm, glistening from the their
aluminium and electron casing; inside them, as in the
beginning of the world in Prometheus' reed, slept fire.
Fire in a silver powder, sixty-five grammes in weight,
ready to slip through six holes at the base of a glittering
tube. So, as the houses were broken to pieces over the
people, sheathed fire descended from heaven to burn
them up. ... The people were worn out by noise, heat and
terror; they lay about like dirty bundles of washing,
mindless, sprawling and immobile. ... Gernika was finished, and as night fell and the motorized police stumbled along the road to ring up Bilbao to say that all was
over, the total furnace that was Gernika began to play
tricks of crimson colour with the night clouds. ... Around
the corpse of the Basques' oldest village caserios [farm-
houses] aflame in the hills made candles. The aviation
had spent the residue of its fire upon them and had
struck many. ... At Bilbao ... we were having dinner ...
when at ten o'clock Antonio Irala rang up. 'Gernika is in
flames,' he said. We got cars, threw our napkins on the
floor, and drove out into the dark towards Gernika. ...*

Irala must be exaggerating, I felt. The whole town cannot be burning. ... It glowed ahead of us, until we lost it against a brighter sky. Fifteen miles south of Gernika the sky began to impress us. It was not the flat dead sky of night; it seemed to move and carry trembling veins of blood; a bloom of life gave it body, flushed its smooth round skin. Nearer it became a gorgeous pink ... and it seemed enormously flat; it was beginning to disgust us. ... [W]e saw a dazed core of militiamen, Batallion Saseta, standing by the roadside, half waiting for, half incapable of understanding orders. The fire of the houses lit up their spent, open faces. In the plaza ... people sat upon broken chairs, lay on rough tables or mattresses wet with water. Mostly women: some hundreds of them were littered around in the open space ... some of the witnesses were quite dumb. They were digging them out of ruined houses—families at a time, dead and blue-black with bruising. Others were brought in from just outside Gernika with machine-gun bullets in their bodies. ... [I]n the center of the town ... [the] streets tightened and intertwined to make the heart of our conflagration. We tried to enter, but the streets were a royal carpet of live coals. ... [T]here were people, they said, to be saved there: there were the frameworks of dozens of cars. But nothing could be done, and we put our hands in our pockets and wondered why on earth the world was so mad and warfare became so easy.[193]

William Foss and Cecil Gerahty, extract from *The Spanish Arena* (1938):

The official report on Guernica has just been published. The report is manifestly restrained, conscientious and true. ... As Salamanca [Franco's wartime headquarters] has stated, and no less than twenty-one foreign journalists had been able to see for themselves, the town had been destroyed by fire from the retreating forces of the Madrid Government on April 26th when the advance lines of the Nationalists [Mola's troops] were within four miles of Guernica. The report of the commission, made up of two magistrates and two civil engineers who examined twenty-two eye-witnesses, states: (1) that Guernica was destroyed by fire; (2) Guernica was attacked by aeroplanes on April 26th and bombed intermittently; (3) the town at the time was occupied by Basque troops; (4) the market was sparsely attended that day because a number of the inhabitants had been warned of an "impending destruction"; (5) the total casualties were less than a hundred; (6) buildings started to burn for two days after the alleged raid; (7) explosions took place all night of April 26th. Most important of all, most of the damage in the streets was caused by subterranean explosions at nine different points. In each case the explosion occurred at the same distance from one of the nine manholes of the main sewer. The story of Guernica's 'wanton bombing' raised the indignation of Britain. It was untrue in almost every particular.[194]

20 · "Spain: one, great, and free"
The Francoist state and Basque culture to the 1960s

T HE TRIUMPH of General Francisco Franco in 1939 marked the victory of violence as a central instrument of political action. Thereafter, violence came to define day-to-day life in Francoist Spain. This was openly cultivated by Francoist political culture, which re-created the most extreme variant of nineteenth-century essentialist Spanish nationalism, calling on aspects of the Castilian Reconquest, the Counter-Reformation of Inquisition Spain, and the Spanish empire to create, in the words of the new regime's central motto, "Spain: one, great, and free." For Franco's domestic crusade, the great cultural enemies were the country's regional dialects. A cultural war was consequently waged against Basque national identity. Indeed, it would not be too much to say that Franco and his regime made a conscious effort to eradicate Basque culture in general. The next forty years in Hegoalde would prove to be a critical time, when there emerged a very real and seemingly invincible threat that Basque identity would be crushed under the weight of the state.

THE FRANCOIST STATE
Politics and Administration: Under the retroactive Law of Political Responsibilities of 1939, anyone who had supported the republic or hindered the eventual triumph of Franco at any time since 1934 could be subject to prosecution. The legislation served as the basis for a massive wave of persecution in the Spanish state in the aftermath of the war, with up to 200,000 people executed and 400,000 imprisoned. It was, above all, a systematic attempt to repress and eradicate *ideas*.

Franco also faced the difficult task of keeping the Carlists and the members of the Falange Española (Spanish Fascists) in line. He had therefore ordered the amalgamation of the two groups into the official state party (modeled on fascist institutions of the era), Falange Española Tradicionalista y de las Juntas de Ofensiva Nacional Sindicalista (FET y de las JONS), in April 1937. Despite the merger, the early years of the new regime were marked by internal power struggles between the Falangists and the armed forces, with Carlist monarchists waiting to capitalize on any disruption to the political order. To compound the problems of the new dictator, he had to contend with a small but persistent clandestine opposition movement within the Spanish state. There was also a period of international isolation, after the victorious Allies withdrew diplomatic relations in 1946 and barred the country from entering the United Nations for its support of Nazi Germany and Fascist Italy during World War II. Domestically, a law of 1943 combined the party and the state into one institution popularly known as the National Movement.

THE 1940s MARKED the most fragile decade of the dictatorship. Franco responded to the effects of international isolation by cementing a closer relationship with the Church to create a new state ideology, national Catholicism, which attracted a broader, if not exactly *popular*, base of support among the people. Franco also appointed a faithful deputy leader, Admiral Luis Carrero Blanco, and came to an agreement with the monarchists. At the end of the decade, the diplomatic isolation of the country waned as the United States began (in 1949) a series of financial-aid payments that would eventually translate formally into a military and economic agreement with the proto-fascist state. In an emerging Cold War atmosphere, Franco's friendships

Hitler welcomed by Franco at Hendaia railway station.
Franco kept a photo of the Führer on his desk until his
death in 1975. Together with Mussolini, he remained a
role model for the Caudillo, even after Spain's acceptance by the western powers in the 1950s.
*Photo by permission of Koldo Mitxelena Kultu-
runea archives.*

---

with Adolf Hitler and Benito Mussolini were forgotten as
the United States—following the line of the Truman
Doctrine of 1947—sought a strategic bulwark against
communism in southern Europe. This subsequently
allowed for the reintegration of the Spanish state into
the international community, and in 1955 the country
was admitted into the United Nations. American aid
continued through the 1950s, in return for which

United States military bases were established on Spanish territory.

Economy: The economic reorganization of the country under Franco was based on the policy of autarky, or self-sufficiency: industrialization that, instead of importing goods, used cheap domestic labor to produce them. It was, in other words, progress at a heavy human cost, with the working classes expected to bear the brunt of the hardship. As Mike Richards observes, "physical and economic repression in the wake of the Spanish civil war were used as a way of disciplining the lower orders of a society and confirming their defeat."[195] The policy proved to be redundant, however. In 1948, industrial production had only just caught up to 1929 levels, and by 1951 it remained at a pre–Civil War mark.

AGRICULTURE was also subject to state control through fixed pricing and marketing. This led to an even harsher standard of living in rural society, where, in real terms, wages fell by 40 percent between 1941 and 1951. The solution for many of the rural poor was urban migration, but the state frowned on the people taking their own initiative in attempting to relocate to the cities, rigidly controlling population movement. Instead, in a strategy aimed at maintaining a large body of surplus labor in the countryside, ready for the state's planned industrial development, Francoist Spain eulogized rural society.

Throughout the 1940s, Franco's economic policies made his country poor and desperate. Work and food were hard to come by, and official rationing (in force between 1939 and 1952, though its effects would last until the beginning of the 1960s) was inadequate. Hunger and disease, especially malaria and typhoid, were common. Franco viewed this as a necessary sacrifice on the road to modernization, with the brunt of the hardship falling, again, on those with the least means to cope with it. "'Progress' in the wake of the Spanish civil war," remarks Richards, "entailed a terroristic reversion to primitivism."[196] Beginning in the late 1950s, however, the dictatorship favored a policy of economic consolidation through liberalization (helped in no small part by American aid), whereby working conditions were improved and state regulation relaxed as Franco sought to reintegrate Spain economically into the international capitalist system. By the early 1960s, the regime had adopted a new policy of industrialization and structured development, so that integrated planning (work, housing, health, and education) were for the first time given priority in the economic policies of the regime. The state was aided in this by the twin factors of the growth of a Spanish tourist industry and the foreign currency flooding into the state from migrant workers, both of which stemmed from the economic boom experienced by postwar Europe in the 1950s and 1960s.

FRANCOISM AS SPANISH NATIONALISM

At the root of Franco's Spanish nationalism was a religious interpretation of Spain's destiny. Thus what in wartime had been a *crusade* translated into an *inquisition* in postwar society, with religion used to justify the extreme violence of the state. Indeed, the Church sanctioned and justified the use of violence as a means of exterminating enemies of the faith.

BUILDING ON the elimination of all other ideologies, the state and the Church attempted to impose their own Catholic moral orthodoxy. The basis of this ideology was a negation of those who had lost the war and all they stood for. Education remained the principal sphere for diffusing these ideas. Francoist education, employing Social Darwinian principles as well as sixteenth-century Catholic educational theory, emphasized the natural inequality and inherently sinful nature of humanity.

LANGUAGE WAS, of course, a key dimension of Franco's national vision. A 1941 decree proscribed the use of "dialects," such as the "inferior" tongues of Catalan and Basque ("the regime carefully chose to refer to these languages as 'dialects,'" states Clare Mar-Molinero[197]), "barbarisms" from foreign languages, and foreign languages themselves.[198] (However, Franco continued to study English privately.) Furthermore, all place and first names had to be Castilianized in an attempt to create the "one nation" vision of the *caudillo* (leader). "All the patriotic rhetoric of the dictatorship centred around the concept of *'lo castellano'* (things Castilian); anything challenging this was considered dangerously subversive," writes Mar-Molinero.[199]

"The distinction between the 'traditional' and the 'popular' was a crucial one in defining cultural policy," argues Carolyn P. Boyd; "tradition not only conferred legitimacy, but it also permitted greater selection and control of the cultural components of national identity that the regime claimed to embody. The popular culture consecrated as 'traditional' distilled and authenticated values and customs supportive of a hierarchical and reactionary social order and a unitary state, while marginalizing those deemed inconsonant with the 'purest and most traditional national essences'. The model of 'traditional culture' against which both popular and elite culture was now measured was Castilian, Catholic, rural, and, in the opening phases of the regime, imperial. To the extent that individual Spaniards or modern popular culture did not conform to this model, they were targeted for 'Hispanicization'."[200]

BASQUE SOCIETY IN FRANCOIST SPAIN

The Civil War ended in Hegoalde in 1937, but would continue for a further two years in the remaining parts of the state loyal to the republic. During those two years, a conscious strategy of state terror was applied to Basque society.

Angel García Sanz-Marcotegui has calculated that around 25,000 Basques died during the war between 1936 and 1939: 16,000 loyal to the republic and 9,000 insurgents.[201] Yet the killing did not cease in 1939, for with the cessation of official hostilities, a period of official state reprisal began. Those suspected of affiliation with pro-republic ideologies were summarily rounded up and executed. The losses were compounded by Franco's incarceration policy. There were perhaps as many as 5,000 to 7,000 Basque political prisoners during the immediate aftermath of war. Finally, out of the approximately half-million people who fled the country as a result of Franco's victory, possibly up to 150,000 were Basque, an extraordinarily high percentage for a minority region within the state as a whole.

TO COMPOUND the sense of defeat and loss within Hegoalde, the new Francoist state officially branded Bizkaia and Gipuzkoa as "traitorous" provinces. Without doubt, this stigmatization carried with it a cultural or ethnic dimension and served to legitimize the state terror imposed on the inhabitants of the two provinces. To a certain extent, these inhabitants were terrorized for being Basque, just as the decision to bomb Gernika (Guernica) in 1937 had been ideological (rather than tactical). Franco's regime continued to distinguish Bizkaia and Gipuzkoa from the rest of the country throughout its existence, imposing, for example, twelve "states of exception" (periods of martial law) between

An ikurriña (Basque flag) of the Beti Aurrera Division of the Sáseta Battallion, Euzko Gudarostea (Basque Army). Symbols are important in rallying individuals together as a group, especially in wartime.
Photo by permission of Abertzaletasunaren Agiritegia.
Sabino Arana Kultur Elkargoa archives.

1956 and 1975. Moreover, a deliberate attempt was made to exterminate all vestiges of Basque culture.

ACCORDING TO Robert P. Clark, "from 1937 to the middle 1950s the Spanish policy was one of total suppression of the [Basque] language. The only university in the Basque provinces was closed. Libraries of social and cultural associations were seized by troops and there was mass burning of books in Euskera. The teaching of the language was prohibited in all schools, public and private. The use of Euskera was prohibited in all public places, including casual conversations in the street, and on the radio and in the printed media. Basque cultural societies and their publications were proscribed. Euskera was prohibited in all religious publications, as well as in religious ceremonies. A decree was issued that required translation into Spanish of all Basque names in civil registries and other official documents, Basque names could not be used in baptism, and all inscriptions in Euskera were ordered removed from tombstones, funeral markers and public buildings."[202]

IN RESPONSE to this repression of all public expression of a separate ethnocultural identity, Basqueness retreated in postwar Spain into the private spheres of family, the local church, and the *cuadrilla* (social group). In the absence of any public space in which to maintain their Basque identity, for many the family became an intimate location of political education. While the Spanish Church hierarchy had sided with Franco and the rebels through the war, many Basque priests had defended the Basque nationalist cause. In the aftermath of war, those priests who had been sympathetic to Basque nationalism were considered traitors. As such, the Spanish authorities imprisoned more than four hundred Basque priests and monks, with sixteen executed for treason. Thereafter, Spanish priests were typically sent to Hegoalde to replace their suspect Basque counterparts. Those in the Basque clergy who did manage to remain in Euskal Herria were often the only source, outside the family, transmitting the Basque language (however clandestinely) to younger generations. *Cuadrillas* of young people also allowed individuals to maintain their Basque culture, and in the postwar Basque society of Hegoalde they became a crucial vehicle for articulating collective responses to Franco's dictatorship.

After the war, the leadership of the Basque nationalist movement went into exile, so that between 1939 and 1945 nationalist activity was restricted entirely to overseas groups. Several attempts were made by newly exiled Basques in France, Great Britain, and the United States, together with more established communities in Argentina, Uruguay, and Mexico, to raise the "Basque question" in the international community. This strategy involved an early commitment to the Allied cause during World War II. In 1941, after negotiations with General Charles de Gaulle's "Free French" organization in London, a Basque military unit was established; however, Winston Churchill's reluctance to test Franco's theoretical neutrality forced the disbandment of the unit the following year. More importantly for the Allies, a spy network was established in Euskal Herria during 1942, to monitor movements between Francoist Spain and German-controlled France. The principal wartime activity of ordinary Basques, however, was that of transporting refugees into the Spanish state and forming isolated pockets of resistance against the Nazi occupiers.

CLARK MAINTAINS that at the very least, several hundred exiles from Hegoalde must have been among the 14,000 Spanish Civil War veterans fighting with the French resistance fighters, the Maquis, in France.[203] In 1944, the Gernikako Batalloa (Gernika Battalion) was created out of Basque nationalist refugees and incorporated into the Eighth Mixed Moroccan-Foreign Regiment of the French state army. It subsequently saw active service in 1945 against the last remnants of German resistance in and around Bordeaux, distinguishing itself at the battle of Pointe-de-Grave. For their part in the battle, the Basques were awarded the Croix de Guerre, the highest French military honor, and were accorded an official reception in Baiona (Bayonne) for

"One Fatherland, One State, One Caudillo" Francisco Franco, Spanish dictator. The caudillo portrayed himself as the physical embodiment of a single, unitary Spain. *Photo by permission of Koldo Mitxelena Kulturunea archives.*

their efforts. The unit continued to serve until March 1946, when it was disbanded.

Given their active role in the Allied war effort, there was good reason for the exiled Basque community to feel optimistic about the possibility of international pressure being brought to bear on the Francoist regime. In 1945, the exiled Basque government met for the first time since the Civil War. A subsequent agreement between exiled political groups from the Spanish state reaffirmed the legality of the Second Republic and the Basque Statute of Autonomy. The president of the exiled government, José Antonio Aguirre y Lecube, had settled in Washington, D.C., in 1945,[204] from where he began lobbying the United States to help the Basque cause against Franco. After 1945, the Euzko Alderdi Jeltzalea-Partido Nacionalista Vasco (EAJ-PNV; Basque Nationalist Party) also began organizing a clandestine infrastructure within Hegoalde to coordinate resistance against the dictator.

THEREAFTER, between 1945 and 1947, a series of symbolic acts designed to unsettle the Francoist authorities were carried out: the *ikurriña* (Basque national flag, which had been banned under the regime) was planted on highly visible locations such as church steeples and monuments; nationalist slogans and the prohibited word "Euzkadi" were daubed on walls; and a statue of General Emilio Mola in Bilbo (Bilbao) was blown up in 1946. In 1947, some members of the resistance managed to interrupt the broadcast of a Donostia (San Sebastián) radio station with some words in Euskara proclaiming freedom for Euskal Herria. That same year, 120,000 people peacefully congregated in the four capitals of Hegoalde to celebrate the *aberri eguna* (Basque national day). A few days later, two bombs (presumably planted by Basque nationalist activists) exploded in Gernika on

the tenth anniversary of the town's destruction. The
Spanish state's response was severe: Between 1946 and
1947, a number of arrests led to the imprisonment of
many and execution of some.

The initial period of resistance to the Francoist state
culminated between 1947 and 1951. In May 1947, a
widespread general strike in Hegoalde was convened to
protest the harsh conditions imposed by the dictatorship. The strike began among the miners and steel
workers of Bizkaia, but quickly spread to Gipuzkoa. However, with the exception of 15,000 workers in Madrid,
the rest of the state did not respond. With three-quarters
of the Bizkaian workforce out on strike, the government
sent in troops to patrol the streets of Bilbo, and by the
second week of May the protest was all but over. There
followed a wave of industrial protests in a concerted
attempt to unsettle the state, culminating in another
general strike in 1951. In late April of that year, 250,000
workers in Bizkaia and Gipuzkoa (nearly all the workforce in the two provinces) walked out, although the
arrests of many forced their comrades back soon after.
The strike took a decidedly violent turn in Gipuzkoa,
with clashes between strikers and police in Donostia
and Tolosa. The repressive response of the authorities
provoked sympathy strikes in Gasteiz (Vitoria) and
Iruñea (Pamplona), which also turned into violent
clashes between police and workers. However, as in the
1947 protest, the rest of the Spanish state did not support the Basque action, and this ultimately allowed
Franco to concentrate the authorities at his disposal in
Hegoalde.

ABROAD, AGUIRRE met with American State Department officials in 1950 to discuss the country's
policy toward the Spanish state and to lobby for a
renewed commitment on the part of the international

community to bring down the Franco regime. However, unbeknownst to him at the time, American (and Western) policy was already in the process of an about-turn, as mentioned previously, that would ease international relations with Francoist Spain. Amid the power play of international diplomacy, Euskal Herria, despite the support demonstrated to the Allied cause by many Basques throughout World War II, remained an insignificant "region" between the two more important states of France and Spain.

From the 1950s on, Hegoalde underwent a series of rapid social and economic changes that left the exiled leadership isolated from the day-to-day reality of Basque society. A new generation of Basque nationalists, who knew nothing of the experience of war and little of the clandestine activity of the 1940s, was emerging at the same time. They would increasingly reject the path of international diplomacy in favor of direct confrontation with a state intent on eliminating their culture (discussed in greater detail in Chapter 21).

THE INDUSTRIALIZATION that began in the mid-1950s encouraged waves of migrants (previously restricted to their economically depressed rural areas) to converge on the centers of development, prominent among which were the towns and cities of Hegoalde, including the new urban centers of Araba and Nafarroa. By the 1960s, remarks Clark, population movement toward the region "reached flood proportions."[205] Between 1951 and 1970, the four provinces of Hegoalde gained around 200,000 new residents, principally from the western provinces of the Spanish state. The four capital cities of the region experienced rapid growth: Between 1957 and 1970, Gasteiz grew at an annual rate of 9.37 percent, followed by Bilbo (5.25 percent) and Iruñea (4.25 percent). Donostia's growth was more limited, due to its unique socio-economic position as a tourist and administrative center, with industry diffused into nearby Gipuzkoan towns such as Eibar, Tolosa, Errenteria (Rentería), and Irun.

It was not hard to see why Hegoalde experienced such massive population change during the period: By 1969, the provinces of Gipuzkoa, Araba, and Bizkaia ranked first, second, and third in the Spanish state in terms of per-capita income, with Nafarroa coming in seventh. This second great wave of migration into Hegoalde (after that of the late nineteenth century) led to a less homogeneous population than ever (indeed, by the mid-1970s about one-third of the workforce in Hegoalde had been born outside the Basque Country) and, together with the conscious efforts made by the regime, a decreasing level of Basque-language knowledge and use. Culturally, it seemed as if a distinctively separate Basque ethnocultural identity was on the wane.

BY THE 1960s, the Spanish state had changed dramatically. The international isolation and random, widespread state terror experienced from the late 1930s to the early 1950s had gone. Reborn as a solid opponent of communism, Franco had carefully cultivated Western support to gain both economic aid and a cautious foothold in the international community. By the early to mid-1960s, Franco's fascist dictatorship (with its severely repressive tactics, including imprisonment, torture, and execution) had evolved into a more pragmatic regime. Although still a dictatorship, and more than able to employ brutal repressive methods when needed, the Spanish state relaxed many of its former restrictions. For example, it allowed the *private* teaching of languages other than Castilian and selective publication in these languages.

A Gudari (basque nationalist soldier) with ikurriña or Basque flag. As with French nation-building during World War One, Basque nationalists used the Spanish Civil War to promote a sense of loyalty to Euskal Herria. *By permission of Abertzaletasunaren Agiritegia. Sabino Arana Kultur Elkargoa archives.*

Mar-Molinero argues: "To some extent, this reflects the confidence of the Franco regime, as it judged that it had little to fear from unflattering views published in non-Castilian languages, given the inevitably limited readership. The regime deliberately encouraged a certain type of media coverage in non-Castilian languages of a sort which might in fact seem to trivialize their cultures—reports on dance competitions or local fiestas or how to cook local dishes—leaving 'serious' news and politics to be reported in Castilian."[206]

BUT FOR clandestine political developments, this might indeed have been the case. However, the existence of a distinctively Basque national identity had been neither exterminated nor relegated to cooking reports, for at the very moment that the Franco regime emerged from the crisis years of the 1940s, a renewed political movement would emerge to doggedly upset the otherwise resurgent dictatorship.

Lesson twenty

REQUIRED READING

Robert P. Clark, *The Basques: The Franco Years and Beyond* (Reno: University of Nevada Press, 1979), pp. 79–106.

José Antonio de Aguirre, *Escape via Berlin: Eluding Franco in Hitler's Europe* (Reno and Las Vegas: University of Nevada Press, 1991), pp. 23–61.

SUGGESTED READING

Michael Richards, "Constructing the Nationalist State: Self-Sufficiency and Regeneration in the Early Franco Years," in Clare Mar-Molinero and Angel Smith, eds., *Nationalism and the Nation in the Iberian Penin-*

sula: Competing and Conflicting Identities (Oxford
and Washington, D.C.: Berg, 1996), pp. 149–67.

Mike Richards, "'Terror and Progress': Industrialization,
Modernity, and the Making of Francoism," in Helen
Graham and Jo Labanyi, eds., *Spanish Cultural
Studies: An Introduction* (Oxford: Oxford University
Press, 1995), pp. 173–82.

Jo Labanyi, "Censorship or the Fear of Mass Culture," in
Helen Graham and Jo Labanyi, eds., *Spanish Cultural
Studies: An Introduction* (Oxford: Oxford University
Press, 1995), pp. 207–14.

LEARNING OBJECTIVES

1. To understand the structure of the Francoist state.
2. To explore the role of violence in the new regime.

WRITTEN LESSON FOR SUBMISSION

1. In what ways did Franco's Spanish nationalism represent a continuation of past incarnations of the ideology? List specific elements in your answer.
2. Critically analyze the assigned text by José Antonio de Aguirre. What does it reveal about the nature of wartime Europe? What, in your opinion, are the most *important* and *interesting* points disclosed by the text? Why would you highlight these points?

21 · Political violence
ETA and Basque nationalism during the Franco years

"THE POSTWAR generation of Basque nationalists,"
observe Francisco J. Llera, José M. Mata, and Cynthia L. Irvin, "are the children of a century and a half of
civil wars and symbolic violence."[207] In this chapter, we
will see how Euzkadi ta Askatasuna (ETA; "Euzkadi"—
the name coined by Sabino de Arana y Goiri to refer to
the Basque Country—and Freedom) emerged as the
product of historical experience in Euskal Herria. We
will thus trace the emergence and development of the
organization from post–Civil War society to the death of
Francisco Franco in 1975. Thereafter, we will engage in
critical reflection about the nature of Basque political
violence.

THE BIRTH AND DEVELOPMENT OF EKIN, 1947–59
Between 1947 and 1951, despite the successful mobilization of Basque workers in protest against the Spanish
state, many activists were arrested and imprisoned. Such
was the experience, also, of a student group by the name
of Euzko Ikasle Alkartasuna (EIA; Society of Basque Students). Unversed in the ways of clandestine organization, virtually its entire leadership was arrested in 1950.
Thereafter, the remaining members of the group
(together with those who served their prison sentences
and were able to return to their studies) were determined not to make the same mistakes they had made
during the late 1940s. At the same time, the clandestine
network of the Euzko Alderdi Jeltzalea-Partido Nacionalista Vasco (EAJ-PNV; Basque Nationalist Party) had also
been severely weakened, leaving a number of young
activists to organize their own activities independently
of established groups.

During the academic year of 1951–52, one such group of young people, principally composed of engineering students, some of whom had been active in EIA, began meeting on an informal basis in Bilbo (Bilbao) for secret discussion in Euskara about common interests and Basque culture in general. They were, in the main, upper-middle-class male students from urban Spanish-speaking families in Bilbo and Donostia (San Sebastián), and constituted a group of around eleven members. Gradually, the group began to take on a more formal organization, with each member concentrating his efforts (the group was composed of only males at this time) on researching one particular field of Basque history and culture. The results of these efforts were then published in an internal newsletter by the name of *Ekin* (a Basque verb implying the act of doing something).

BETWEEN 1951 and 1953, the group, which increasingly came to term itself by the name of the newsletter, dedicated its time to the intellectual investigation and publication of Basque historical and cultural information. At the same time, it came to conceive of outright independence as the only real goal of Basque nationalism, and it distanced itself from what it saw as the vague self-determination policy and general inaction of the EAJ-PNV. In doing so, the young activists thought of themselves as more faithful to the original precepts of Basque nationalism, that they were true *radicals* returning to the roots of the political problem between Euskal Herria and the Spanish and French states. The group also borrowed heavily from the existential ideas prevalent in European intellectual thought at the time, and looked to the growing number of predominantly "third-world" *national* liberation struggles against Western imperial powers as an example (as opposed to the tactic of international diplomacy).

ETA built up an organizational infrastructure of a couple
of hundred activists and relied wholly on the theoretical
tactic of symbolic violence. However by the late 1960s
and beyond this symbolism would be replaced by an all-
too-real and progressively tragic call-to-arms.

B Y 1953, AN alternative vision of Basque nationalism
had thus been established, opposed in several distinct ways to that of the EAJ-PNV. That year, the Ekin
group edited the findings of the previous two years into
seven publications known as the *Cuadernos Ekin* (Ekin
Notebooks), works that would serve as the ideological
basis of the new movement. Robert P. Clark observes
that two basic differences from the EAJ-PNV ideology
marked the new organization: an insistence on the

importance of Euskara in defining Basqueness and the goal of creating an independent Basque republic. To this, I would add the nonconfessional nature of the group, as opposed to the Christian democracy of the EAJ-PNV.[208]

IN 1953, EKIN (having lost four members of the original group of students) counted two cells, representing Bizkaia and Gipuzkoa. The purpose of the group at this time was twofold: First, it would serve as an educational organization aimed at diffusing Basque language, history, and culture, together with information about contemporary intellectual and political developments. Second, learning from the mistake of EIA, it proposed the creation of a truly clandestine Basque nationalist political organization. From 1953 on, with a growing affiliation, the group began to attract the attention of the EAJ-PNV. Having already incorporated the remaining activists of EIA into its fold, the EAJ-PNV was naturally interested in the activities of Ekin, and, however suspicious they were of each other, the two organizations established a dialogue. In Gipuzkoa, this took the form of a close relationship between Ekin and Eusko Gaztedi (EG; Basque Youth), the youth wing of the EAJ-PNV. Ultimately, this led to an amalgamation of the two in 1956, under the name Eusko Gaztedi del Interior (EGI; Basque Youth of the Interior)—"interior" meaning within the Spanish state.

In 1956, another wave of industrial protest gripped the Spanish state, and once again the capitals of Hegoalde staged of much of the action. In mid-April, 3,000 workers in Iruñea (Pamplona) began a strike that spread soon after to both Gipuzkoa and Bizkaia. By the end of the month, 40,000 workers were on strike in Bilbo, and thereafter the protest spread to Gasteiz (Vitoria). To the former Ekin members now in EGI, the industrial unrest of Hegoalde confirmed the need to build up ties to working-class organizations in order to foment a social revolution, but their rhetoric was too extreme for the EAJ-PNV leadership.

IN 1957, EGI members met with the party leadership in its Parisian exile, in an attempt to resolve obvious differences between the youth wing and the main party. The meeting ended in disaster, however, as the EGI members felt snubbed by the EAJ-PNV hierarchy (though not, ironically, by EAJ-PNV's leader, José Antonio Aguirre y Lecube), and the older members regarded their younger counterparts as lacking a pragmatic approach to the problems of Euskal Herria. Thereafter, many members of the youth organization determined to follow the path charted by Ekin, not that of the EAJ-PNV. Further problems ensued, and a second crisis meeting was held in Paris in the spring of 1958, but the two sides were once again unsuccessful in resolving their basic differences. Members of the EGI began to go their separate ways, with the group splitting roughly in half between those still loyal to the EAJ-PNV (predominantly those in Bizkaia) and those more attracted by Ekin's program (predominantly those in Gipuzkoa). Throughout the following year, both factions continued to use the acronym EGI, until in 1959 the Ekin-inspired group came up with a new name: Euzkadi ta Askatasuna (ETA).

ETA'S FIRST INCARNATION, 1959–67

During the initial period of its existence, from 1959 to 1968, ETA built up an organizational infrastructure with a couple of hundred activists and relied wholly on the theoretical tactic of symbolic violence. In 1961, it attempted its first *ekintza* (action): On July 18, the anniversary of the Spanish military uprising in 1936, an unsuccessful attempt was made to derail a series of trains carrying Francoist sympathizers to a rally in Donostia to celebrate the anniversary. The state quickly responded. One hundred and ten Basques were arrested, tortured, and sentenced to jail terms up to twenty years long. A further group was forced into exile in the French state (predominantly Iparralde).

In 1962, the group held its first organizational assembly (in the comparative safety of the French state). There, it was formally agreed that the organization would develop along the lines of an armed national-liberation movement, as had successfully appeared in countries from Israel to Algeria. As such, ETA's program called for a revolutionary war, and increasingly the group invoked Marxist ideology to justify the need for insurrection. During this time, a new wave of industrial protest had gripped the Basque Country, and the changing fabric of Basque society—in particular, the large number of non-Basque workers now involved in Hegoalde's labor movement—forced a critical rethinking of ETA's commitment to social, as well as cultural, needs.

BETWEEN 1963 and 1964, in a successful operation to sever the new organization, the Spanish state's security forces managed, with relative ease, to identify and crush the group. ETA would learn from this that only a highly clandestine structural organization would be capable of withstanding the all-pervasive control of the Franco dictatorship, and at the watershed third assembly of 1964 (also held in France), the group reorganized along these lines. By this time, a new generation of young activists had enlisted in ETA. Socially and culturally distinct from the group's founders, they would set in place a series of changes, both ideological and organizational, within ETA. Specifically, the group definitively broke with the EAJ-PNV, at the same time defining their organization as anticapitalist and anti-imperialist.

By the time of the fifth assembly, held during 1966 and 1967, a series of different factions had emerged within ETA, with the group divided into (for want of better expressions) *cultural, social,* and *anticolonial* activists.[209] The cultural activists emphasized the need to pursue a national struggle as a way of safeguarding and promoting Basque culture, especially Euskara. The social militants took less of an interest in cultural matters, preferring to concentrate on ETA's struggle to liberate the working classes from the industrial oligarchy (both Basque and Spanish) of the state. The anticolonial faction of the group—in many respects incorporating ideas from the other two branches—viewed ETA's struggle as a war of national liberation from colonial oppressors, namely the Spanish state.

THE FIFTH assembly proved to be a critical moment for the tactics of group, and one in which the "old guard" (many of the former Ekin members) tended their resignations from ETA. Specifically, they disagreed with the clearly evolving guerrilla-tactical strategy and Marxist-Leninist political ideology of the organization. Thereafter, the new-look ETA isolated the remaining moderates in the group and made a commitment to open confrontation with representatives of the Spanish state, typically members of the popularly hated Civil Guard.

THE VIOLENT TURN OF ETA, 1967–75

From the spring of 1967 on, a series of confrontations took place between ETA activists and the Civil Guard. Typically, the confrontations occurred after an ETA *ekintza* (a bank robbery to secure money to buy

Basque soldiers at the funeral of a fallen colleague. The coffin is draped with an ikurriña (Basque flag), leaving no doubt as the soldiers' primary national identity.
By permission of Abertzaletasunaren Agiritegia. Sabino Arana Kultur Elkargoa archives.

---

weapons, for example, or the blowing up of an unoccupied building) and subsequent police or Civil Guard roadblocks. Several ETA members were wounded during these confrontations, and in November 1967 the Civil Guard killed a sixteen-year-old boy, wrongly suspected of being an ETA militant, in Nafarroa. Through the spring of 1968, a series of arrests were carried out in brutal fashion, and in Gasteiz one ETA activist lost an eye during a police beating. In 1968, a shoot-out took place near the village of Aduna in Gipuzkoa, resulting in the death of a Civil Guard, José Pardines. As the car carrying the ETA members involved fled, it ran into another roadblock and one of its occupiers, Txabi Etxe-barrieta, was hauled from the vehicle and shot dead. Its other occupier, Iñaki Sarasqueta, managed to flee, although he was eventually caught and sentenced to fifty-eight years in jail.

The Basque public response to the deaths was one of sympathy for Etxebarrieta. Mass demonstrations were held in towns and cities across Hegoalde, from Bilbo to Iruñea. Etxebarrieta became the martyr for ETA's cause, and the organization's ranks swelled with huge numbers of new recruits. ETA's response to Etxebarrieta's death was the assassination of Melitón Manzanas, a police inspector in the Gipuzkoan border town of Irun well known as a sadistic torturer of prisoners. In turn, the government declared martial law in Gipuzkoa and rounded up many suspects. Finally, it decided to prosecute fourteen members of ETA and two priests for what it considered their part in the events of 1968.

BETWEEN 1968 and 1970, Spanish security forces successfully neutralized ETA's leadership and organization through a wave of mass arrests and incarcerations. However, although the group's military wing had effectively been made inoperative, the state's widespread repressive tactics actually served to radicalize the Basque population, leading to a greater level of popular support for, and recruitment to, the group. This was evident when, in December 1970, the fourteen people supposedly implicated in the Manzanas assassination went to military trial in Burgos. The prosecution requested the death penalty for six of their number, but a massive sway of public opinion against the state (both domestically and internationally) and the bad publicity that the trial had generated for the Franco regime forced the authorities to back down. The death penalties were commuted to life sentences.

The Burgos trial acted as a catalyst for the Basque nationalist movement in general and ETA in particular. Although much of the group's infrastructure had been depleted by the state crackdown during the 1968–70 period, and despite the fact that it continued to be plagued by ideological and tactical differences, after 1970 ETA received many new recruits, including a new wave of former EGI members and many working-class youths from the industrial towns of Hegoalde. As a result, ETA became much more of an urban guerrilla movement than before, and during the next four years (until the death of Franco) the group engaged the security forces in increasingly sophisticated ways.

By 1970, ETA had split into two factions, ETA-V (a group committed to a Basque ethno-cultural nationalist ideology and armed insurrection following national-liberation models) and ETA-VI (a leftist group less interested in Basque cultural activism and more committed to ideological reflection and revolutionary socialism). Although ETA-VI entered the new decade as, theoretically, the more powerful of the two factions—it controlled the organizational apparatus, for example—it was ETA-V that gradually emerged as the more dynamic of the two, mobilizing large numbers of young Basques during the early 1970s with daring *ekintzak*. By 1973, ETA was imploding under this ideological and tactical division, which was played out in an increasing divergence between the organization's military and labor fronts. That year, ETA undertook its most audacious action to date, assassinating Admiral Carrero Blanco, Franco's right-hand man and chosen successor.

In 1974, the labor front split from ETA to form the Langile Abertzale Iraultzaileen Alderdia (LAIA; Patriotic Revolutionary Workers' Party). That same year, ETA was further divided as the military front split into two

Poster for the film Operación Ogro (Operation Ogre) (1979) about the assassination of Admiral Carrero Blanco, Franco's right-hand man, in 1973. In the immediate aftermath of the dictatorship a flood of movies treated Basque relations with the former regime in a relatively open way.

Photo by permission of Koldo Mitxelena Kulturunea archives.

factions: ETA(m) (military), which remained committed to armed struggle as the principal vehicle of independence, and ETA(pm) (politico-military), which adopted a Marxist class-struggle program.

IN APRIL 1975, the Spanish government imposed the last, but one of the most severe, measures of martial law in Hegoalde, leading to the detention, imprisonment, and torture of thousands of Basques. That September, as a result of the arrests, two Basque youths were executed, together with three members of Grupos de Resistencia Antifascista Primero de Octubre (GRAPO; The First of October Anti-Fascist Resistance Groups), a left-wing Spanish armed-resistance group, an event that provoked the recalling of several European ambassadors from Madrid. As a result of the persecution, several civil and armed groups in the Basque Country created a coalition known as Koordinadora Abertzale Sozialista (KAS; Socialist Nationalist Coordinating Council) as a platform for lobbying for the amnesty of all political prisoners and exiles. However, that same year, on November 20, Franco died after a five-week illness, and prince Juan Carlos (Franco's chosen successor in the wake of Blanco's death) was crowned king on November 22. This brought one period of ETA's history—and supposedly the defining *raison d'être* of the group (Franco's dictatorship)—to an end. Between 1968 and 1975, ETA assassinated thirty-four people. The group would now be faced with the implications of a transition to Spanish democracy.

SOME CRITICAL OBSERVATIONS ABOUT BASQUE POLITICAL VIOLENCE

Llera, Mata, and Irvin maintain that a subculture of violent resistance emerged in Hegoalde as a result of the "continuous and pervasive application of coercive force"

by the Franco regime, which "effectively limited its discourse with Basques to one of violence."[210] This
"causes and consequences" approach (critiqued by
William A. Douglass and Joseba Zulaika[211]) would
present a basic historical summary of the armed Basque
group thus: The violence of ETA emerged as a consequence of the violence of the Francoist state, and consequently the group should have disappeared with democ-
ratization and the legitimization "of institutional means
to achieve collective aims."[212] We will explore the effec-
tiveness of such institutional means in greater detail in
the following chapter, but for the moment let us critically evaluate this conceptual idea.

VALUE JUDGMENT seems to pervade the study of terrorism, perhaps more than in other field of academic
inquiry. By starting from a basic conceptual notion that
ETA was and still is a *terrorist* group that had some legitimacy during the Franco dictatorship, but that should
have disappeared during a democratic transition, it is
difficult to analyze Basque political violence without
drawing on moral, rather than critical academic conclusions. The reason, then, that a critical approach to the
study of Basque political violence has been introduced
at this historical juncture is that it fosters academic
inquiry by enabling the researcher to disassociate him-
or herself from the "ought to be" obligations (predeter-
mined categorizations or value judgments devoid of
individually thought-out opinion) highlighted by Douglass and Zulaika.[213]

Following the argument of Douglass and Zulaika, I
would contend that most explanations of ETA and
Basque political violence have been incomplete, due to
"ought to be" value judgments being brought to
analysis of the phenomenon. Thus, as I have argued
elsewhere,[214] we might first of all ascribe ETA a three-

fold historical genealogy: as a congruent component of
the development of Basque nationalism in general; as a
fluid response to the evolving social, economic, political,
and cultural context of post–Civil War Basque society;
and as a reflection of the intellectual preoccupations of
post–World War II European society. At its origin, ETA,
far from proposing the immediate use of arms in a violent war against the Spanish state, was more concerned
with critical self-reflection about the meaning of Basque
national identity and the interplay between Basque and
Spanish identities throughout history. It took the
extremes of a dictatorship to provoke a violent response,
but to simplify ETA as merely a product of the dictatorship is, in my opinion, misleading. Indeed, ETA had a
twenty-year nonviolent history that does not seem to fit
in with the neat explanations of much terrorism theory.
It would be more accurate to look at the conceptual basis
by which Ekin and ETA emerged as a cultural dynamic
between Spanish and Basque nationalisms, or as competing cultural and ideological claims to individual and
group identity. As we have seen, these concerns have
been a historical constant in Basque society during the
entire modern period, with several examples of clashes,
physically violent or otherwise, between the competing
sides.

GIVEN THIS history of confrontation between the
Spanish state and Basque militants, violence in
Hegoalde is, as Begoña Aretxaga puts it, "a fantastic
reality" more than "ideological product." That is not to
say, she explains, that it is *illusory*; "it means that in
the Basque Country the experience of violence corre-
sponds to a *different* mode of reality, one whose visibility [historically also, in my opinion] is that of the
invisible, a spectral mode not unlike that of witch-
craft."[215] This *fantasy* has been played out historically

in the subjugation of Basque culture to the needs of
state building, with Basque culture (and, most obviously, its language) being relegated to another world of
rustic savagery. Defined as primitive and savage, some
Basques thus took it upon themselves to react in what
for the state was a primitive and savage way. Historically, as Aretxaga maintains, this "hall of mirrors" effect
has been a consistent factor in defining the cultural
struggle between Basque and Spanish or French identities.

Lesson twenty-one

REQUIRED READING

William A. Douglass and Joseba Zulaika, "On the Inter-
    pretation of Terrorist Violence: ETA and the Basque
    Political Process," *Comparative Studies in Society
    and History* 32, no. 2 (April 1990), pp. 238–57.
Begoña Aretxaga, "A Hall of Mirrors: On the Spectral
    Character of Basque Political Violence," in William A.
    Douglass, Carmelo Urza, Linda White, and Joseba
    Zulaika, eds., *Basque Politics and Nationalism on the
    Eve of the Millennium* (Reno: Basque Studies Pro-
    gram, 1999), pp. 115–26.

SUGGESTED READING

Robert P. Clark, *The Basque Insurgents: ETA, 1952–1980*
    (Madison: University of Wisconsin Press, 1984),
    pp. 28–56.
Cameron Watson, "Imagining ETA," in William A. Dou-
    glass, Carmelo Urza, Linda White, and Joseba Zulaika,
    eds., *Basque Politics and Nationalism on the Eve of
    the Millennium* (Reno: Basque Studies Program,
    1999), pp. 94–114.

Cameron Watson, "Sacred Earth, Symbolic Blood: A Cultural History of Basque Political Violence" (Ph.D. diss., University of Nevada, Reno, 1996), pp. 547–83.

Francisco J. Llera, José M. Mata, and Cynthia L. Irvin, "ETA: From Secret Army to Social Movement—The Post-Franco Schism of the Basque Nationalist Movement," *Terrorism and Political Violence* 5, no. 3 (autumn 1995), pp. 106–34.

LEARNING OBJECTIVES

1. To account for the emergence and development of ETA from its origins during the early 1950s through to the death of Francisco Franco.
2. To place ETA within the context of the history of Basque nationalism.
3. To make some preliminary considerations about the critical analysis of Basque political violence.

WRITTEN LESSON FOR SUBMISSION

1. Critically compare and contrast the article by Francisco J. Llera, José M. Mata, and Cynthia L. Irvin with that by William A. Douglass and Joseba Zulaika. What common observations do the authors draw? How do they differ in their approaches? Which (if either) of the two articles do you find the most persuasive, and why?
2. In reading Begoña Aretxaga's analysis of the Otegi incident, how do you feel this contemporary event mirrors historical experiences in the Basque Country? Think about some of the theoretical issues Aretxaga raises when framing your answer.

22 · Spain's second transition, 1975–82

TOWARD THE end of the twentieth century, the struggle between the Spanish state, with its dedication to national integration, and those elements of Basque political culture wanting to preserve regional power or even declare independence, would, having grown over the previous two hundred years, now accelerate and diversify—to such an extent that, on the eve of the new millennium, Basque political culture might reasonably be considered one of the most complex and vexing in western Europe. In the following four chapters, we will primarily consider political events in Euskal Herria through the division of Hegoalde and Iparralde. I do not want to deny that there remained obvious links between the two regions of Euskal Herria during this time, but it seems more expedient to treat political events separately, arriving at a general comparison toward the end of Chapter 25. Furthermore, as identity is the primary focus of this investigation of Basque history, it is not possible to escape the issue of political violence.

THE UNCERTAINTY, 1975–77

Between the death of Francisco Franco in 1975 and the democratic elections of June 1977 (the first in the Spanish state since February 1936), a period of intense social and political activity took place. To say that Spain became a democracy on the death of Franco would be misleading, for the framework of the dictatorship (censorship and police repression, for example) remained in place. During this period, ETA(pm) gradually renounced its armed struggle, believing that social and political progress were now theoretically possible through systematic means. King Juan Carlos immedi-

ately granted a general amnesty to many of the thousands of political prisoners in Spanish jails, although
the pardon was principally applied to those who had
been tried for lesser crimes (such as the dissemination
of illegal propaganda or for "illicit association")
together with many common criminals; about three
hundred (principally Basque) political prisoners being
held on suspicion of terrorism were unaffected.

Then, in the spring of 1976, tensions between the state
and the Basque provinces erupted in open confrontation. On March 3, workers in Gasteiz (Vitoria) proclaimed a "day of struggle," resulting in a peaceful mass
demonstration by about 80 percent of the city's workforce in support of a strike over pay demands in several
firms. Under the orders of Manuel Fraga, Franco's
former Minister of the Interior, the police were sent to
violently crush the demonstration. Two people were
killed and a dozen seriously wounded. Thereafter, the
violence escalated, with police tactics more reminiscent
of Franco's dictatorship than of a new Spain. By the end
of the fourth day, the state security forces had killed five
demonstrators. In a subsequent March demonstration
throughout Hegoalde, the police killed yet another pro-
tester, this time in Bilbo (Bilbao). The confrontation
continued for several weeks and dissipated through lack
of energy rather than through resolution. Throughout
the spring, Hegoalde was consumed by political violence
as both ETA and Spanish nationalist right-wing groups
engaged in a wave of assassinations.

B Y THE SUMMER, however, the king felt that enough
progress had been made to name a provisional government, and Adolfo Suárez became acting premier. He
immediately presented a new plan of amnesty for all
political prisoners not convicted of terrorism or guerrilla activities, and this was eventually accepted by the

Mauser semi-automatic pistol, 1937. This remarkable
gun was a weapon of choice by the Basque army. A
wooden holster doubles as a rifle stock.
Photo by permission of Abertzaletasunaren Agiritegia.
Sabino Arana Kultur Elkargoa archives.

king. However, many Basque nationalists, as Robert P.
Clark observes,[216] were dismayed by the government's
failure to recognize that the first such violent action had
been Franco's military uprising, and that many people
guilty of atrocities in support of the Francoist regime
were not subject to the same laws. One of the features of
the Spanish transition was becoming increasingly clear,
however: The Spanish political Right continued to exert
a significant influence in the country—perhaps *the*

dominant influence of the transition period—and any agreement toward democracy would be based on a *selective* forgetting of the past; that is to say, while enemies of the Francoist state remained in jail, many Francoists would remain free.

That summer, a young Basque was killed by the Spanish police in the town of Hondarribia (Fuentarrabía) in Gipuzkoa. A strike ensued across the province in protest against the general policy of the police, spreading throughout Hegoalde through early fall. The protest culminated in a day of mass demonstrations throughout the region on September 27, with an estimated 700,000 people out on the streets (an extraordinary figure considering the total population of Hegoalde). On October 4, ETA(m) responded to the death of the young Basque by killing the president of the Provincial Assembly of Gipuzkoa, Juan de Araluce, its most high-profile victim since Carrero Blanco. This in turn provoked a backlash by right-wing gangs (totaling about one thousand people) in Donostia (San Sebastián), who went on a rampage after a demonstration in the wake of the assassination, smashing up shops and bars and beating passersby in the Gipuzkoan capital. The police made no effort to control the demonstration. A week later, similar incidents occurred in the Bizkaian town of Durango, where right-wing militants repeatedly attacked local people without police intervention of any kind.

IN NOVEMBER, Suárez recommended that the country should actively seek a democratic transition. A December referendum approved the measure by a large margin throughout the state, except in Bizkaia and Gipuzkoa, where only 50 and 42 percent, respectively, voted in the affirmative, due to the fact that the reform agreement included a provision to maintain several elements of the former Francoist regime, such as the police, judiciary, and military. In December 1976, the Partido Socialista Obrero Español (PSOE; Spanish Socialist Workers Party) held its twenty-seventh congress, where it accepted the transition program of Suárez. The most reluctant partners in the "new" Spain remained the Basques. In 1977, a deal of sorts was struck, whereby the Spanish armed forces accepted the legalization of the Partido Comunista de España (PCE; Communist Party of Spain), and the PCE accepted the monarchy, flag, and territorial unity of the state.

THE EUZKO Alderdi Jeltzalea-Partido Nacionalista Vasco (EAJ-PNV; Basque Nationalist Party) cautiously entered negotiations with the state's other political parties over the question of when to hold general elections. Meanwhile, the Koordinadora Abertzale Sozialista (KAS; Socialist Nationalist Coordinating Council) was split between ETA(pm) militants, who favored participation in the elections, and those of ETA(m), who opposed the move. A significant group of Basque political prisoners still remained in Spanish jails through 1977, causing further tension between the state and Hegoalde. In the spring of 1977, a new political party, Euskadiko Ezkerra (EE; Basque Left), comprised of ETA(pm) militants, came into existence to participate in the new process. Meanwhile, the remaining groups in KAS steadfastly refused participation. The result of the June 1977 poll was a victory for the Unión de Centro Democrático (UCD; Union of the Democratic Center), a party created by members of the Francoist government and headed by Suárez, while the PSOE came to form the official opposition. In Hegoalde, the EAJ-PNV and the PSOE triumphed well above all other parties.

TOWARD THE CONSTITUTION AND A BASQUE STATUTE OF AUTONOMY, 1977–80

Following the election, the Madrid political elite drew up plans for a new constitution, including provisions to formally recognize the Spanish state as a *multinational* country. The Constitutional Subcommittee met from late 1977 through early 1978, but neither of the Basque nationalist parties (EAJ-PNV and EE) was represented. The results were presented in January 1978, and the Basque nationalist parties responded with lengthy and detailed proposed amendments. At the same time, the EAJ-PNV and the PSOE in Hegoalde drafted a preliminary plan for the creation of an autonomous Basque region. There remained widespread skepticism on the part of many Basques, however. The Spanish transition to democracy had been undertaken at the price of forgetting past injustices and of creating a professional political class detached from the day-to-day realities of Spanish society in general and Basque society in particular.

IN THE FALL of 1977, ETA(m) began a renewed campaign, with an intensity never before experienced. Through the following year, ETA stated that it would only cease the armed struggle if the Spanish state would negotiate five points drawn up by KAS in February 1978: amnesty for all Basque political prisoners; the legalization of pro–Basque independence parties; the withdrawal of the Spanish police force from Hegoalde; an acceptance by Madrid of the right of self-determination, together with the inclusion of Nafarroa within the new autonomy statute; and the improvement of basic living conditions for the working classes. In the spring of 1978, another Basque nationalist party was created to work for the implementation of the so-called "KAS alternative," Herri Batasuna (HB; Popular Unity). Madrid remained hostile to negotiation, however. In August 1978, a new antiterrorist bill gave wide-ranging powers to the state security forces to combat the threat of ETA.

As autonomy negotiations continued through 1978, it was clear that a basic difference of opinion existed between the state and Basque nationalists of all political persuasions. First, the question of whether Nafarroa should be included in a Basque autonomous region occupied the central point of debate. Both the Basque nationalists and the PSOE favored incorporation, but the Unión del Pueblo Navarro (UPN; Union of the Nafarroan People)—the dominant party of the province, linked to the central UCD—rejected the plan. Given its ties to Madrid, UPN's wishes prevailed, and thereafter the creation of the Basque Autonomous Community (comprised of Araba, Bizkaia, and Gipuzkoa) and the Foral Community of Nafarroa would add yet another frontier to the Basque political landscape.

S ECOND, FROM the Basque nationalist perspective, there could be no autonomy without recognition by the Right of self-determination, but this was never on the agenda for Madrid. Indeed, the draft constitution maintained within its provisions the *indissoluble* unity of Spain with sovereignty only residing in the Spanish nation. This was reflected most clearly in those sections of the constitution dealing with language. The first clause of Article 3 states, "all Spaniards have the duty to know [Castilian] and the right to use it." As Clare Mar-Molinero observes, "few if any national constitutions worldwide prescribe the *duty* to know a language."[217] Further, by the second clause of this article, the "other" languages of the state are accorded co-official status *within their own territorial space.*

"This clear geographical limitation," argues Mar-Molinero, "means realistically that the future role of

Recognizing many of the mistakes of his forebears, King Juan Carlos successfully oversaw the transition to democracy by placating the most powerful sectors of Spanish society in a general agreement to forget the sins of the past and look only to the future.
Photo by permission of Euskaldunon Egunkaria *archives.*

---

minority languages will always take second place to Castilian. It could even be argued that it contravenes the spirit of later articles of the Constitution which claim equality for all Spanish citizens. Those Spanish citizens whose mother-tongue is not Castilian could argue that they do not have equal linguistic rights with those who are Castilian mother-tongue speakers."[218]

INDEED, ARTICLE 8 of the same constitution adds that "the mission of the armed forces is to guarantee the sovereignty and independence of Spain, to protect its territorial integrity and to oversee the implementation of the Constitution," thereby backing up the geographical demarcation with military force. The linguistic provisions of the constitution reflected widespread opinion among many Spaniards. In an interview with the Spanish prime minister, the journal *Paris Match* questioned Suárez whether, under the new autonomous provisions, it would be possible to complete a university degree in Euskara. His response was telling: "Your question, forgive me, is idiotic. First of all, find me professors who can teach nuclear chemistry in Basque."[219] The fact that there is no such subject as nuclear chemistry apparently did not concern the normally erudite prime minister.

BY NOT RECOGNIZING the sovereign nature of the autonomous regions, the Spanish transition failed to implement a truly federal state. Furthermore, Basque appeals to the international community were as fruitless as they had ever been. Although the right to self-determination of "all peoples" had been legally established by the international community (including the Spanish state)—in Articles 1(2) and 55 of the United Nations Charter of 1946; United Nations General Assembly Resolutions 1514 and 2625; the United Nations International Covenant on Economic, Social, and Cultural Rights of 1966; and the United Nations International Covenant on Civil and Political Rights, also of 1966—these provisions were carefully worded so that they would only be applied to developing countries in the process of decolonization, a useful escape clause for Western states plagued by troublesome minorities.

In December 1978, a referendum to ratify the draft text of the constitution was held throughout the state. The *abertzale* (Basque nationalist) parties—the EAJ-PNV, EE, and HB—urged Basques either to vote against the proposition or to abstain. While the proposition was approved statewide by a 60 percent favorable vote, affirmative votes in the four provinces of Hegoalde totaled about 35 percent. The referendum revealed the extraordinary geo-political complexity of the four southern Basque provinces, highlighting the lack of social integration within the region as a whole. For example, border areas of Hegoalde, from western Bizkaia through southern Araba and Nafarroa, mirrored their adjoining "Spanish" provinces by voting predominantly in favor of the measure, whereas the core area of support for Basque nationalism—from Bilbo eastward, including northern Araba and all Gipuzkoa into northwestern Nafarroa—returned a mostly negative vote. What was clear, however, was that the majority of Basques did not accept the new Spanish constitution, the foundation on which modern democratic Spain was subsequently built.

IN THE MARCH 1979 general elections, the EAJ-PNV were the clear winners in the embryonic Basque Autonomous Community, followed by HB (surprisingly, for most observers), the PSOE, and the UCD. In October, a referendum in the autonomous community ratified the Statute of Autonomy (by the slim affirmative vote of 53 percent), and in the subsequent first autonomous elections, held in March 1980, the 1979 general election results were repeated, with the EAJ-PNV candidate, the Nafarroan Carlos Garaikoetxea, becoming the first *lehendakari* (Basque president) since José Antonio Aguirre y Lecube to take office. Article 6 of the new autonomy statute established Euskara as a co-official language with Spanish in the autonomous community. That same March, the foral election results of Nafarroa reflected a growing polarization in the province between the majority UPN and a minority composed of Basque nationalists, the PSOE, and Carlist remnants. The law creating the Foral Community of Nafarroa (thereby

Anti-Suarez poster, c.1980. "Enough tricks! Work, Amnesty and Freedom. Out with Suarez!" The Spanish prime minister is depicted urinating on the sacred Tree of Gernika.
Illustration: Koldo Mitxelena Kulturunea archives.

separating the provinces of Hegoalde) was passed in 1982, without being put to a referendum.

IN TERMS OF political violence in Hegoalde, ETA's activity did not cease, but rather increased in the post-Franco period. Between 1975 and 1980, ETA claimed 253 victims. In 1979, the same year that the first autonomous elections were held in the Basque Autonomous Community, a number of shadowy right-wing groups, such as the Alianza Anticommunista Apostólica (AAA; Apostolic Anticommunist Alliance) and the Guerrilleros de Cristo Rey (Warriors of Christ the King), came into existence with the declared intent of combating ETA, adding to the already existent official policy against the armed Basque organization. In July, AAA assassinated an ex–ETA member's wife, seriously injuring the ex-member himself in the attack, in Baiona (Bayonne). Similarly, a collective by the name of Batallón Vasco Español (Spanish Basque Battalion) claimed twenty-two killings (including one child) between 1979 and 1981. In the case of two female victims, rape preceded death. The Spanish authorities made few attempts to resolve these crimes (and, indeed, one of the police chiefs responsible for not investigating the murders was promoted to head up police intelligence during the socialist administration of Felipe Gonzalez in the 1980s).[220] These activities culminated in the mid-1980s with the activity of the Grupos Antiterroristas de Liberación (GAL; Antiterrorist Liberation Groups), discussed in the following chapter.

THE NEW UNCERTAINTY, 1980–82

Meanwhile, in Madrid the fortunes of the UCD government had deteriorated to such an extent that it was increasingly under attack from all sectors of Spanish society. In January 1981, Suárez resigned under

increasing pressure, and thereafter the country plunged
into a chain of crises. That year, the new head of state,
King Juan Carlos, visited Gernika (Guernica), to protests
by various representatives of HB. ETA then kidnapped
the chief engineer of the nuclear plant at Lemoiz in
Bizkaia, demanding the dismantling of the plant in
return for his release. When this was not immediately
forthcoming, the engineer was killed. In a subsequent
police operation, an ETA militant was arrested and tortured, and died soon after in prison. A judicial action
against the police officers responsible for the militant's
death gave rise to a wave of indignation among the
Spanish Right.

THIS INDIGNATION was most obviously expressed in
the plotting of three distinct military conspiracies:
one by military officers opposed to the constitution;
another by those who wished to implicate the king in a
coup; and one by a group who planned to incorporate
the PSOE into a military-led government. (Miscalcula-
tions and a lack of coordination between the three
groups would cause them, ultimately, to be unsuccessful.) On February 23, 1981, some Civil Guards implicated in the first conspiracy occupied the Spanish parliament under the leadership of Lieutenant Colonel
Antonio Tejero. This provoked large popular demonstrations in the Spanish state in support of the constitution,
but in Hegoalde the response was more muted. The
indifference of Basques to the constitution, coupled with
popular feeling that the so-called "Basque problem" had
been a root cause of military discontent, gradually led to
a growing Spanish opinion that Basques—and not the
former members of the Franco establishment—were the
principal source of instability in the new country. Thereafter, the Spanish army was sent to patrol the borders of
Hegoalde in an operation not dissimilar to British policy

toward Northern Ireland, and a new law was passed that stiffened antiterrorist measures, under which those who supported what the state considered terrorism (not just those direct *involved* in it) would be strictly punished.

At the same time, the UCD and the PSOE collaborated on a bill that eventually became the "Ley Orgánica de Armonización del Proceso Autonómico" (Organic Law for the Harmonization of the Autonomy Process), by which central state laws would take preeminence over autonomous ones. The Basque government argued that such a law effectively went against the constitution, which supposedly guaranteed their autonomy, and the EAJ-PNV led a campaign of resistance against the bill. In 1983, Spain's Supreme Court upheld the Basque nationalist complaint and agreed that the measures were indeed unconstitutional. However, the PSOE continued to support similar measures. Basque nationalist confrontation with central government continued through 1985, until the Basque autonomous region was accorded its own treasury and therefore the right to self-finance its institutions. This provoked a debate within the hegemonic political party of the Basque government, the EAJ-PNV, over whether the new financial structure should be centrally controlled or placed in the hands of each of the three provinces. The issue raised a number of tensions within the party, resulting in the formation of a breakaway group, Eusko Alkartasuna (EA; Basque Solidarity), led by the president of the Basque Autonomous Community (though he resigned his post), Garaikoetxea.

THE EARLY 1980s marked a particularly intensive wave of action by both ETA and the forces of counterinsurgency, with a strong military presence in Hegoalde. From 1982 on, HB made repeated offers to mediate negotiations between the state authorities and ETA. The continued military presence in Hegoalde was increasingly resented by many Basques with no affiliation to, or solidarity with, the actions of ETA.

Lesson twenty-two

Note: Chapters 22 and 23 should be considered jointly. The reading lists and learning objectives that appear below and the written assignment in Lesson 23 all refer to the material covered in both Chapters 22 and 23.

REQUIRED READING (FOR CHAPTERS 22 AND 23)

Cyrus Ernesto Zirakzadeh, "Economic Changes and Surges in Micro-Nationalist Voting in Scotland and the Basque Region of Spain," *Comparative Studies in Society and History* 31, no. 2 (April 1989), pp. 318–39.

Robert P. Clark, "Negotiations for Basque Self Determination in Spain," in I. William Zartman, ed., *Elusive Peace: Negotiating an End to Civil Wars* (Washington, D.C.: Brookings Institution, 1995), pp. 59–76.

Pedro Ibarra and Antonio Rivas, "Environmental Public Discourse in the Basque Country: The Conflict of the Leizaran Motorway," in David Sciulli, ed., *Comparative Social Research*, Supplement 2: *Normative Social Action* (Greenwich, Conn., and London: JAI Press, 1996), pp. 139–51.

Jacqueline Urla, "Outlaw Language: Creating Alternative Public Spheres in Basque Free Radio," in Lisa Lowe and David Lloyd, eds., *The Politics of Culture in the Shadow of Capital* (Durham and London: Duke University Press, 1997), pp. 280–300.

SUGGESTED READING (FOR CHAPTERS 22 AND 23)

Daniel Philpott, "In Defense of Self-Determination," *Ethics* 105, no. 2 (January 1995), pp. 352–85.

Michael von Tangen Page, "The Spanish Basque Country, 1969–97," in *Prisons, Peace and Terrorism: Penal Policy in the Reduction of Political Violence in Northern Ireland, Italy and the Spanish Basque Country, 1968–97* (New York: St. Martin's Press, 1998), pp. 119–44.

Pauliina Raento, "Political Mobilization and Place-Specificity: Radical Nationalist Street Campaigning in the Spanish Basque Country," *Space & Polity* 1, no. 2 (1992), pp. 191–204.

LEARNING OBJECTIVES (FOR CHAPTERS 22 AND 23)

1. To trace social and political developments in Hegoalde between 1975 and 2002.
2. To critically examine the nature of the Spanish transition to democracy.
3. To examine the extent to which activism took place beyond the purely political realm during this period.
4. To explore various proposals for ending the political conflict in Euskal Herria.

23 · Spain's second transition, 1982–2002

THE PSOE IN POWER, 1982–96

In the general elections of October 1982, the Partido Socialista Obrero Español (PSOE; Spanish Socialist Workers Party) was the undisputed winner, eliciting a widespread feeling among the Spanish population as a whole that at last the country would rid itself of the vestiges of Francoism and modernize itself socially. There was hope that the victory would end the strong public presence of the military, for example, as well as the practice of torture; several prominent PSOE members had publicly criticized its continued use by the Spanish National Police and the Civil Guard (a prescient political and social issue throughout the state through the early years of the transition). The triumph of the PSOE marked the end of this transitory phase of the post-Franco Spanish state. The impending entry of the country into the European Economic Community was eagerly anticipated, as the ravaging effects of the decline in heavy industry were being increasingly felt in the form of rising unemployment. This was especially true in Bizkaia and Gipuzkoa, where the economy centered on heavy industry. Indeed, as Cyrus Ernesto Zirakzadeh points out, the rising economic instability correlated with a growing Basque nationalist vote in Hegoalde (from 29.8 percent in the general elections of 1977 to 47.6 percent in 1982).[221]

MUCH WAS expected of the PSOE in terms of a new regional policy, especially given its alliance with the Euzko Alderdi Jeltzalea-Partido Nacionalista Vasco (EAJ-PNV; Basque Nationalist Party) during the last years of the Second Republic and within the anti-Franco opposition movement. Yet as a member of the multi-

A new anti-terrorist bill gave wide-ranging powers to the state security forces. From then on fire would be met with fire.

---

party commission that drew up the new Spanish constitution of 1978, the PSOE no longer showed support for the idea of a wide-ranging Basque autonomy, which it had pragmatically adopted during the Second Republic; instead, it now favored the limited and subordinate role ascribed by the new Spanish state after 1978. After election to government, the party revealed itself to be closer to the Unión de Centro Democrático (UCD; Union of the Democratic Center), the party of many ex-Francoists, than to its former allies in foreign exile and domestic repression—Catalan and Basque nationalists, for example.

In 1983, the socialist government, headed by Felipe González, formulated a strategic plan to counteract radical Basque nationalism, including the sanctioned use of increasingly coercive measures against widespread sectors of the Basque population. For example, between the coming to power of the PSOE in 1982 and 1990, 484 cases of torture of political prisoners (comprising beatings, physical exhaustion, and asphyxiation, together with sexual and psychological violence) were reported to the Spanish authorities. Moreover, during the period from 1983 to 1986 members of the Grupos Antiterroristas de Liberación (GAL; Antiterrorist Liberation Groups) killed twenty-six Basques; it subsequently emerged that the group had been partly sponsored by both the official state security services and the PSOE government.[222] The creation of the GAL was intended to intimidate ETA into giving up the armed struggle, but this clearly didn't work. ETA had killed forty-four people in 1982 before the emergence of the GAL and maintained a similar rate through the years that the government-organized group operated (from 1983 to 1986). In 1987, ETA claimed a further fifty-four victims.

IN JANUARY 1985, a new *lehendakari* (president) of the Basque Autonomous Community, José Antonio Ardanza, was appointed by the EAJ-PNV to replace the deposed Carlos Garaikoetxea. At the same time, to compensate for the widespread defection of members to Garaikoetxea's newly formed Eusko Alkartasuna (EA; Basque Solidarity), the hegemonic Basque nationalist party entered into an alliance with the PSOE of the Basque Country. During this initial period of the rupture between the EAJ-PNV and EA, from 1985 to 1989, the principal Basque nationalist party lost much electoral ground; thereafter, however, it would steadily recover, attaining a reasonably strong position by the beginning of the 1990s. Indeed, through electoral bargaining with a weakening PSOE in Madrid, the EAJ-PNV was able to serve as a powerbroker through the late 1980s and early 1990s, and as a result secured a number of concessions for the autonomous community from the central authority.

IN 1985, EUSKADIKO Ezkerra (EE; Basque Left), the party formed by ex–ETA(pm) members, began a period of intense self-reflection due to its poor electoral performance in comparison to that of the other Basque nationalist parties, the EAJ-PNV and Herri Batasuna (HB; Popular Unity). The party benefited from the split between the EAJ-PNV and EA, but it was felt that a new direction was needed; thereafter, EE gradually moved out of the Basque nationalist orbit toward accommodation with the PSOE. (Indeed, during the early 1990s it was officially integrated into the PSOE of the Basque Country.) HB clearly emerged as the most outspoken proponent of self-determination during the 1980s, with the EAJ-PNV opting for a more pragmatic strategy of accommodation with the state system, even if it did not entirely agree with it.

During this same period, throughout the Spanish state, a great deal of cultural (and, indeed, "political") activity occurred outside the official political sphere,[223] reflecting in part a rejection of the post-Franco system. Indeed, social activity of this kind, such as a growing environmental movement and the creation of independent local radio stations, was particularly noticeable in Hegoalde, creating, in effect, a veritable *counter*political culture, often (though not always) intimately connected with the so-called *abertzale* (patriotic) Left, or

"A real government for a real people: Vote PNV/EAJ"
Campaign poster for the 1980 Basque Autonomous elections. The dynamic and affable Carlos Garaikoetxea was seen as the ideal candidate for the EAJ, a party associated with a sober, conservative image.
Photo by permission of Koldo Mitxelena Kulturunea archives.

rather those sectors associated with electoral support for HB.

In the 1980s, Nafarroa followed a distinctive political course, with the consolidation of rightist power by the Unión del Pueblo Navarro (UPN; Union of the Nafarroan People) and the gradual movement away from the question of Basque unity by the PSOE, both of which occurred within a framework of cultivating a Nafarroan identity culturally separate from that of the Basque Country. There was also a radicalization of Basque nationalist affiliation within the province, so that HB remained the principal *abertzale* voice after 1982 (followed by EA), to a greater degree than in the three provinces to the west.

NAFARROA CLEARLY split politically along cultural and geographical lines, with the northwestern Basque-speaking mountainous zone returning a solid *abertzale* vote, the middle culturally mixed zone returning a number of independents (with various political affiliations, but usually with a strong Nafarroan-identity element), and the southern plains, historically the most Hispanicized and Castilian-speaking zone, emerging as the bastion of UPN support. Indeed, these divisions were reflected in the establishment of a special linguistic law by the Foral Community of Nafarroa, which gave full co-official status to Euskara in the so-called "Basque-speaking" zone (the northwestern area of the province), some official status to the language in the so-called "mixed" zone (the middle section of the province, including the capital), and no official status to the language in the "non-Basque-speaking" southern zone.

During the late 1980s, two significant changes took place in the Basque political landscape. Until that time, the basic position of ETA had been that a cessation of its violence would be the *object*, not the *precondition* of negotiations with the Spanish state, but this changed with its declaration of a temporary truce in 1988. Between 1988 and 1989, there was a tense political stand-off between ETA and Madrid over the terms of a more permanent or lasting truce / negotiation agreement. Often Madrid publicly stated that it would not negotiate with ETA until it had laid down its arms permanently, but, as was the case in Northern Ireland, secret meetings had already taken place. Indeed, Robert P. Clark estimates that between twenty and thirty attempts to negotiate a lasting cease-fire took place between November 1975 and July 1989.[224] While settlement seemed close at hand in 1988–89, negotiations ultimately broke down. At the same time, in early 1988, all the political parties in the Basque Autonomous Community, with some reservations on the part of EA and the abstention of HB, signed the Ajuria Enea Pact (named after the autonomous Basque seat of government), a definitive official statement against ETA. The pact committed the Basque government to mobilizing its resources in favor of a "social reaction against terrorism." This was mirrored that same year in the Foral Community of Nafarroa by a similar arrangement, known as "The Roundtable for Peace in Nafarroa."

THE SECOND significant transformation affecting the Basque political landscape was the wave of change engulfing Europe at the end of the decade in the wake of the fall of the Soviet Union. This provoked an intense European debate about nationality and national self-determination, which encouraged the EAJ-PNV to introduce a motion in the Basque parliament calling for a nonbonding resolution on the right of self-determination for the Basque Country. This was supported by the Basque nationalists, EA, EE (hesitantly), and HB, but provoked widespread indignation among the Spanish nationalist parties—the PSOE and PP—as well as from the king and the armed forces. The resultant debate ended with a Basque parliamentary motion in favor of the right to self-determination being approved in 1990 through an electoral agreement between the EAJ-PNV, EA, and EE. HB abstained from approving the final text, although many of its militants agreed with its basic tenets. The PSOE vehemently opposed the motion.

AGAIN, IN 1992 and 1993, ETA offered several proposals for a truce in return for talks with the government, but these initiatives were repeatedly ignored by Madrid. Both the official response of the Spanish government and ETA's offers were most likely the result of a noteworthy series of setbacks for the Basque group during the early 1990s. In March 1992, February 1993, and again in June 1994, several high-profile arrests of ETA leaders in exile were carried out by French police, leading to lengthy prison sentences. At the same time, the continued use of violence by ETA was generating less support among Basques than it had done ten years previously, for example. This encouraged Madrid to pursue a hard-line, non-negotiating stance, oblivious to the fact that although support for ETA had waned, it still represented a significant minority within Euskal Herria. (HB, the political party closest to the general goals of ETA, regularly polled between 15 and 20 percent in Basque elections.) As such, a stalemate of sorts existed during the early 1990s. Whereas a widespread social movement in Hegoalde in favor of a negotiated peace settlement (along the lines of similar movements in Northern Ireland) resulted in the creation of organizations such as Elkarri, Madrid favored a more hard-line policy supporting the use of traditional police tactics to "defeat" terrorism.

THE RECRUDESCENCE OF THE SPANISH RIGHT: THE PP
IN GOVERNMENT, 1996–2002

In the general elections of March 1996, fourteen years of
PSOE rule in the Spanish state came to an end after a
long series of political and financial scandals. The victorious Partido Popular (PP; Popular Party) was led by an
unassuming tax inspector by the name of José María
Aznar, a dramatic contrast with the flamboyant
González. The PP was a conservative political alliance
formed out of the Coalición Popular (CP; People's Coalition), the heir to the Alianza Popular (AP; Popular
Alliance), with Franco's ex-Minister of the Interior,
Manuel Fraga (the former head of AP who had been
responsible for sending troops onto the streets of
Gasteiz (Vitoria) in 1976), as its president. The credentials of the PP were therefore solidly on the extreme
right of the political spectrum. Indeed, Aznar had been a
Francoist in his youth but now publicly proclaimed in
favor of Spanish democracy. The PP's narrow victory
meant that government alliances had to be brokered,
and once again the EAJ-PNV assumed a crucial role,
gaining a political leverage within the state reminiscent
of the party's prominence in the 1930s. Initially, the PP
and the EAJ-PNV established cordial relations, but these
would break down in the remainder of the decade.

B Y THE 1990s, the moderate *abertzale* parties saw the
European Union as a means of bypassing the
increasingly restrictive avenue of the Spanish state
(especially after the triumph of the PP). Indeed, ethnonationalist movements pinning their hopes on a potential new "Europe of Nations" was a common feature
throughout the continent during this period. We will
explore the possibility of *re-creating* Basque political and
cultural identity through Europe in the final chapter of
this book.

Lieutenant Colonel Antonio Tejero of the Spanish Civil Guard. The failure of his attempted military coup in February 1981 strengthened the position of both the king and the constitution within Spanish society. *Photo by permission of* Euskaldunon Egunkaria *archives.*

In 1995, ETA presented the "Alternatiba Demokratikoa" ("Democratic Alternative"), which, in a significant policy shift, called for a referendum to decide the question of Basque self-determination as the one basic precondition for the laying down of its arms. A video explaining the new proposal (which showed hooded ETA members talking to the camera) was aired during an electoral broadcast by HB. This resulted in

the arrest and incarceration of HB's entire leadership.
Thereafter, a renewed period of violence by the armed
group culminated in the kidnapping and later killing
(after the impossible demand of repatriating all Basque
prisoners to jails in Hegoalde within forty-eight hours
was not met) of a young PP representative from Bizkaia,
Miguel Angel Blanco, in the summer of 1997. The bru-
tality of the Blanco assassination provoked large-scale
and widespread demonstrations in Hegoalde, but soon a
backlash against Basque culture and a rise in Spanish
nationalism (with a concomitant increase in popularity
of the PP) took place throughout Spain.

F OR MANY Basque nationalist political groups, the
time had come to seek a new course of action toward
abertzale goals. Since the early 1990s, the Elkarri peace
movement had been sponsoring a series of meetings
and debates between representatives of the *abertzale*
political parties (as well as any other interested groups),
and in October 1997 the two Basque nationalist labor
unions, Eusko Langileen Alkartasuna (ELA; Basque
Workers' Solidarity) and Langile Abertzalean Batzordea
(LAB; Nationalist Workers' Commission), arrived at a
tentative agreement as a potential precursor to an
accord between their respective affiliated political parties, the EAJ-PNV and HB. This was followed in September 1998 by an unconditional and indefinite cease-
fire on the part of ETA. During the next fourteen
months, a number of new initiatives flowered through a
tentative political alliance among the Basque nationalist
parties: Udalbiltza, an organization fostering the integration of municipal authorities in Hegoalde and Iparralde;
Batera, a common political platform devoted to the repatriation of Basque political prisoners to Euskal Herria
(according to United Nations stipulations); and, most
importantly, the Lizarra-Garazi political agreement

signed by both *abertzale* and non–Basque nationalist
political and social agents. The Lizarra-Garazi agreement, drawing inspiration from the Northern Irish
peace process, proposed dialogue and negotiation as the
only effective framework for a lasting solution to the
conflict; supported the right of Basques to a vote on the
question of self-determination; and included a basic declaration against violence as a means of achieving political goals.

In early 1995, a schism within the Nafarroan UPN led
to the creation of a new political formation, the Conver-
gencia Democrática de Navarra (CDN; Democratic Con-
vergence of Nafarroa). The CDN represented a moderate
Nafarroan-identity–inclined group that was willing to
reach some form of accommodation with the important
Basque nationalist minority in the foral community.
This went against the hard-line approach of the UPN,
which increasingly mirrored its electoral ally, the PP, in
demonizing all forms of Basque nationalism as a "Balka-
nizing" influence in the Spanish state, a tactic employed
with some enthusiasm by the recently elected president
of the foral community, Miguel Sanz of the UPN. Indeed,
a growing intransigence and even hostility on the part of
the UPN toward specifically Basque cultural traits (supported by the party's solid electoral majority among the
population of southern Nafarroa) has been a feature of
Nafarroan politics through the 1990s.

JEREMY MCCLANCY notes, "rather than diminishing,
the UPN's attitude seems to be catching, as shown by
the increasingly anti-*vasquista*, unashamedly
españolista [Spanish nationalist] stance of the Araban
party, Unidad Alavesa [UA]. Indeed the slogan by the
party in the campaign for the regional elections of 1999
was 'Alava, like Navarra.'"[225]

"Itxaropenak: Bake Prozesua Irlandan. Afganistanen Aurkako Erasoak" ("Hopes: Irish Peace Process. Strikes Against Afghanistan"). Cartoonist Martintxo of Euskaldunon Egunkaria casts an ironic view on different potential approaches to solving the so-called Basque problem.
Illustration by permission of Euskaldunon Egunkaria archives.

WITHOUT DOUBT, there has been a long historical trend of Hispanicization in Araba, especially in the province's south, much like that of the southern zone of Nafarroa. By the late twentieth century, Araba had (unlike Nafarroa), lost virtually all its mother-tongue Basque speakers. Yet the growth of the UPN and UA also mirrored the political redefining of the extreme Spanish Right in the late 1980s (through a selective forgetting of its Francoist past), with the creation and subsequent growth of the PP. By the mid-1990s, even in Hegoalde, it was once more politically acceptable to be a right-wing

españolista, as evinced in the extraordinary growth of
the PP in the traditional Basque nationalist heartlands
of Bizkaia and Gipuzkoa (at the expense of the PSOE).
This was principally due to an increased weariness
with, translated into hostility against, the specter of
Basque political violence, together with an effective
PP-generated campaign linking all forms of Basque
nationalism with the violence, and, perhaps as much as
anything else, the passage of time. Young voters in the
late 1990s were unaware of the legacy left by Franco,
which had kept the Spanish Right out of power for so
many years.

A NEW SPIRIT of cooperation and confidence seemed
to sweep Basque nationalism with the Lizarra-
Garazi agreement, at least during 1999. A new *lehendakari*, Juan José Ibarretxe, came into office in January
and presided over the tentative all-*abertzale* electoral
agreement, which included members of Euskal Herritarrok (EH; Basque Compatriots), the party that had
emerged out of HB as the voice of the Basque nationalist
Left. In the June elections for the provincial and foral
councils of Hegoalde, the Basque nationalists returned
impressive results, particularly EH. At the same time,
results for the PP / UPN confirmed the parties' electoral
rise through the 1990s, whereas the PSOE could only
maintain its exisiting level of support.

The success of EH was generally put down to the continuing ETA cease-fire, but at the end of 1999 this came
to an end, with ETA blaming inactivity on the part of
both the EAJ-PNV / EA and the Spanish government for
its cessation. In early 2000, the armed group once again
began a series of assassinations, and the conflict, which
had for fourteen months seemed distant, returned with
a vengeance. In the spring Spanish general elections, the
PP was returned with an increased and absolute

majority, heralding a new period of inaction toward a negotiated peace settlement.

With the return to arms of ETA now focusing almost entirely on so-called "easy" targets (local councillors of the PP and PSOE, journalists hostile to ETA, and the like), the PP, both in the Basque Autonomous Community and in Madrid, unquestionably strengthened by the breaking of the cease-fire, began to call for autonomous elections, accusing the governing EAJ-PNV / EA alliance of falling into the trap of a false ETA ceasefire by signing the Lizarra-Garazi agreement. Through 2000, the animosity of the PP attacks on the Basque government, supported by the PSOE (especially its regional component in the Basque Autonomous Community), rose to unprecedented levels, as the two principal Spanish parties accused moderate Basque nationalists of collusion with ETA by holding the same basic goal—namely, independence for Euskal Herria. For many commentators in political and media circles, the message was that the EAJ-PNV and EA were complicit in the violence of ETA.[226]

FINALLY, THE autonomous Basque government of Juan José Ibarretxe called regional elections for May 2001. In the run-up to the elections, opinion polls confidently predicted sweeping gains for the PP / PSOE anti–Basque nationalist alliance, with a distinct possibility that Jaime Mayor Oreja, the tough ex–Minister of the Interior in Madrid and now leader of the Basque PP, might even become the new *lehendakari*. However, on May 13, the electorate of the Basque Autonomous Community astounded most Spanish commentators by returning a massive vote for the EAJ-PNV / EA coalition (which received more than 600,000 votes among 1,812,000 eligible voters), in an impressive (and enviable for many Western democracies) overall turnout of

79.9 percent of the electorate. The PP confirmed its position as the second major force in the Basque Autonomous Community. Izquierda Unida (IU; United Left) recorded its biggest ever vote in the Basque Autonomous Community and was subsequently rewarded with representation in a coalition government with the moderate Basque nationalists. The Basque PSOE received considerably fewer votes than it had in the June 1999 regional elections, but the biggest loss was experienced by EH, which fell from its highest ever polling in the 1999 elections to its lowest result, receiving 140,000 fewer votes.

IN THE PERIOD following the May 2001 autonomous elections, a reinvigorated Ibarretxe administration sought to press ahead for more devolved regional authority, in particular the full completion of the Statute of Autonomy of 1979, the stipulations of which had still not been fully carried out. In the meantime, the PP / PSOE alliance in the Basque Autonomous Community moderated its attacks on Basque nationalism in general, but refused a Basque government proposal for a negotiated end to the conflict.

At the same time, the PP government in Madrid, supported by the PSOE, began to consider the possibility of outlawing the party considered ETA's political wing, Batasuna (Unity), formerly known as Euskal Herritarrok and renamed in June 2001. A central tenet of this policy was that Batasuna, like its previous incarnations EH and HB, refused to condemn ETA assassinations, lamenting instead the general loss of life associated with the conflict as a whole. This argument seemed to enjoy public support (if one judges by the polls), yet the PP's refusal to condemn Franco's uprising did not seem to engender the same hostility among the Spanish electorate.[227] Despite protests from the EAJ-PNV, EA, and IU, as well as major reservations on the part of many of Spain's political parties, this proposal came into force in the late summer and fall of 2002. The leading figure in the judicial assault on Batasuna was Judge Baltazar Garzón, an investigating magistrate of the Audiencia Nacional (a special national court dealing with terrorism- and drug-related cases). As 2002 drew to a close, Garzón's edicts regarding Batasuna began to call into question the line between the executive and judiciary branches of the Spanish state. Indeed, a conservative Spanish newspaper supportive of the outlawing of Batasuna was even prompted to publish an editorial that observed of one such edict that it "turn[ed] out to be more characteristic of a literary or political essay than a judicial resolution, [where] Garzón anticipat[ed] ... some conclusions and later [sought] arguments to corroborate them."[228]

TWO MAIN issues occupied Basque political culture after the death of Franco in 1975: the constitutional settlement of the post-Franco Spanish state and the political violence of ETA. The complexity of both these issues is evident from the preceding narrative. I will not attempt to offer answers to the questions engendered by the post-1975 events; at best, I can propose a series of conclusions, without in any way offering these reflections as a political *certainty* of contemporary Basque history.

One of the key problems of the Basque conflict with Madrid is the official relationship (administrative, judicial, legal, fiscal, penitentiary, etc.) between Hegoalde and the state. Indeed, this dimension of the conflict has long historical roots. By the end of the twentieth century, many of the Spanish state's contemporaries had moved toward devolved forms of government. In terms of regional power among European states, Spain falls between federal states, which recognize regions as sover-

Miguel Angel Blanco. ETA's assassination of the young Partido Popular politician in 1997 led to widespread condemnation of the use of political violence and a renewed effort on the part of the Spanish government to crack down on the Basque organization.
Photo by permission of Euskaldunon Egunkaria *archives.*

---

eign entities and have a relatively greater degree of regional decision-making authority and minimal power residing in the center (such as Belgium, where two nations effectively coexist within one state; Germany,

where multilateral relations exist between the Länder, or
regions, and the federal government; and Switzerland,
where a great deal of power is vested in the cantons) and
unitary countries, where, although a limited degree of
devolved administrative authority might exist, state
authority principally emanates from the center and the
state is the sole source of sovereignty (France, for
example). Spain certainly does not, as Raymond Carr
curiously argues, possess the most decentralized constitution in Europe.[229] Recent changes to the (unwritten)
British constitution make the United Kingdom, formerly
a unitary state par excellence, somewhat akin to Spain in
terms of regional authority. (Interestingly, though, if the
newly devolved Scottish parliament were to vote for a
plebiscite on self-determination among the Scottish
people, it could legally do so, unlike its regional counterparts in Spain.) This general trend seems to be in
keeping with a belief among member states of the European Union that if the so-called "European experiment"
is to succeed, they will have to sacrifice at least some of
their centralized power (although much of this change
may well be less for altruistic reasons than for pragmatic
political considerations). In the Spanish state, however,
the autonomous experiment would seem not to have
worked as well as many people had envisaged. Much of
the problem, I suspect, lies in the ambiguous nature of
the Spanish constitution, which, while granting a series
of autonomous rights, also maintains a rigid definition
of state unity that appears guaranteed to provoke tension and hostility between center and periphery.

AT THE END of the 1990s, the increasing tendency on
the part of the PP government to speak of the invio-
lable nature of the Spanish constitution—a language
bolstered by an increased electoral majority within the
Spanish state—seemed to be more political rhetoric

than an argument of constitutional substance. Apart from the fact that the precursor of the PP, the AP, opposed this same constitution at the time it was being introduced, the very nature of membership in the European Union means that constituent states have had to make constitutional amendments acknowledging the increasing trend toward an integrated continent. Indeed, the Spanish state seemed to have adapted to this process more comfortably than other countries within Europe, amending its constitution, for example, to incorporate the provisions of the Maastricht Treaty. (According to this treaty, all European Union citizens were now theoretically able to stand as candidates in elections in all the countries that had signed the agreement; a European single currency came into effect in January 2002; and common foreign and defense policies would be generated among the member states.) Madrid's fear of ceding more autonomous concessions, especially evident among the PP administration during the late 1990s, was highlighted very visibly in 1999, when a proposal by the Basque Autonomous Government to host a symbolic meeting of the Kurdish National Parliament was met with the threatening response that Madrid would take "all necessary steps" to prevent the meeting.

POLITICAL violence, as we have seen, is a complex issue that has consumed Basque political culture for most of the modern period. In Hegoalde, the problem of political violence has been used to justify a heavy police presence. At the close of the 1990s, there were perhaps as many as seven uniformed officers for every thousand people in the four provinces, a rate that negates the need for a high army presence (as was the case in Northern Ireland). This was justified by Madrid as the single means for countering the threat of political violence, and yet it would seem that, despite the arrests of

"Basque Labyrinth: Exit" Martintxo, Euskaldunon
Egunkaria, July 26, 2001. Early in the new millennium,
some Basque political commentators could see little way
out of the conflict.
Illustration by permission of Euskaldunon Egunkaria
archives.

the early 1990s, the "police solution" has not been effective in removing ETA from Basque life. By the turn of
the new millennium, in the thirty or so years that it had
engaged in direct actions, ETA had assassinated around
eight hundred people. In the same period, perhaps half
as many people were killed by the forces of the state.

THE MURKY history of political violence in post-
Franco Spain seemingly affected not only Basque,
but Spanish politics as a whole. In the GAL scandal, not
only have leading members of the PSOE been legally

implicated, but Paddy Woodworth notes that a general of the Spanish armed forces who was a prinicipal organizer of Madrid's antiterrorist campaign in the 1980s has hinted that, if forced to testify in the GAL affair, he would reveal the details of links between current PP members and the anti-ETA death squads of the late 1970s. "An appalling vista opens up," states Woodworth, "that the entire Spanish democratic establishment has had some involvement in state terrorism."[230]

THE PLIGHT of prisoners associated with the Basque conflict is also a serious political issue. There are currently (in October 2002) around six hundred Basque political prisoners dispersed in jails throughout Spain and France. Not all of them are killers, nor are they all ETA members. Indeed, not all are Basque. By the same token, it is difficult to classify all of them as "prisoners of conscience." The policy of dispersion—separating ETA prisoners from one another and moving them continuously and without warning to either families or attorneys—is regarded by Madrid as an important security measure to prevent prison conspiracies and to keep hardliners from others who might be willing to give up their struggle, but is illegal according to the mandates of the United Nations, which stipulate that political prisoners should be jailed within a reasonable distance of their families. For the radical Basque nationalist Left, the repatriation of these prisoners would serve as a basis from which to start a negotiated settlement to the conflict.

Most people in Hegoalde, it would appear from opinion polls, disagree with the use of force on either side of the conflict and believe that a negotiated settlement is the only solution. Interestingly, the two biggest stumbling blocks to such a settlement seem to have been ETA and the government in Madrid. A perverse symmetry seems to have emerged between ETA and the post-Franco Spanish political class, created during the transition, despite the wishes of the majority of Basque citizens in Hegoalde.

As OF OCTOBER 2002, despite the changes generated by the fourteen-month cease-fire in 1998–99, there appears to be no movement on either side. ETA made its intentions clear with a return to direct action in early 2000 and a subsequent period of violence that witnessed the assassinations of, among others, Fernando Buesa, a leading politican of the Basque PSOE, and Ernest Lluch, a Catalan member and former government minister of the PSOE, who had been a leading proponent of a nego-tiated settlement in the Basque conflict. Similarly, the PP government, bolstered by a strong electoral base both in the Spanish state and in Hegoalde, refused to acknowledge the fundamentally political nature of the conflict in Hegoalde, a prerequisite for negotiations from ETA's point of view.

"In the Basque case," argues William A. Douglass, "it is clear that the unwillingness of all parties to negotiate has led to both prolongation and gridlock, a kind of Iberian Cold War that has resisted resolution for more than half a century irrespective of whether or not Spain's political system was autocratic or democratic." Should any negotiation take place, he continues, "not only would minds (on both sides) have to be opened [but] a far more generous spirit than that obtaining at present would have to prevail."[231]

Lesson twenty-three

WRITTEN LESSON FOR SUBMISSION (FOR CHAPTERS 22 AND 23)

1. Critically examine the articles by Jacqueline Urla, Pauliina Raento, and Pedro Ibarra and Antonio Rivas. What do they reveal about the nature of social, cultural, and political activism in Hegoalde during the transition? To what extent does the information provided seem to substantiate the claim that *another* political culture emerged during this time, outside of that formally created by the political elite? Explain your answer.
2. To what extent, in your opinion, would an acknowledgment of the right to self-determination resolve the so-called Basque conflict?

24 · Iparralde, 1945–81

THE POLITICAL culture of post-World War II Iparralde revolved around four key issues: the continuing demographic decline of the rural interior and the question of how to deal with the problem; modest but growing calls for the establishment of a single Basque *département* as a necessary means of safeguarding the social, economic, and cultural life of the region; the emergence of a specifically Basque political movement that seemed to display an even greater propensity to fission than that of Hegoalde; and political violence.

THE FRENCH FOURTH REPUBLIC

In 1945, liberated France voted overwhelmingly against reviving the discredited Third Republic. As a consequence, the task of reconstructing postwar French society fell initially to the new Fourth Republic. The reconstruction was hampered by two problems: that of reconciling the divisions in French society engendered by widespread collaboration during the war, and, perhaps as a consequence of this, the lack of a suitably dynamic political class to oversee the change. If one figure stood head and shoulders above the rest, it was the idiosyncratic military leader General Charles de Gaulle, who had led the "official" wartime resistance as head of the Free French in London. During the war, de Gaulle had attracted a large following, who saw in his personality an essence of Frenchness. This cult of identity, even greater than that of Franco in Spain, would come to define a powerful sense of French national identity through to the late twentieth century.

Through a combination of luck and skill, de Gaulle outmaneuvered all potential rivals for power during the closing stages of the war. Thereafter, he alone presided

over the provisional government of 1945 while a constituent assembly drafted the charter of the new
republic. In January 1946, however, he resigned in
protest over the fact that, in his opinion, the new
republic resembled too closely the prewar regime. It had
been de Gaulle's intention all along to replace what he
saw as the weakness of the parliamentary system with a
stronger executive body. With the withdrawal of de
Gaulle, the Fourth Republic was created and run by
three political formations: the Parti Communiste
Français (PCF; French Communist Party), the Section
Française de l'International Ouvrière (SFIO; French Section of the Workers' International), which in 1969
changed its name to the Parti Socialiste (PS; Socialist
Party), and the Mouvement Républicain Populaire
(MRP; Popular Republican Movement, a Christian
Democratic party that subsequently disbanded in 1967),
with power exercised, as de Gaulle had feared, principally from the Chamber of Deputies.

FOR THE NEXT twelve years, as had occurred in the
Third Republic, a series of mostly centrist parliamentary coalitions ran the new French state. While this
made strong central government and policy formation
impossible, a broad consensus did emerge over the
needs to plan and diversify the economy and to extend
social-welfare services. The government also launched
an ambitious policy of economic modernization in the
public sector, while the private sector, preferring a
degree of cooperation with central government to unreg-
ulated competition, participated in the modernization
program. As a concomitant policy to industrial decentralization, the Fourth Republic also tentatively approved
an administrative *deconcentration*, which created, to
some extent, a context in which more decentralizing
political movements could attempt to build up new

constituencies. Indeed, some of the center-left governments of the Fourth Republic were even sympathetic to
moderate regional demands.[232]

IPARRALDE DURING THE FOURTH REPUBLIC
Society and Economy: With the demographic trend
toward migration out of the economically marginalized,
small mixed-farming communities of the rural interior,
a growing need for cooperative farming emerged.
Formal cooperatives, rare before the war, flourished in
the period between 1949 and 1964, the most well-known
of which was Lur Berri, based in Donapaleu (Saint-
Palais), Nafarroa Beherea. The very success of Lur Berri,
however, aroused accusations from other cooperatives
that it was, in effect, operating in a business rather than
cooperative spirit. (By 1990, for example, it had 271 full-
time employees, with a further 140 part-time staff members.) After the war, agriculture in Iparralde began a cautious process of modernization that would mark its
development through to the end of the century, yet this
was often too little and too late to save the rural
economy from losing its most precious resource: its
people.

BASQUE industrial development remained connected
to the coast, with the modest exception of shoe-
manufacturing businesses in several interior towns such
as Hazparne (Hasparren) and Maule (Mauléon). In 1954,
the industrial sector employed 12,000 people, or 26 percent of the active population. Industry in Iparralde
remained a family concern, with a number of interests
owned and operated by the same families that had
founded them. This, in many ways, added to both stagnation and decline in certain sectors as family-run businesses, content for several generations with locally generated custom, had little incentive to expand or develop

In August 1983, Popo Larre disappeared after a shoot-out between gendarmes and IK militants. Graffiti in Baiona, Lapurdi, asks "What are the gendarmerie and the police hiding? What did they do to Popo?" His whereabouts are still a mystery, prompting many a call for an official inquiry. Iparralde is littered with graffiti asking "Where is Popo?" ("Nun da Popo?")
Photo by the author.

and were therefore ill prepared for the serious demographic decline of the region. For example, the fish-canning industry declined seriously after 1950 with depleted fish stocks in the traditional preserve of the Bay of Biscay; between 1956 and 1962, the number of fish-canning factories on the coast of Iparralde went from twenty to thirteen. The shoe-manufacturing industry suffered from a number of internal structural faults, such as outdated technology, poor marketing, and a lack of investment, which led to an overall decline between the 1950s and the 1970s. Tourism continued to exert a strong economic influence in Iparralde through the 1950s, with, for example, the establishment of the first regular direct flight between London and Miarritze (Biarritz) in 1954.

HOWEVER, the most striking socio-economic phenomenon continued to be the rural exodus plaguing the interior. Between the mid-1930s and the mid-1950s, rural Iparralde's population declined from nearly 93,000 to about 84,000, a loss of around 10 percent of its inhabitants, more or less the same rate as that established at the beginning of the century.

Politics: A formal Basque nationalist movement emerged in Iparralde during the 1940s. From the start, however, there were signs that it would fragment. In general terms, it faced, in the immediate aftermath of the war, a degree of both suspicion and indifference on the part of the electorate. The only success of any kind for Basquist candidates in the first postwar legislative ballot was the election of Jean Etcheverry-Ainchart as a "Basque candidate" for Baigorri (Saint-Etienne-de-Baigorry). Shortly after his election, Etcheverry-Ainchart introduced a plan (devised in the main by the activist Marc Légasse) for an autonomy statute for Iparralde within the new republic. Despite their poor showing in the 1945 elections, Basque nationalists worried the state authorities, and in 1946 Légasse was arrested for threatening the security of the state (by urging, through posters, abstention in legislative elections that year). During the subsequent trial, Légasse was questioned in detail about the autonomy plan he had devised, confirming for many that this was the real reason behind the arrest. Furthermore, in 1948, during an international folk festival in Miarritze, the deputy mayor of the town removed a Basque flag from the proceedings for fear it might offend Spanish participants.

D ESPITE, OR maybe as a result of, the foregoing problems, a renewed movement in favor of maintaining and promoting Basque culture emerged in the late 1940s. In 1947, under the guidance of Father Pierre Lafitte, the Association des Etudiants Basques (Association of Basque Students) was created to coordinate and promote a new series of Basque cultural festivals aimed at imparting a mixture of Catholic social and Basque cultural values. The group was composed of the young elite of Iparralde's bourgeoisie, socially and politically conservative and not *abertzale* (Basque nationalist) as such, but with a strong sense of Basque cultural identity. In 1953, the association changed its name to Embata, referring to the ocean breezes that precede storms on the Basque coastline. As the 1950s progressed, the group, now settling into professional careers in Iparralde, gradually adopted a more political outlook, influenced most likely by the social and political changes sweeping the French state and western Europe at the time.

THE FRENCH LOSS OF EMPIRE

No other European power tried as forcefully as the French state to hold onto empire after World War II.

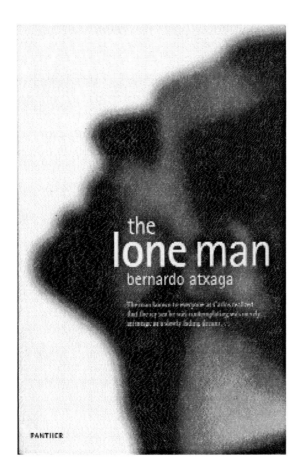

the
lone man
bernardo atxaga

The man known to everyone at Carlos realised that for up just he was contemplating with no idly attempts at a slowly fading dream...

PANTHER

Bernardo Atxaga is an internationally renowned author who often lectures throughout Europe and North America.

During the sixteen years after the war, the country was engaged in one colonial conflict after another, in repeated and increasingly desperate attempts to hold onto the last vestiges of its overseas dominions. Between 1946 and 1954, the French waged a protracted war in Indochina that left a bitter legacy (ultimately leading to United States involvement in Vietnam in the 1960s). Thereafter, it continued its struggles against the colonies with an even more bitter struggle in Algeria between 1954 and 1961. During the second conflict in particular, the difficulties of waging a colonial struggle, against a hostile local population and in inhospitable territory, resulted in the French army employing increasingly brutal tactics. The French state was divided over the issue, between those of the Left, who saw the conflict as cruel and worthless, and the not inconsiderable reactionary Right, who saw it as a combination of French imperial strength and anticommunism at the height of the Cold War.

IN 1958, THE WAR in Algeria took an especially vicious turn as French settlers took over control of the struggle against the Algerians, determined to win at all costs. They proceeded to seize the island of Corsica (sparking a reaction among the local population that ultimately led to the emergence of a Corsican ethnonationalist movement and the use of political violence in its struggle), and even threatened to invade the French state itself. It was at this moment that de Gaulle returned to the political scene, guaranteeing to save the Fourth Republic. Instead, he abolished it, withdrawing from Algeria, and instituting the Fifth Republic in the image he had designed in 1945: an authoritarian, conservative, and French nationalist state.

────────

DE GAULLE, FRENCH NATIONALISM, AND THE FIFTH REPUBLIC

De Gaulle's notion of an *eternal* France, perpetuated through speeches, statements, and the like, implied a confident grandeur. It combined Napoleonic efficiency and power with the aesthetic achievement of the pre–World War II *belle époque*. Jacobinism also lay at the heart of his national policy: "One interpretation of the Jacobin notion of nationhood," notes John Loughlin, "is that the individual's personality can develop only within the wider context of French culture. In other words, minority languages and cultures, *by themselves*, are insufficient to bring about this development."[233]

De Gaulle's principal European policy once he was in office was designed to solidify an agreement with West Germany whereby the two dominant states of the Common Market would attempt to control the process of European integration. To this end, a historic treaty was signed in 1963 that effectively ended the bitter rivalry between the two countries. Thereafter, de Gaulle's pro–European-integration policy rested on securing French national interests in the continent and elsewhere. Indeed, from the outset, he insisted that the new Europe must be a *federation of nation-states*; an idea that, to this day, many still cynically believe is the real agenda of European integration.

DOMESTICALLY, as Loughlin points out, de Gaulle's accession actually served to galvanize regional sentiment among certain sectors as the theory of internal colonialism was popularized.[234] During and after the 1960s, then, two fundamentally different visions of French state identity emerged. On the one hand, Gaullism emphasized the absolute unity and indivisibility of the state, whereas the minority ethnonationalists (Bretons, Corsicans, Basques, etc.) began to think of

France as a kind of prison that held together its disparate people by force. This framed a growing ideological discrepancy, especially between "official" and "popular" visions of French national identity. In particular,
the new French Left began to embrace elements of the
latter ideology, which gave much hope among the
declared nationalist movements that administrative
reorganization would take place once the Left achieved
political power in the French state. Thus, as we shall
later see, François Mitterrand gained the support of
many minorities during his electoral campaign leading
up to the 1981 elections.

IN MAY 1968, the French state exploded in popular
social protest. The protest began as a student movement against what was seen as an educational system
that served as a vehicle for producing an uncritical and
compliant citizenry. As the scale of the protest escalated,
the state responded with force. This in turn provoked a
sympathy strike among workers, who were also
protesting the pitiful wage increases of the 1960s in
light of the general economic recovery of the country. By
late May, ten million people were on strike in the
French state, in a genuinely popular spontaneous political statement. The country was paralyzed and many
thought de Gaulle was finished. There was, however, a
fundamental difference in the protests waged by students and workers—namely, one was based on social
and the other on economic grievances—and the French
leader recognized this. The majority of the workers
accepted a generous pay rise in June 1968, and this effectively isolated the students. In elections held toward the
end of that month, a public backlash against the crisis
generated by the protest returned de Gaulle to power.
For the first time in French democratic history, one
party, the Gaullists, received an absolute majority in the

French parliament. Although he emerged triumphant, the general was astute enough to realize that he presided over a radically changing society—one that he would eventually not be able to control as easily. A year later, at the age of seventy-nine, he left office.

IPARRALDE IN THE 1960s AND 1970s
A mood of quiet decline captured Iparralde during this time. The population shift from rural to urban areas continued unabated, with the urban population growing from 121,000 to 134,000 between 1954 and 1962, and expanding to 163,000 by 1968. Concomitantly, the region continued to decline economically throughout the 1960s and 1970s. This was most visible in the rural interior, where the shoe-manufacturing industry underwent a severe crisis in the 1970s. Even the tourist industry began to change, as a trend toward the buying and construction of secondary homes, principally by the northern French middle classes, became popular in the 1970s. This led to a sharp rise in property prices, particularly on the coast, forcing many locals—farmers, for example—out of the market.

ONE OF THE first effects of de Gaulle's Fifth Republic for Iparralde was the renaming of the Basses-Pyrénées *département* to "Pyrénées-Atlantiques"—a symbolic attempt, perhaps, to water down the geographic identity of the region. During the 1950s, Embata had become more politicized, and this was probably even more true after the death of the exiled *lehendakari* José Antonio Aguirre y Lecube in 1960. A reported 5,000 people attended his funeral in Donibane-Lohizune (St. Jean-de-Luz). Thereafter, Embata decided to establish both a central office and a newspaper, which began circulation toward the end of 1960 (that same year modifying the name of both the group and newspaper to

A poster of Ezkerreko Mugimendu Abertzalea (Basque Patriotic Movement of the Left) (EMA) from the mid 1980s leaving no doubt about the party's objection to the appropriation of rural farm land for leisure pursuits of the wealthy.

Illustration: Koldo Mitxelena Kulturunea archives.

Enbata). The heightened political tone of this Basque
cultural publication retained a conservative perspective,
invoking much Aranist sentiment. As an important
addition, it also began to debate the issue of colonialism, a central political question within the French
state at the time.

The result of the ideological reorientation of the early
1960s was an impending confrontation between clerical
and secular visions of the Basque movement in Iparralde. Between 1960 and 1963, the Enbata movement
remained little more than a collective charged with producing their newspaper. In April 1963, however, it formally constituted itself as a political organization dedicated to Basque nationalist aims, including the recognition of Basque culture by the French state. The group
did not advocate outright separatism, but instead called
for a single Basque *département* as the best guarantor of
Euskara and Basque cultural identity in general. This
secular vision also, importantly, established a link
between economic decline and the threat to Basque culture in Iparralde by emphasizing the connection
between this culture and traditional (and now drastically
declining) agricultural activity.

DESPITE THE moderation of the group's proposals,
conservative reaction in Iparralde was harsh; the
group was accused of the threatening charge of separatism. Through the 1960s, then, Enbata developed a
carefully constructed political program aimed at
avoiding state charges of separatism—a particularly
serious charge with severe consequences under de
Gaulle's republic—while reclaiming the right to foster
and promote Basque culture. The greatest obstacle for
the new movement was actually in achieving an electoral
foothold in Iparralde. Indeed, the region remained a
solid bastion of conservatism, as evinced by the high

degree of support from the (overwhelmingly Basque-speaking) interior for de Gaulle. "It was not that the Basque electorate had changed substantially from that of a century before," observes James E. Jacob, "but rather that the political context had changed around them"[235]; the conservative, ruralist values of Gaullism proved especially vote-catching in Iparralde during the 1960s and 1970s.

IN CONTRAST, as Jacob points out, most of the new Basque nationalist groups emerging in Iparralde from the 1960s on tended to adopt both the ideologies and conflicts of similar movements in Hegoalde, a trend reinforced by the increasing contacts established with Basque nationalists fleeing the Spanish state during the decade, most obviously militants of ETA.[236] Indeed, Enbata established early and strong links to ETA, and the effect of these ties would influence the movement in Iparralde. One effect was the embracing of the rhetoric of national liberation struggles, such as those of Indochina and Algeria, which the French state had fought so hard to suppress. This therefore pitted all expressions of Basque nationalism against the most virulent forms of state nationalism that the Fifth Republic could develop. Faced with such overwhelming odds, there was little that the Basque nationalist movement of Iparralde could achieve in real terms, beyond, perhaps, raising the social or cultural conscience of those willing to listen.

In the 1967 French legislative (general) elections, Enbata candidates polled around 5 percent in both coastal and interior regions, reflecting the low degree of Basque nationalist political mobilization at the time. This was emphasized even more in the 1968 legislative elections to reaffirm Gaullist France in the wake of the 1968 uprising, when the Enbata vote fell to around

2 percent. Thereafter, from the late 1960s on, the movement began to split apart due to the various explanations offered for its electoral failure.

IN THE WAKE of the events of 1968 in Paris, a new radicalized youth movement emerged to redefine Basque nationalism in Iparralde. This movement, divided between a host of different groups, was particularly influenced by the rising tide of ETA militants and refugees seeking shelter in Iparralde. In 1972, this resulted in a series of hunger strikes, in favor of the refugees and against French state repression, by several young militants from Iparralde. The overall effect of the changes of the late 1960s and early 1970s was for Enbata to move toward the political left. As early as 1971, it defined itself as a "Basque Socialist Party," and in the increased climate of French state suspicion toward, and repression of, Spanish state Basque refugees, this would become the platform on which the movement would mobilize throughout the 1970s.

The new strategy was hardly appropriate in a region long dominated by conservative political customs, however. By 1973–74, the Enbata movement would all but disappear as a political organization. In its wake, there emerged two clear tendencies within the Basque political movement of Iparralde: an openly socialist formation, Herriko Alderdi Sozialista (HAS; Popular Socialist Party), and a radical group following the example of ETA, Iparretarrak (IK; "Those of the North").

HAS took part in the electoral process and condemned the use of political violence, but openly pressed for Basque unification of Hegoalde and Iparralde. In 1975, it merged with a minority counterpart in Hegoalde, Euskal Alderdi Sozialista (EAS; Basque Socialist Party), to form Euskal Herriko Alderdi Sozialista (EHAS; Socialist Party of the Basque Country). The ideological orientation of

Donibane-Garazi, Nafarroa Beherea, in the 1960s. In the 1960s the rural interior of Iparralde, faced with a decline in agriculture and population exodus, attempted to renew its tourist industry through beautifying its townscapes.
By permission of the "Les Amis de la Vieille Navarre" Association archives.

EHAS was based on the concept of internal colonialism by the French state in Iparralde, and the need for a national liberation movement to free the region of this imperial domination. In the 1977 municipal elections, EHAS gained encouraging results in both urban Baiona (Bayonne) and smaller rural towns, which, by the late 1970s, were suffering the dramatic effects of depopulation. Yet little substantial gain was subsequently forthcoming, for in the legislative elections of 1978 EHAS candidates could only poll between 3 and 4 percent of the vote. By the late 1970s, then, the EHAS movement, like Enbata before it, had failed to break out of the constraint of being a minority political formation within Iparralde. By the watershed 1981 election of Mitterrand to office, the group had effectively been disbanded.

IPARRETARRAK came into being as a result of the well-established contact between ETA refugees and young politically conscious Basques in Iparralde during the 1960s and 1970s. It committed its first act of political violence in 1973, yet it would never reach the virulence of ETA, limiting most of its *ekintzak* (actions) to low-intensity activities aimed at disrupting rather than overthrowing society. In many ways, the symbolic violence of IK was as much an instrument of political mobilization as anything else, with its major targets (initially) being tourist-development projects that increased the depopulation trend of the rural interior (by encouraging young Basques to go to the coast in search of work), forced land values to rise as rich non-Basques bought both vacation and retirement property in the region (further alienating the local population), and made condescending gestures toward Basque culture, packaging it as a tourist commodity while developers retained all the economic profits for themselves. After 1973, the group lay dormant until 1977, when it renewed a series of attacks on tourist-industry targets, such as the offices of property developers. At the same time, however, political targets were being considered, and this strategy would be adopted from 1979 on (discussed in Chapter 25).

Lesson twenty-four

Note: Chapters 24 and 25 should be considered jointly. The reading lists and learning objectives that appear below and the written assignment in Lesson 25 all refer to the material covered in both Chapters 24 and 25.

REQUIRED READING (FOR CHAPTERS 24 AND 25)

James E. Jacob, "The Future of Basque Nationalism in France," in William A. Douglass, Carmelo Urza, Linda White, and Joseba Zulaika, eds., *Basque Politics and Nationalism on the Eve of the Millennium* (Reno: Basque Studies Program, 1999), pp. 155–74.

John Loughlin, "A New Deal for France's Regions and Linguistic Minorities," *West European Politics* 8, no. 3 (July 1985), pp. 101–13.

Jean-Jacques Cheval, "Local Radio and Regional Languages in Southwestern France," in Stephen Harold Riggins, ed., *Ethnic Minority Media: An International Perspective* (Newbury Park, London, and New Delhi: Sage Publications, 1992), pp. 165–95.

Sandra Ott, *The Circle of the Mountains: A Basque Shepherding Community* (Reno: University of Nevada Press, 1993), pp. 1–30 and 213–24.

James E. Jacob, *Hills of Conflict: Basque Nationalism in France* (Reno, Las Vegas, and London: University of Nevada Press, 1994), pp. 386–402.

Thomas D. Lancaster, "Comparative Nationalism: The Basques in Spain and France," *European Journal of Political Research* 15 (1987), pp. 561–90.

SUGGESTED READING (FOR CHAPTERS 24 AND 25)

Herve Michel, "Government or Governance? The Case of the French Local Political System," *West European Politics* 21, no. 3 (July 1998), pp. 146–69.

Sarah Waters, "New Social Movement Politics in France: The Rise of Civic Forms of Mobilisation," *West European Politics* 21, no. 3 (July 1998), pp. 170–86.

LEARNING OBJECTIVES (FOR CHAPTERS 24 AND 25)
1. To trace the social, economic, and political evolution of Iparralde within post–World War II French society.
2. To examine the fortunes of Basque nationalism in Iparralde during the same period.
3. To critically explore the role of political violence within broader social and political developments in Iparralde.

25 · Iparralde, 1981–2002

CHALLENGES TO FRENCH NATIONAL IDENTITY
After World War II, immigration to France occurred on a large scale, encouraged by successive governments in order to fill the menial jobs that French workers increasingly refused to do. Immigrants flooded into the country from Spain, Portugal, and Italy, and, increasingly, from its former colonial possessions in North and West Africa. Hostility toward non-European immigrants was intensified by the struggle in Algeria and the subsequent declaration of Algerian independence in 1962, which provoked the rise of small groups of extreme right-wing groups dedicated to fomenting street violence with immigrant youths. This culminated in the 1980s with the rise of Jean-Marie Le Pen's Front National (FN; National Front), the most successful far-right party in western Europe during the decade, with a version of French nationalism based almost exclusively on anti-immigrant rhetoric and allusions to Holocaust revisionism.

By 1988, the FN had achieved 14 percent of the vote in the state as a whole, with a regional stronghold in the south of the country, home to many North African immigrants as well as one of Le Pen's strongest constituencies, the former French settlers of Algeria. Le Pen did much to galvanize an antiracist lobby in response to his views, provoking a growth in social activism within the French state from the mid-1980s on. Among these new social movements were Basque groups increasingly concentrating on single-issue political goals, such as the introduction of the Basque language into the school curriculum or the creation of a single Basque *département*. It is also worth noting that, despite being a bastion of

Father Pierre Lafitte. In both Iparralde and Hegoalde the Church played an important role in defending and promoting Basque culture.
Photo by permission of Koldo Mitxelena Kulturunea archives.

conservative voting tendencies and, increasingly, a declining economy, Iparralde never gave much electoral support to the FN. Indeed, Basque nationalism remained a stronger political force in Iparralde than the French variant of the FN, up to and including the shock presidential elections of 2002, when Le Pen resurfaced to mount a serious challenge for the ultimate political office of France.

THE MITTERRAND YEARS, 1981–95

In May 1981, François Mitterrand, leader of the French socialists, was elected to the presidency of the French state. It was a watershed moment, for conservatives had governed the country, in various guises, since the implementation of General Charles de Gaulle's Fifth Republic in 1958: Georges Pompidou (1969–74) and Valéry Giscard d'Estaing (1974–81) had followed de Gaulle's resignation. As with the impending triumph of the socialists in the Spanish state, France was filled with a sense of optimism at the proposed reforms of the new premier.

MITTERRAND began confidently enough, raising wages in order to encourage spending as a stimulus to the embattled economy. He also abolished the death penalty and liberalized much of the media. Perhaps the area in which Mitterrand most failed to deliver, though, as John Loughlin observes, was in the realm of political decentralization and educational reform.[237] Indeed, the 1982 laws of decentralization were manifestly "diluted" from the original promises made by Mitterrand "in the process of intercommunal integration organized by the state,"[238] as Herve Michel writes, referring to efforts by the central government to foster cooperation between local authorities while consciously avoiding the development of separate regional political identities.

Soon after, the new leader quickly ran into difficulty as the promised economic stimulus was not forthcoming. The state had run up a debt, and a radical restructuring program was necessary. In 1983, the French state implemented a particularly severe austerity program, encouraging the Right to think that their time had come. This was, indeed, the case in the 1986 elections, when a conservative prime minister, Jacques Chirac, was chosen to share power with President Mitterrand. French politics thus reverted to modest shifts between the moderate Left and Right. Mitterrand, cultivating the role of international statesman, was re-elected as president for a further seven years in 1988.

BY THE EARLY 1990s, a changing Europe threatened the French state's comfortable role at the head of European integration. As James E. Jacob remarks, "in 1991, both France and Spain were greatly troubled by Germany's insistence on independence for Croatia and Slovenia, fearing the precedent it would create for their own restive minorities."[239] However, he explains, at the end of the decade only 350,000 students were studying one of the French state's seven different minority languages with no official status, help, or encouragement. Therefore, one might reasonably conclude that they presented little threat to the state, as evinced also by France's near refusal to admit the existence of these languages within its borders.[240]

IPARRALDE FROM THE 1980s TO THE NEW MILLENNIUM

French society, like that of all western European states, changed dramatically between the mid-1980s and the 1990s. With the end of the Cold War and increasing European integration, a mood of transformation swept the country. One of the manifestations of this change was a renewed social activism and protest within French society—what some have called a "democratic rebirth" or the emergence of a "new civic generation."[241] It is more than likely that several of these state-wide social movements, based, for example, on feminism, environmentalism, and antiracism, influenced a rising level of social activism in Iparralde. Here, however, the activism centered particularly on calls for more sympathetic policies toward Euskara or a single Basque *département*. Whether the idea of "new citizenship" had been wholly embraced in Iparralde by the end of the 1990s is open to question,[242] but there was a noticeable increment in the social activity of specifically Basque-related movements.

As PART OF his policy statement in the run-up to the 1981 elections, Mitterrand had promised the creation of a single Basque *département*, a plan vehemently opposed by the Gaullist Rassemblement pour le Republique (RPR; Union for the Republic) party. As a result of this promise, perhaps, there was an increase in the socialist vote in Iparralde compared to the previous election.[243] Once in office, however, Mitterrand reneged on the promise, despite the historical precedents of the administrative reorganization of Paris in the mid-1960s and Corsica in the mid-1970s. From about 1982 on, then, Basque nationalism in Iparralde fragmented further as separate groups responded in different ways to the Mitterand betrayal, from pragmatic acceptance (and a belief in the need to continue lobbying in favor of Basque issues with the powerful political interests of France) to an outright rejection of ever relying on Paris to cede more regional authority. However, in general, Basque nationalism in Iparralde moved away from the more radical postures of the past in search of a political center ground. At the same time, there were tentative steps to extend the party political culture of Hegoalde to its northern neighbor. "In *abertzale* circles," concludes Jacob, "the prevailing opinion was that France had sacrificed the idea of a Basque department on the alter of Spanish-French diplomacy."[244] Certainly, the French state began to take a more serious interest in the activities of Basque refugees from the Spanish state at about this time.

B ETWEEN THE late 1970s and early 1980s, Iparretarrak (IK; "Those of the North") began to include French government representatives in Iparralde and law enforcement agents among its targets. In 1982, the group carried out its most serious attack to date, assassinating a French CRS (Compagnie Républicaine de Sécurité; the state security police) officer on patrol and wounding his colleague, who later died from the wounds, in Baigorri (Saint-Etienne-de-Baigorry). The principal suspect in the attack was an IK militant, Philippe Bidart, who had been on the run since 1981 after a hold-up. Throughout the 1980s, Bidart, a resident of Baigorri, was considered public enemy number one by French authorities, but proved to be an elusive figure for the security forces despite his daring ventures into public life. In some circles, he earned a Robin Hood–like renown, embodying the nuisance (more than threat) that IK proved to be for the French state throughout the decade.

In 1983, a shoot-out took place between French police and IK militants—Bidart was thought to be among them—in the region neighboring Iparralde, Les Landes. A *gendarme* (regular police officer) was killed and the four militants escaped (although one, Jean-Louis "Popo" Larre, was never heard from again, leading to speculation that he had been executed by either IK itself or agents of the French security forces). From this time on,

Manuel Fraga, former minister of Franco and later one of the founders and first leader of the Partido Popular (PP), the governing Spanish political party at the end of the 1990s.
Photo by permission of Euskaldunon Egunkaria *archives.*

---

it was clear that IK was accelerating its actions. Targets now routinely included police stations and army barracks, as well as the homes and cars of political representatives, though not, in the main, people themselves. This violence coincided with activity by the Grupos Antiterroristas de Liberación (GAL; Antiterrorist Liberation Groups), directed against ETA refugees in

Iparralde, to make the region, during the mid-1980s, a battleground of sorts. Indeed, by 1985 the GAL had moved from meticulously planned attacks on specific targets to acts of indiscriminate violence, killing French and Spanish citizens alike in bars and hotels.

DURING THIS period, ETA's insistence that IK share a common front with the Hegoalde group was rejected, leading to a divergence between the two organizations from this time on. In many ways, IK's *ekintzak* (actions) annoyed the French authorities into increasingly persecuting ETA refugees in Iparralde, who since the 1960s had enjoyed a relatively safe haven in the region. The French state gradually abandoned its asylum practice for Basque political refugees and began, from the early to mid-1980s, working more closely with Spanish security forces in terrorist counterinsurgency operations. This culminated, as we have noted, in the major police operations in Iparralde during the late 1980s and early 1990s that severely damaged the organizational infrastructure of both ETA and IK.

The first of the new Basque nationalist parties created in Iparralde during the 1980s was Ezkerreko Mugi-mendu Abertzalea (EMA; Basque Patriotic Movement of the Left), established at the end of 1985. As its name suggests, it followed a typically left-wing progressive model, but it promoted a more ambiguous policy toward the use of political violence than had previous Basque nationalist groups, some of which had been openly supportive of it. EMA polled disappointingly in the 1986 legislative and regional elections, gaining only 3.77 and 4.21 percent of the votes, respectively. In June 1986, the creation of Euskal Batasuna (EB; Basque Unity) was announced. Despite its close ties to HB in Hegoalde (a political group who remained ambiguous about ETA's armed struggle), the party came out against the use of political violence as a tactic in the Basque nationalist struggle. In November 1986, the leader of Eusko Alkartasuna (EA; Basque Solidarity) in Hegoalde, Carlos Garaikoetxea, announced that his party was establishing a section in Iparralde that would pursue the same political platform as the main branch.

In 1988, the three Basque nationalist parties—EMA, EB, and EA—joined together in a common electoral alliance for the French legislative elections that year. While this united *abertzale* front received only around 5 percent of the vote, it was clearly the third political force of Iparralde, surpassing the PCF (Communist Party) and the FN (National Front). The moderate success of the alliance was repeated soon after, in the 1988 cantonal elections, when it won more than 7 percent of the vote in Iparralde, behind the Parti Socialiste (PS; Socialist Party) and a coalition of the moderate French Right comprised of the RPR and the Union pour le Démocratie Française (UDF; Union for French Democracy), who received 27 and 59 percent, respectively. These modest successes culminated in the 1989 municipal elections, when three Basque nationalist councillors were elected in the Lapurdian coastal towns of Baiona (Bayonne), Miarritze (Biarritz), and Hendaia (Hendaye).

MEANWHILE, outside the realm of electoral politics, IK continued an increased period of activity, specifically targeting state symbols such as the police. IK's most spectacular action, however, was the liberation of two of its militants from prison in Pau in mid-December 1986. Between March and June 1987, IK mounted three attacks, against a police station in Donibane-Garazi (Saint-Jean-Pied-de-Port) and police vehicles in Hazparne (Hasparren) and Maule (Mauléon). In July 1987, Prime Minister Chirac visited Baiona and condemned both the violence of IK and the

Phillipe Bidart, a leading member of Iparretarrak (IK).
After moving into hiding in 1981, he spent seven years
evading capture by the security forces, effectively
becoming France's public enemy number one.
Photo by permission of Gatuzain archives.

separatist inclinations of Basque nationalists. According
to French authorities, IK had been responsible for more
than sixty attacks between its appearance in 1973 and
mid-July 1987. In a growing alliance with its neighbor to
the south, the state thus resolved to crack down on
Basque political violence. That summer, the police
began a series of arrests that would soon lead to the dismantling of IK as an effective group.

IN THE FALL, the whole southwestern region of the
state was flooded with police as the authorities
increasingly closed in on the IK leader, Bidart. Finally,
in February 1988, the authorities announced his capture, together with that of four accomplices, in Boucau,
an industrial suburb of Baiona. Sixteen leading members were now in custody, and their long-delayed trial
began in early 1991. It was clear that the organization
had suffered from the arrest of its principal coordina-
tors, but despite these arrests, IK activists continued
their low-intensity attacks through the early 1990s.

IPARRALDE AT CENTURY'S END

Society and Economy: In 1990, the industrial sector in
Iparralde employed just over 17,000 people, with the
largest single industrial employer being construction.
The construction industry was linked, of course, to the
tertiary activity of tourism, which saw steady growth
from the mid-1970s through the 1990s, lending to the
rural exodus and encouraging yet more urbanization
(despite an industrial downturn during the 1990s).
Indeed, the service sector in general (including, of
course, tourism) accounted for just over 70 percent of
employment in Iparralde by 1999, with agriculture
accounting for just under 10 percent.[245] By the 1990s,
Baiona, Miarritze, and Angelu (Anglet) formed a coter-
minous urban nucleus comprising their combined

populations of 40,000, 29,000, and 33,000, respectively. Donibane-Lohizune (St. Jean-de-Luz) and Hendaia both surpassed the 10,000-inhabitant level (with 13,000 and 12,000, respectively), whereas interior towns such as Hazparne, Maule, and Kanbo (Cambo-les-Bains) hovered around the 5,000-inhabitant mark.

IN TOTAL, by the 1990s, the urban population stood at 177,000 inhabitants, the majority of whom were concentrated on the coast, compared to a rural population of 65,000. Without doubt, agriculture, and consequently rural culture, had progressively lost much of the social cohesion it had once enjoyed, as evinced by the serious population decline in Zuberoa and Nafarroa Beherea between 1975 and 1999 (17 and 10 percent, respectively).[246] Another phenomenon apparent through the 1990s was the relocation of Hegoalde residents, principally those working in and around Donostia (San Sebastián), to southern coastal Lapurdi, especially Hendaia, where property values remained lower than those of the southern Basque Country.

Politics: By the beginning of the 1990s, the organizational structure of IK had been dealt a serious blow by the arrest of its principal leadership, and IK *ekintzak*, continuing at a low intensity, proved more of a nuisance than anything else. It seemed apparent that direct confrontation on a level of that in Hegoalde remained a distant reality. In more formal political channels, the situation for Basque nationalism had deteriorated with the rupture of the electoral alliance between moderate and radical Basque nationalists that had gained moderate successes in the late 1980s. Yet two important developments were to take place: In 1988, a new party, Abertzaleen Batasuna (AB; Nationalist Unity), was formed out of an agreement between EMA and EB. Over the next decade and beyond, this party would prove to be the most successful Basque nationalist formation in Iparralde. Then, in an interesting development in May 1990, the Iparralde section of the Euzko Alderdi Jeltzalea-Partido Nacionaliste Basque (EAJ-PNB; Basque Nationalist Party) finally formed a section in Iparralde with the express purpose of taking an active part in the political life of the northern Basque Country. Although less militant than AB, the EAJ-PNB possessed the infrastructure and financial backing that could be put to productive use should unity once again be fostered.

IN THE 1993, 1997, and 2002 general (legislative, as opposed to presidential) elections, AB obtained 5.5, 6.4, and 5.91 percent of the votes, respectively. In the same period, EA managed to gain 1.1 percent of the votes in 1993 (the EAJ-PNB did not take part in this election), and, in coalition with the EAJ-PNB, 2.9 percent in both the 1997 and the 2002 elections. In electoral terms, the Basque nationalist vote represented around 10 percent of the total in Iparralde at the dawn of the new millennium, which marked some degree of advance from the beginnings of Basque nationalism in France during the 1960s. That said, this advance was slow and Basque nationalism found it difficult to break the two-party hold on the electorate of Iparralde. For example, in the legislative elections of 2002, an RPR-UDF coalition achieved 42.2 perecent of the vote, while the PS managed 25.2 percent. Presently, then, the *abertzale* vote is the third or fourth political force in the region, but it remains a somewhat "unknown" quantity. For example, Jean-Jacques Cheval states that "regional political claims are not well developed" in Iparralde,[247] which seems curious given the surprisingly *well-developed* movement for a single *département*.

Between the mid-1970s and the early 1990s, an increasing cycle of violence and repression led to a changing political landscape in Iparralde.[248] Following the reorganization of the *abertzale* political parties in the 1980s, the Basque nationalist vote actually increased substantially in the 1990s. This may have been due to the political violence employed by both ETA and IK—or, more accurately, the repression this engendered—or was perhaps the result of a wider malaise within the French state reflecting changing cultural identities at the end of the twentieth century; indeed, it may have been a combination of the two. Low-level violence (vandalism and the like), perpetrated for contrasting political reasons, continued to occur in Iparralde through the 1990s and into the new millennium. Between 2001 and 2002, for example, attacks were perpetrated on the property of police officers, EAJ-PNB sympathizers, and the familes of Basque political prisoners.

ONE OF THE repeated problems for the numerous groups that have tried to establish Basque nationalism as a significant political force in Iparralde since the 1930s has been a basic indifference and even hostility among the electorate. Beyond local politics, traditionally subordinated in a unitary state like that of France, Basque nationalism has found it hard to break into the political mainstream. And yet at the end of the twentieth century, as the Basque nationalist movement concentrated on key issues such as a single *département* and the need to promote the use of the Basque language in education, it appeared to galvanize support like never before. Embracing the single-issue approach seems to have been a good tactic for Basque nationalism in Iparralde. In 1990, nearly half the municipal councils of the region voted in favor of a single *département*. Using this vote, and sensing a slight upturn in the fortunes of

"Language Game: To develop words in Basque and English, 3-7 year olds, Game of Letters." Multilingual promotion is a present-day reality of Euskal Herria. Developing English-language skills is particularly important and increasingly pursued through the medium of Basque.

Basque nationalism, in 1997 AB made a specific decision to concentrate on two issues: the creation of a single Basque *département* and full legal status for Euskara in Iparralde.[249]

The movement for a single Basque département gained momentum through cross-party support (from individuals rather than from the parties themselves), and in October 1999, 13,000 people, or over 5 percent of the population of Iparralde (a percentage equivalent to over three million of the French population as a whole), demonstrated in favor of the issue in Baiona. "In France," argues Sarah Waters, "more than any other Western European country it seems, protest constitutes a fundamental mechanism of political change and renewal."250 At the end of the 1990s, it was clear, from both opinion polls and an escalating social movement in favor of the issue, that the inhabitants of Iparralde were generally favorable to the idea of a single départe-ment. Thereafter, a series of negotiations between an all-party pro-département lobby from Iparralde and the French government took place, but in the spring of 2000, the French state, citing Spanish objections to the move as one of the reasons (specifically, that it would incite more Basque nationalist violence in Hegoalde), refused a widespread petition by various social groups, political parties (abertzale and non-abertzale), and elected officials in favor of the issue. Interestingly, at the same time that this peaceful campaign in favor of a single Basque département failed, the French govern-ment began a series of plans to grant more autonomous rule to the island of Corsica after a thirty-year violent campaign waged by Corsican nationalists. It would seem that, at the end of the century, the states of Europe were rallying their collective energies to preserve the power bases carefully built up over the previous two hundred years (or one hundred years, in the Spanish case).

CHEVAL ARGUES, in relation to France during the 1980s: "Recent administrative measures that pro-vide time for regional languages in national educational programs remain timid and do not amount, according to regionalist militants, to the historic measures of restoration, which they demand in compensation for what some have called a real *ethnocide*. As for the media, they have ignored regional languages for a long time."[251]

Similarly, the French Ministry of Education has met repeated calls for the creation of a university in Iparralde with silence. Events in Hegoalde, according to Jacob, such as the emergence of Basque nationalism, the effect of the Franco dictatorship, and the activity of ETA, have been critical in determining the relationship between Basque and French culture.[252] He states further that "the history of Basque nationalism in France has been a part of the political history of France as well. The nature of Basque political mobilization since before the Revolution has been a reflection of the growth of French institutions and the growth of a national myth which has driven the process of nation- and state-building in France. ... [T]he use of force has been a historic tool in the state's effort to tame its society—to create the French nation from which it ostensibly derives its own legitimacy."[253]

AT THE END of the 1990s, Iparralde seemed to have gained little practical benefit from its political allegiance to the French state's most conservative political ideologies. Rural depopulation, property values in certain areas rising beyond the means of local inhabitants, and a declining reliance on the primary agricultural sector had uprooted Basque society to such an extent that a critical rethinking was necessary on the part of those residents who wished to remain in the region rather than leaving for another region of France or, more typically, for Paris in order to find work and a better standard of living. This rethinking may, in part,

explain the tentative increment in the Basque nationalist vote and the widespread acceptance and, indeed,
support of issues like the calls for official recognition of
Euskara and for a single *département*. In a poll conducted in Iparralde in September 2000, 62 percent of
those questioned were in favor of the compulsory
teaching of Euskara in French Basque schools and 66
percent were favorable to the creation of a Basque
département. Whatever the reasons, it would seem that
at the end of the century the inhabitants of Iparralde,
like their neighbors to the south, were critically
rethinking what it meant to be Basque.

Lesson twenty-five

WRITTEN LESSON FOR SUBMISSION (FOR CHAPTERS 24
AND 25)

1. Write a critical review of the article by Thomas D.
   Lancaster. Use your knowledge of Basque nationalism
   in Euskal Herria to analyze Lancaster's argument.
   What, in your opinion, are the strengths and weaknesses of the article? Explain your choices.
2. Going into the new millennium, which of the two
   Basque ethnonational movements (that of Hegoalde
   or that of Iparralde) has more cause for optimism?
   Why?

26 · The dawn of the new millennium

OW CAN we hope to explore Basque culture and
society at the dawn of the new millennium in one
chapter when the theme could (and does) occupy the
space of a whole book? We cannot, of course, explore
every aspect of the subject here. Instead, after a brief
summary of some of the principal cultural developments in Euskal Herria during the late twentieth century, we will concentrate on two facets of modern Basque
culture—literature and popular music in Euskara—
emphasizing in particular the emergence of a *postmodern* Basque culture.

When considering cultural developments at the end of
the twentieth century, it is worth remembering that with
the fall of Franco, a relaxation of Jacobinism, and a general renewal of interest in the dynamism of peripheral
(rather than monolithic, centralized) culture, multiple
cultural traditions surfaced in the Basque Country. Consequently, a question immediately springs to mind:
What constitutes a specifically Basque culture? Were
Miguel de Unamuno y Jugo, Ramiro de Maeztu, and Pío
Baroja Basque or Spanish writers, or both? Literature
seems to be the thorniest of the cultural fields when it
comes to this question, given its reliance on language as
the conduit of its production. While it would be easy to
assign a sense of "Basqueness" simply to cultural artifacts produced in Euskara, the distinction is more complex. As Jesús María Lasagabaster states, people use the
term "Basque cinema" to refer to a genre that is almost
entirely produced in Castilian.[254] Indeed, a growing
tension between Castilian and *Euskaldun* (Basque-
speaking) cultures came to mark late-twentieth-century
developments.

TWO BROTHERS

Bernardo Atxaga

"Among the most terrenk, moving, ribald and accomplished lyrical of contemporary writers"
AMANDA HOPKINSON, Independent on Sunday

Bernardo Atxaga's works have acquired widespread recognition and praise for their lyrical qualities.

BASQUE CULTURAL DEVELOPMENTS DURING THE LATE
TWENTIETH CENTURY: AN OVERVIEW

The Castilian Tradition: Increasingly from the 1950s on,
modern Basque culture was divided along Euskara /
Castilian lines. The dominant figures of modern Basque
culture during this time were those of the Castilian-
speaking world, though all were firmly opposed to the
Franco regime. The ethnologist and cultural historian
Julio Caro Baroja represents the intellectual bridge
between the work of figures like Telesforo de Aranzadi y
Unamuno, Resurrección María de Azkue, and José
Miguel de Barandiarán and late-twentieth-century investigations of Basque culture. He also represents a point of
intersection between the worlds of art (his uncle Ricardo
Baroja was an artist of renown), literature (through
another uncle, the novelist Pío Baroja), and social science. On the advice of his uncle Pío, Julio Caro Baroja
assisted Aranzadi and Barandiarán in their fieldwork
during the 1930s. Over the next twenty years, he refined
his own particular ethnographic research to produce, in
1949, the influential work *Los vascos* (*The Basques*),
which quickly became the standard reference for investigations of Basque culture. In it, for the first time within
the academic study of the Basques, Caro Baroja affirmed
the importance of *culture* as a driving motivation behind
human identity. His conclusions also asserted the *historical unity* of Euskal Herria.

PERHAPS THE most gifted Castilian-language poet in
the Spanish state during this period was Gabriel
Celaya (a pseudonym for Rafael Múgica). Born in Her-
nani, Gipuzkoa, he inherited the mantle of Federico
García Lorca as the leader of a new movement of *social*
poetry. A member of the Partido Comunista de España
(PCE; Spanish Communist Party), he observed that
"poetry is a weapon loaded with the future."[255] Further,

in one poem he stated: "[W]e Basques only speak when something from inside / requires courage. / We Basques, when we speak, it's to say something that if it cannot be sung, is shouted. / We Basques do not like to blend fairly nice words. / We tough Basques drag along a chirping verse. / We Basques fight. We Basques punch, stirring up life. / We Basques are serious. Seriousness is our work. / Seriousness is our happiness. / We Basques are men of truth, not little children / playing tricks"[256]

Another of post–Civil War Spain's principal poets was Blas de Otero. Born in Bilbo (Bilbao), Otero became an exponent of "uprooted poetry," reflecting the Unamunian tradition of personal anguish. In the poem "España" ("Spain"), he wrote of Bilbo: "[C]ity where I was born, misty lap / of my childhood, damp with rain / and smoked with priests; / tonight / I cannot sleep, and I think about your protégés, / time lived among your streets overtakes me and I'm calling you from Madrid, / because only you maintain my expression, / you give sense to my steps."[257]

IN THE POST-FRANCO period, Basque writers continued to work in Castilian. At the end of the twentieth century, Basque women writers working in Castilian, such as the novelist Lucía Etxeberria from Bizkaia and the poet Julia Otxoa from Gipuzkoa, were especially prominent. Interestingly, one of France's leading authors in the 1990s (in French) was also Basque: Marie Darrieussecq from Lapurdi, who earned widespread critical and commercial success with her 1996 novel *Truismes* (translated into English as *Pig Tales*).

The Emergence of a Euskaldun Tradition: The modern novel in Euskara emerged during the 1950s and 1960s in the work of two pioneers: José Luis Alvarez Enparantza (alias Txillardegi) and Ramon Saizarbitoria.

As Lasagabaster notes, their work represented more than just an aesthetic or cultural change, but a political rebellion of sorts.[258] Not only did it flout the strict measures of the dictatorship suppressing the Basque language, but it also criticized the sense of Basque identity cultivated and promoted by the hegemonic political party, the Euzko Alderdi Jeltzalea-Partido Nacionalista Vasco (EAJ-PNV; Basque Nationalist Party). The contexts of their novels, for example, were not the bucolic ruralist paradise of traditional Basque nationalist myth, but a (similarly mythically constructed) gritty urban world.

THE WORK of Txillardegi and Saizarbitoria inspired a flowering of Basque authors, such as Angel Lertxundi from Gipuzkoa, who was influenced by the Magic Realism of Latin American literature; Dominique ("Txomin") Peillen from Zuberoa, who embraced the genre of detective fiction; and the Gipuzkoan Arantxa Urretavizcaya, who led the way for other female postwar writers, including the Zuberoan feminist writer Itxaro Borda and the Nafarroan Laura Mintegi in the 1980s. This initial period of the flowering of Basque literature culminated in the work of Bernardo Atxaga (pseudonym for Joseba Irasu), whose *Obabakoak* (meaning "the people and things of Obaba," 1988) not only heralded a postmodern turn in Basque literature, but received wide critical acclaim, both *nationally* (within Spain) and *internationally*, winning the 1989 Spanish National Literary Prize and being a finalist for the 1990 European Literary Prize. As of 1999, it had been translated into twenty-one languages, selling 43,000 copies in Basque, 75,000 in Castilian, and 18,900 in English. By the 1990s, Atxaga's work was therefore routinely translated into many languages. In terms of international acclaim, Atxaga was followed by Mariasun Landa, the premier Basque author in the genre of children's literature.

As Javier Cillero Goiriastuena notes, the existence in the late 1990s of a Basque-speaking society versed in multimedia forms provided a fertile breeding ground for the development of new Basque literary forms (detective and crime fiction, erotic literature, and so on). Among the generation of Basque writers using these new forms are Harkaitz Cano, Ur Apalategi, and Jasone Osoro.[259]

TXILLARDEGI and Saizarbitoria had begun a new trend by expressing sensitivity (a quality never previously developed in the written use of Euskara) in their novels. This was mirrored in the poetry of two of their contemporaries who also used sensitivity: the Bilbo-born Gabriel Aresti and the Zuberoan Jon Mirande. As *euskaldunberriak* (people who had learned Basque as adults), Aresti's and Mirande's achievements—like those of Txillardegi, another *eukaldunberri*—were quite remarkable. Drawing inspiration from both Celaya and Otero, Aresti initiated a new wave of *euskaldun* poetry in 1964 with the work *Harri eta Herri* (Stone and People), which affirmed the social and political role that Basque-speaking culture had assumed in the 1950s. In contrast to the serious character of the poetry of Aresti, Mirande's work, both in prose and poetry, tended to rely on irony and black humor. Nevertheless, Mirande also sent an obvious socio-political message through his work concerning the survival of Basque culture amid the threat of extermination on the part of the Franco regime.

The expression of Basque culture that gained the most recognition internationally during and after the 1950s, perhaps, was the blossoming Basque school of sculpture. At the forefront of this school was Jorge de Oteiza Embil. Born in Orio, Gipuzkoa, Oteiza originally studied medicine, but later opted for an artistic career, concen-

One of the current border crossing points between the French and Spanish states at Hendaia (Lapurdi)/Irun (Gipuzkoa). For the most part, traversing these two countries does not involve any kind of official regulation.
Photo by the author.

trating on sculpture during an eleven-year stay in Latin America between the mid-1930s and mid-1940s. His abstract work gradually gained him a premier reputation internationally, and in the 1950s he led a Vatican-funded project to design the new basilica in the holy town of Arantzazu (Aránzazu), Gipuzkoa, working with other emergent Basque sculptors, such as Néstor Basterretxea Arzadun. The revolutionary design of the basilica represented a cultural and political statement on the part of the Basque artists, who, like their literary contemporaries, were interested in moving away from the bucolic pastoral themes of previous Basque art, preferring instead to provoke or even unsettle the spectator. Oteiza's artistic output culminated in 1957, when he won the prestigious International Prize for Sculpture at the Bienal de São Paolo. Thereafter, he devoted his time to philosophical inquiries into Basque history and culture. The resultant findings of this investigation—in particular, his theory of *disoccupation*, whereby the act of emptying or disoccupying an occupied space leads to the acquisition of freedom or the "nothing" from which "everything" might be subsequently attained—did much to influence new generations of politically conscious Basque artists, writers, and musicians.

L IKE OTEIZA, Eduardo Chillida acquired a growing international recognition in the 1950s. He won the Prize for Sculpture at the Biennale di Venezia in 1958, and in 1959 a retrospective exhibition of his work toured the United States. Unlike Oteiza, however, Chillida continued to develop his own sculpting style through the 1960s and 1970s, becoming, by century's end, the most prolific and internationally recognized Basque artist. In August 2002, Chillida died, and a measure of his popularity among Basques was revealed when thousands of people turned out in Donostia to pay their last respects to the sculptor.

According to Lasagabaster, "cinema is, beyond any doubt, the flagship of recent Basque culture."[260] Within the genre of "Basque cinema" developed in the post-Franco period, he lists the work of the directors Pedro Olea, Imanol Uribe, Juanma Bajo Ulloa, and Julio Medem. To this list, Jaume Martí-Olivella adds Montxo

Armendáriz (nominated for an Oscar for his *Secreteos del corazón* [*Secrets of the Heart*], released in 1997), Arantxa Lazcano, Antxon Eceiza, Ana Díez, Daniel Calparsoro, and Alex de la Iglesia.[261] However, as Martí-Olivella emphasizes, many problems have arisen in defining the exact qualities of a specifically Basque cinema. Indeed, for Daniel Calparsoro, "there is no entity called Basque cinema, zero."[262]

MODERN BASQUE film emerged with the remarkable 1968 documentary *Ama Lur* (*Mother Earth*), co-written and directed by the sculptor Basterretxea and Fernando Larruquert. Narrated in both Euskara and Castilian, *Ama Lur* presented, in moving fashion, a history of Basque culture for an audience whose younger members, children of Franco, would never have seen many of the images shown. Thereafter, contemporary Basque cinema came to reflect the social and political crises of Euskal Herria in the post-Franco period. Early examples of this trend include Uribe's *La fuga de Segovia* (*Escape from Segovia*, 1981), an accurate portrayal, based on a true story, of the mass escape of ETA prisoners from Segovia prison in 1976. Uribe's later *Días contados* (*Numbered Days*, 1995) also took ETA as its central theme, although it was less realist in style than his earlier films, while Calparsoro's *Salto al vacío* (*Jump Into the Void*, 1995) treated the socio-economic decline of Hegoalde. More ironic, quirky, and nuanced films, such as Bajo Ulloa's *Alas de mariposa* (*Butterfly Wings*, 1991), Medem's *Vacas* (*Cows*, 1992), and Lazcano's *Urte illunak* (*The Dark Years*, 1992) have also been a feature of late-twentieth-century Basque film production.

Perhaps the most spectacular single cultural or artistic innovation to occur in the Basque Country at the end of the twentieth century was the construction of the

Pre-history and history blend in the marketing strategy of the Sara caves (Lapurdi) to define a specifically Basque historical reality.

Guggenheim Museum in Bilbo. In a deal signed in 1992 by the Basque Autonomous Government and the Solomon R. Guggenheim Foundation of New York, the former agreed to subsidize the building of a franchise museum in Bilbo as an attempt to revitalize the city's flagging economy. Controversial architect Frank O. Gehry was commissioned to design the structure, and the result was an architectural masterpiece crowned by a

flowing titanium form, located along the former industrial artery of the city, the Nerbioi river. Since its completion in the fall of 1997, the project has had great economic success, though if the heavy debt incurred by the
Basque government to fund the museum is to be paid
off, it will need to continue this success. It was hoped
that a major project of this type would help reinvent the
Basque city for the new millennium. This remains to be
seen.

INTO THE POPULAR

During the 1960s, two *bertsolariak* (improvisational versifiers), Jon Lopategi and John Azpillaga, radicalized the
art form to encompass direct political protest in their
duels. Indeed, in the 1960s, *bertsolaritza* began to trans-
form itself into a leading form of Basque protest against
the Franco regime. Through to the 1980s, *bertsolaritza*
also renewed its structural foundations, with the establishment of specific schools in which to study the art
form, the publication of verses, and the creation of professional competitions. By the 1990s, individual *bertsolariak* had branched out into publishing works of literature and musical composition. Lopategi and Azpillaga
were followed by successive waves of *bertsolariak*,
including Xabier Amuriza, Sebastián Lizaso, Andoni
Egaña, Xabier Pérez (alias "Euzkitze"), and Jon Sarasua.
THE MOST important developments within contemporary *bertsolaritza* have been the inclusion of
women into this traditionally male preserve, the
increasing political radicalization of the art form, and a
new generation of *bertsolariak* from Iparralde. Among
the prominent female *bertsolariak* during the 1990s
were Estitxu Arocena, Maddalen Lujanbio, and Oihane
Enbeita (great-granddaughter of the mythic *bertsolari*
"Urretxindor"). These women, together with young

male *bertsolariak* such as Unai Iturriaga and Jon Maia, as well as Amets Arzalluz and Sustrai Colina from Iparralde, have also been active spokespeople for various social and political causes, such as the repatriation of Basque political prisoners.[263]

PROFESSIONAL sports continued to remain at the forefront of Basque popular culture, as elsewhere, through the late twentieth century. In the early 1980s, the two professional Basque soccer teams, Real Sociedad and Athletic Bilbao, enjoyed a particularly spectacular run of success (with, it should be emphasized, entirely home-grown players), together claiming the Spanish league championship—against great odds—four years in a row between 1981 and 1984 (Real Sociedad in 1980–81 and 1981–82, Athletic Bilbao in 1982–83 and 1983–84). By 2000, four Basque teams—the two previously mentioned plus Alavés from Gasteiz (Vitoria) and Osasuna from Iruñea (Pamplona)—were competing in the Spanish state's twenty-strong first division. Moreover two Basques from Lapurdi, Bixente Lizarazu and Didier Deschamps, were members of the French state's victorious World Cup–winning team in 1998. Other Basque sporting figures of note during the era included Miguel Indurain from Atarrabia (Villaba), Nafarroa, who won cycling's Tour de France a staggering five times in a row; the golfer José María Olazabal from Hondarribia (Fuentarrabía), Gipuzkoa, who has won both the Ryder Cup (with the European team) and the U.S. Masters tournament; Julian Retegi from Eratsun (Erasun), Nafarroa, a champion *pilota* (handball) player who retired in 2001 after more than a quarter-century at the top of the sport; Iñaki Perurena from Leitza (Leiza), Nafarroa, the most famous *harrijotzaile* (stone lifter) in the world of traditional Basque sports; and the cyclist

Joanne Somarriba from Sopela (Sopelana), Bizkaia, the two-time winner of the women's Tour de France.

Sport also became a site of political contest at the end of the twentieth century, with the passing of a recommendation by the autonomous Basque parliament in 1998 that Euskal Herria be allowed to field its own international sports teams and the creation of Euskal Selekzioaren Aldeko Iritzi Taldea (ESAIT; Organization Reclaiming a Basque National Selection), a group actively lobbying for specifically Basque participation in a number of international sports.

PARALLEL TO the artistic and literary regeneration of the 1950s and 1960s, a flowering of Basque music took place in the 1960s, led by popular theater and music groups like Ez Dok Amairu and musicians such as Mikel Laboa, Xabier Lete, and, later, Benito Lertxundi and Amaia Zubiria, who tended toward reviving and updating popular folk music while adding their own social and political commentary to much of the work. Their emergence in Hegoalde was paralleled in Iparralde by the likes of Erramun Martikorena. By the 1970s, this movement had become a veritable institution, and a major rebellion against it—influenced in part by the events of post-Franco Spain and in part by the international cultural manifestations of youth protest, such as punk and reggae—took place in the form of an explosion of almost entirely *euskaldun* popular music. Unlike Lasagabaster, I would point to this movement as the most dynamic expression of Basque culture at the end of the twentieth century.

Building on the emergence of Basque rock music, principally in Iparralde in the late 1970s—with groups such as Niko Etxart and Minxoriak (an anagram of a previous name of the group, Ximinorak, meaning "Monkeys in Anoraks") from Zuberoa and Errobi from

Caption missing. Cycling is a part of the Basque tradition of competitive exertion. Popular interest in the sport is based on a peculiar Basque affinity for trials of endurance. The supreme exponent of this quality at the end of the twentieth century was the Nafarroan cyclist Miguel Indurain.
Drawing from David Carlson: Ready-to-use sports illustrations.

Lapurdi—the countercultural or subcultural genre of Basque "radical rock" (as it came to be known) acted as an important sphere for Basque-identity cultural mobilization and, specifically, for left-wing *abertzale* political mobilization between 1982 and 1989. Punk music in the Basque Country emerged under the same conditions— economic hardship, leading to widespread social discontent—as had its British model.

BY THE EARLY 1980s, nearly two-thirds of the Spanish state's youth were unemployed, a figure that was even higher in some parts of Hegoalde, where heavy industry had been especially affected by the economic downturn. Principal among the first radical rock groups to emerge were Barricada (Barricade) from Nafarroa and Eskorbuto (Scurvy) from Bizkaia, whose nihilist and anarchist directives were aimed against the existing social order as a whole; La Polla Records (Cock Records) from Araba, who had a more specifically defined combative stance; and Kortatu (named after an ETA member killed by the Spanish police) from Gipuzkoa and Hertzainak (The Police), who exemplified a leftist *abertzale* position. The majority of these groups recorded their music in Spanish, but some, such as Kortatu (which, with a new line-up, changed its name to Negu Gorriak, or Hard Winter) evolved into writing lyrics in Euskara, as did a new generation of groups, such as Patxa (a diminutive of the word *patxarana*, a Basque liqueur) from Lapurdi and Su ta Gar (At a Fever Pitch) from Gipuzkoa. Others, like Hertzainak, increasingly introduced irony into their social and political messages, while Itoitz (named after a place in Nafarroa) from Gipuzkoa blended a more melodic pop-based sound into their own version of Basque new wave music.[264] While the songs of these bands were mainly expressed in Euskara, other Basque groups, principally in the pop genre, were also successful at a Spanish level. These groups included Duncan Dhu in the 1980s and 1990s and La Oreja de Van Gogh (Van Gogh's Ear) at the end of the 1990s.

By the 1990s, an explosion of musical forms had taken place in Euskal Herria, with all musical genres represented, from ska (Skalariak from Iruñea, for example) and rap (Selekta Kolektiboa, or Selekta Collective, made up of members from both Iparralde and Hegoalde) to techno (Basque Electronic Diaspora, a musical collective of musicians from both Iparralde and Hegoalde based in international cities such as London and Paris) and the musical blending of Negu Gorriak. Another interesting development that took place during the decade was the emergence of "triki-pop," a musical form blending traditional accordion or *trikitixa* rhythms with pop music, exemplified by the Gipuzkoan duo Alaitz eta Maider. The common thread of the 1990s explosion in popular music was a commitment to progressive social and often "alternative" values, the Basque language, and, for the most part, the *abertzale* Left's political project.[265]

BASQUE CULTURE at the end of the twentieth century was a vibrant mix of old and new forms, trilingual, and multicultural. There now existed a platform or model from which cultural expression could be developed and expanded; increasingly, this model was a combination of both Basque (traditional culture plus the important changes of the 1960s) and international (both marginal and mainstream elements from universal or global cultural forms) influences, excluding Spanish or French developments.

Lesson twenty-six

REQUIRED READING

Jesús María Lasagabaster, "Introduction," in Jesús María Lasagabaster, ed., *Contemporary Basque Fiction: An Anthology* (Reno: University of Nevada Press, 1990), pp. 1–23.

Javier Cillero Goiriastuena, "*Contemporary Basque Fiction* Revisited," in William A. Douglass, Carmelo Urza, Linda White, and Joseba Zulaika, eds., *Basque Cultural Studies* (Reno: Basque Studies Program, 1998), pp. 84–105.

Linda White, "Mission for the Millennium: Gendering and Engendering Literature for the Next Thousand Years," in William A. Douglass, Carmelo Urza, Linda White, and Joseba Zulaika, eds., *Basque Cultural Studies* (Reno: Basque Studies Program, 1998), pp. 134–48.

Christian Lahusen, "The Aesthetic of Radicalism: The Relationship between Punk and the Patriotic Nationalist Movement of the Basque Country," *Popular Music* 12, no. 3 (October 1993), pp. 263–80.

Sharryn Kasmir, "From the Margins: Punk Rock and the Repositioning of Ethnicity and Gender in Basque Identity," in William A. Douglass, Carmelo Urza, Linda White, and Joseba Zulaika, eds., *Basque Cultural Studies* (Reno: Basque Studies Program, 1998), pp. 178–204.

SUGGESTED READING

Jesús María Lasagabaster, "The Promotion of Cultural Production in Basque," in Helen Graham and Jo Labanyi, eds., *Spanish Cultural Studies: An Introduction* (Oxford: Oxford University Press, 1995), pp. 351–55.

Jaume Martí-Olivella, "Invisible Otherness: From Migrant Subjects to the Subject of Immigration in Basque Cinema," in William A. Douglass, Carmelo Urza, Linda White, and Joseba Zulaika, eds., *Basque Cultural Studies* (Reno: Basque Studies Program, 1998), pp. 205–26.

LEARNING OBJECTIVES
1. To explore the varied nature of Basque cultural expression at the dawn of the new millennium.
2. To critically reflect on these varieties of cultural expression, especially in regard to the meaning of "culture."
3. To examine the historical transformation of Basque cultural forms.

WRITTEN LESSON FOR SUBMISSION
Document Question 5
Compare and contrast the following three texts to critically examine the evolution of artistic expression within Basque culture. All three texts were originally written in Euskara at different times of recent Basque historical experience—the 1960s, 1980s, and 1990s, respectively. What does each of the texts tell us about the nature of Basque identity? What (if any) are the social, political, and / or cultural *messages* of the texts? What common themes do you discern in the texts? How do they differ? What is *your* critical reaction to the texts?

Gabriel Aresti, extract from "Nire Aitaren Etxea" ("The House of My Father," 1964):
I shall defend
the house of my father
against wolves,
against drought,

---

against usury,
against the law,
I shall defend
The house of my father.

They will take my weapons
and with my hands I shall defend
the house of my father;
they will cut off my hands
and with my arms I will defend
the house of my father.
They will leave me
armless,
without shoulders,
without a chest
and with my soul I shall defend
the house of my father.
I shall die,
my soul will be lost,
my descendants will be lost,
but the house of my father
will still be standing.[266]

Bernardo Atxaga, extract from *Obabakoak* (1988):
I write in a strange language. Its verbs,
the structure of its relative clauses,
the words it uses to designate ancient things
—rivers, plants, birds—
have no sisters anywhere on Earth.
A house is etxe, *a bee* erle, *death* heriotz.
The sun of the long winters we call eguzki *or* eki;
the sun of the sweet, rainy springs is also
—as you'd expect—called eguzki *or* eki
(it's a strange language but not that strange).

Born, they say, in the megalithic age,
it survived, this stubborn language, by withdrawing,
by hiding away like a hedgehog in a place,
which, thanks to the traces it left behind there,
the world named the Basque Country or Euskal Herria.
Yet isolation could never have been absolute
—cat is katu, *pipe is* pipa, *logic is* lojika—
rather, as the prince of detectives would have said,
the hedgehog, my dear Watson, crept out of its hiding
   place
(to visit, above all, Rome and all its progeny).

The language of a tiny nation, so small
you cannot even find it on the map,
it never strolled in the gardens of the Court
or past the marble statues of government buildings;
in four centuries it produced only a hundred books ...
the first in 1545; the most important in 1643;
the Calvinist New Testament in 1571;
the complete Catholic Bible around 1860.
Its sleep was long, its bibliography brief
(but in the twentieth century the hedgehog awoke).[267]

Negu Gorriak, "Aizu" ("Listen to Me," 1995):
We were born between the years 60 and 64, for those who
   know.
We were the ones who were blown away by the introduc-
   tion of heroine.
The economic crisis of 1979 also hit us hard.
Listening to punk music, they classified us as a "high
   risk" group. ... Listen to me ... condemned to suffer,
   my friend.
Talk long and deep about life.
Listen to me ... I love deepness, my friend.
Let's be healthy together.

Nights have never been longer and dawn's never been so far away, when the social structure is eating us away.
We've got to stop crying.
We mustn't drop out or be useless—that would be a waste of our capacity, even though our spinal column is bent.
If you've got some extra dignity stored up, listen to me ... look into my eyes, my friend.
They still sparkle.
Listen to me ... stay here with us, my friend ... our son wants to hear you.
Listen to me ... you who are condemned to suffer, my friend ... you still have a sparkle.
Listen to me, talk long and deep about life, my friend, our son wants to hear you.[268]

Basque identity today
Conclusion

"The issue of identity formation (and maintenance) is particularly acute within Basque society and culture. Sometimes touted as western Europe's oldest people and speaking a language that thus far remains the sole known representative of its own language family, Basques would seem to be living, indisputable representatives of their own ethnic and cultural reality. However, the absence of a Basque nation-state in a world politically defined in terms of such units ... conspire[s] to pose and confound the issues of Basque authenticity and identity."[269]

These comments seem to be as applicable today as they might have been two or three hundred years ago. Napoleon Bonaparte is reported to have commented that "ground can always be recovered, but time never."[270] Has Basque identity lost *time*? Undeniably, both through state pressure and personal choice, many Basques have relinquished or relegated a sense of their separate identity in favor of the greater and more powerful national claims of being French or Spanish. Given the either / or cultural, social, and political constructions of the modern world stemming from Enlightenment rationalism (see Chapter 3), it has been difficult for Basques to ever win any particular "battle," given the overwhelming nature of their "opponents." (The violent metaphor here seems sadly appropriate.) Yet Basque culture and identity have never quite disappeared altogether, and now, in a somewhat "shaken" modern world (for some, a *post*modern world), they seem to be thriving. What should we make of this? Let us first consider what is often taken to be the cornerstone of any identity: language.

Basque Speakers in 1996 [271]

Area	Population	Basque speakers	Some knowledge of Basque
Basque Autonomous Community	1,778,400	448,200 (25.2%)	290,200 (16.3%)
Foral Community of Nafarroa	437,200	42,100 (9.6%)	42,800 (9.8%)
Hegoalde	2,215,600	490,300 (22.1%)	333,000 (15%)
Iparralde	212,400	56,200 (26.5%)	19,800 (9.3%)
Euskal Herria	2,428,000	546,500 (22.5%)	352,800 (14.5%)

EUSKARA: THE SURVIVAL OF A PREMODERN LANGUAGE
IN A POSTMODERN WORLD
In the late nineteenth century (according to an 1868 estimate by Ladislao de Velasco), just over half of the
approximately 900,000 inhabitants of the seven
provinces of Euskal Herria (470,000, or 52 percent) were
Basque speakers. In a survey published in 1996
(reflecting the sociolinguistic situation of the early
1990s), out of Euskal Herria's total population of just
under two and a half million people, there were over
half a million Basque speakers (22.5 percent of the total
population) and a further 352,800 people (or 14.5 percent of the total population) with some knowledge of

Euskara. What conclusions might we draw from this about Basque identity? How does language affect political or cultural orientation?

AN INITIAL reading of the table on page 435 reveals, possibly, some interesting conclusions: A greater percentage of Basque speakers were to be found in Iparralde than in Hegoalde. If historically France has been an example of "strong" state building compared to the "weaker" integration of Spain, how do we explain the relatively stronger survival of Basque in Iparralde? This cannot be altogether due to the effect of the Franco dictatorship, although certainly this was an important factor. Probably more critical—and this is telling in a cultural history such as this—has been the distinct socio-economic development of Hegoalde. Hegoalde became a *modern* society (in economic and therefore social terms) between the late nineteenth and early twentieth centuries, and in the process of this modernization, Castilian became the medium of business and therefore of economic success, stability, or even just survival. This crucial change, perhaps even more than political developments, resulted in a social transformation whereby knowledge of Basque had declined to a rate of one in five by the 1990s.

By the same token, the statistic that around one in four Basques of Iparralde spoke Euskara in 1996 might imply that Basque nationalism would be a stronger political phenomenon in the north than in the south. However, we know that this is not the case. For a variety of reasons—social, political, cultural, and economic— the Basque language is actually in a *stronger* position in Hegoalde than in Iparralde, having much to do with the solid official status of, significant economic aid for, and strong socio-political connotations of the use of Euskara.

Pagoa Brew-Pub, Oiartzun, Gipuzkoa. For those businesses operating in and around the border between the
French and Spanish states, multi- rather than merely
bilingualism is a practical reality.

For example, according to prematriculation figures for the Basque Autonomous Community's public education system for the 2002–03 school year, 61.25 percent of three-year-olds and 56.81 percent of six-year-olds were enrolled for the linguistic model of education whereby classes are conducted entirely in Euskara, with Castilian taught as a separate subject; a further 30.12 and 32.26 percent, respectively, were enrolled in a model whereby an equal level of teaching takes place in both Euskara and Castilian.[272] Similarly, matriculation figures for the public education system in Nafarroa at the end of the 1990s reveal that 33.9 percent of three-year-olds and 41 percent of six-year-olds were enrolled in the predominantly Euskara or bilingual options.[273] Ironically, during this period, the UPN (the governing party of Nafarroa at that time and an affiliate of the statewide PP) instituted a policy of dismantling whatever minority status Euskara had in the so-called "mixed" and "non–Basque-speaking" areas of the province, in as many fields as it could. For example, Article 16 of Foral Decree 372, passed in 2000, states that all signs in and on public buildings in the "mixed" zone are to be in Castilian only. This passing of this decree led to the extraordinary sight of public employees physically removing Euskara from signs, plaques, and so on, in an effort to extinguish Euskara from public sight.

THE ABOVE incentives, either positive or negative, were mostly absent in Iparralde. If anything, Euskara was mostly ignored by central and local government bodies. In fact, while the number of Basque speakers was substantially growing in the south (with an estimated increase of 200,000 new Basque speakers during the 1990s), the reverse was true in the north. While a significant social movement for the defense and promotion of Euskara had grown over the previous thirty years in Iparralde—in part through the work of organizations like Seaska ("Cradle"; the organization responsible for the development of Basque-language schools) and Alfabetatze eta Euskalduntze Koordinakundea (AEK; Coordination of Education and Literacy in Euskara, the organization founded in Hegoalde for the teaching of Basque to adults)—it was still a struggle, for at the end of the 1990s, there continued to be little incentive (beyond not inconsiderable cultural reasons) to make Basque *viable* in Iparralde.

BY CONTRAST, Basque-language use had permeated many sections of society, both official and nonofficial, within the Basque Autonomous Community. (Regional government support remained less encouraging in Nafarroa, however, despite significant popular support.) What seems clear from the case in Hegoalde is that, together with official or institutional support, Basque-language use had also been supported during the 1990s by a strong and vibrant culture, from music and literature to sports and the media. Might this, then, be the *critical* variable in maintaining a specifically Basque identity?

BASQUE CULTURE AS AN EXAMPLE FOR THE NEW MILLENNIUM

Much of the rhetoric of the "new Europe" encourages citizens to learn other languages, travel, and to be open and flexible to cultural exchange. For this purpose, a whole series of incentives, from the annual naming of one European city as the "cultural capital" to a single European flag and anthem, have been directed at encouraging the development of a European identity as a general expression of its constituent parts. One might argue that the Basques have been doing this all along. Basque culture has had to adapt to other (usually more

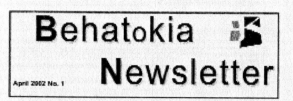

Behatokia

Newsletter

April 2002 No. 1

Behatokia defends the linguistic rights of the citizens of the Basque Country

The Observatory of Linguistic Rights, Behatokia, is a tool promoted by Kontseilua, the Council of Social Organizations in Favour of the Basque language. Behatokia protects the linguistic rights of the citizens of the regions covered by Euskara, the Basque language, and its activities aim to guarantee those rights both in the public and the private spheres.

Currently, Euskara is spoken in a territory administratively divided into two states, Spain and France, and by different entities within both. This territory, Euskal Herria, the Basque Country, involves the historical regions where the Basque language is spoken, currently under different administrations: within Spain, Navarra (Nafarroa) and the Basque Autonomous Community territories of Araba (Araba), Bizkaia (Bizkaia) and Gipuzkoa, and within France, Labourd (Lapurdi), Basse Navarre (Nafarroa Beherea) and Soule (Zuberoa).

The status of Basque, the native language of the Basque Country, is regulated by five different legal regimes. Some grant speakers recognised rights to use the language, when it is considered co-official with the official language of the state, in other cases speakers have certain recognised rights, although Basque is not officially acknowledged; as regards the rest of the speakers, the administration does not grant them any right to use the language, although its existence towards its use may vary.

Therefore, Euskara, the native language of the Basque Country, is not official in all regions, and the linguistic rights of Basque speakers are constantly violated. In the light of this situation:

✔ Behatokia protects and defends the linguistic rights of Basque speakers and condemns their violation.

✔ The aim of Behatokia is to guarantee Basque speakers their right to use the Basque language in Euskal Herria, their right to address the administration in Basque and to receive its services (health, education, justice, information and other services) in Basque, and to guarantee their right to enjoy the services offered by individuals in the language.

The newsletter of Kontseilua, the Council of Social Organizations in Favor of the Basque Language. This organization aims to implement measures designed to normalize the use of Euskara in the public sphere, while at the same time explaining its message in a variety of languages.

dominant) cultural formations. In many ways, this is the basis of Basque culture—the collective ability, forged out of historical necessity, to maintain a cultural identity despite losing what for many other cultures could be considered essential cultural markers.

As Jesús Azcona notes, "Basque society is in the process of becoming a society based on a new legitimation of the collective identity of the people that live there."[274] Thus, Basque culture has increasingly displayed the confidence to revert to a broad sentiment of belonging. To be sure, the use and promotion of Euskara have been important in building up this sentiment, but the very success of the pro-Euskara movement (in Hegoalde, at least) now means that its rigid tenets—*having to* speak Basque all the time—are no longer applicable. Knowledge of Basque is *important* and even *fashionable* (thus making it viable), and this has prepared Basque speakers well for the new millennium. Already possessing a culture of multilingualism, Basque speakers should not only have fewer problems acquiring additional languages (English in particular),[275] but, we might conclude, they are well placed in the race to become *European* or *multicultural*. Certainly the examples of musical and literary trends at the close of the 1990s would seem to bear this out.

As WE HAVE seen throughout this study, questions over Basque identity have been especially pertinent in the history of Euskal Herria, but this should not *mean* anything other than the fact that Basque culture has a propensity for critical reflection. I would contend that, as the new millennium takes shape, Basque culture and identity are as confident and flexible as they can be to face new and unknown challenges. In many ways, those well-known identities that have long enjoyed cultural power and that have thus had less need for cultural reflection (if two or three hundred years may be considered a long time within the overall sweep of human history) are the more nervous aspirants to membership of the new global cultural formations taking shape. England, for example, perhaps the oldest state identity, seems to be in the process of a critical reforming or regaining of its cultural identity, lost historically in the formation of Great Britain. The Scots and the Welsh, not to mention the Irish, have been happily *inventing* their traditions for many generations, and can only look on in wonder at the English attempt. What must the Basques be thinking of their French and Spanish neighbors at the gates of the new millennium?

Final lesson

REQUIRED READING

Joseba Zulaika, "Tropics of Terror: From Guernica's 'Natives' to Global Terrorists," *Social Identities* 4, no. 1 (1998), pp. 93–108.

Jacqueline Urla, "Contesting Modernities: Language Standardization and the Production of an Ancient / Modern Basque Culture," *Critique of Anthropology* 13, no. 2 (1993), pp. 101–18.

Jesús Azcona, "To Be Basque and to Live in Basque Country: The Inequalities of Difference," in Carol J. Greenhouse, ed., *Democracy and Ethnography: Constructing Identities in Multicultural States* (Albany, N.Y.: State University of New York Press, 1998), pp. 163–77.

Manuel Castells, "Globalization, Identity, and the Basque Question," in William A. Douglass, Carmelo Urza, Linda White, and Joseba Zulaika, eds., *Basque Politics and Nationalism on the Eve of the Mill-*

ennium (Reno: Basque Studies Program, 1999),
pp. 22–33.

Andoni Alonso and Iñaki Arzoz, "Basque Identity on the
Internet," in William A. Douglass, Carmelo Urza,
Linda White, and Joseba Zulaika, eds., *Basque Cultural Studies* (Reno: Basque Studies Program, 1998),
pp. 295–312.

SUGGESTED READING

Jacqueline Urla, "Basque Language Revival and Popular
Culture," in William A. Douglass, Carmelo Urza,
Linda White, and Joseba Zulaika, eds., *Basque Cultural Studies* (Reno: Basque Studies Program, 1998),
pp. 44–62.

Tom Nairn, "Nations: Breaking Up Is Hard to Do,"
Marxism Today, November / December 1998,
pp. 40–43.

LEARNING OBJECTIVES

1. To critically consider the meaning of Basque identity
at the beginning of the new millennium.
2. To chart the myriad ways in which this identity has,
or has not, changed since the eighteenth century.
3. To consider the prospects of survival for a specifically
Basque identity in the new millennium.

WRITTEN LESSON FOR SUBMISSION

1. Consider the opening remarks in the introduction to
this book. How do *you* think that Basque identity has
been historically *represented*? What do you now make
of Ian Gibson's and Mark Kurlansky's comments?
How would you frame a brief historical and cultural
introduction to Euskal Herria? Incorporate some
comment on Joseba Zulaika's article "Tropics of

Terror: From Guernica's 'Natives' to Global Terrorists" into your answer.

2. Compare and contrast the articles by Manuel Castells, Jacqueline Urla, and Andoni Alonso and Iñaki Arzoz. What do they tell us about the nature of Basque identity? On what points do they agree, and where do they differ? What is your opinion of the common themes they highlight?

Spelling and Usage

F INDING A common spelling policy for writing about Basque-related topics is somewhat akin to negotiating a particularly difficult minefield. The Basque Country is a trilingual territory, and there are even some specifically English variants for Basque place names. For example, the province of *Vizcaya* (Castilian) might also be written *Bizkaia* (Euskara), *Biscaye* (French), and *Biscay* (English). The French name of another of the Basque provinces, *Navarre*, has passed into English and is more common than its Castilian (*Navarra*) or Euskara (*Nafarroa*) equivalents. Furthermore, some place names that are well-known to an Anglo-literate world (such as *Bilbao* and *Biarritz*) actually have variants (*Bilbo* and *Miarritze*, respectively) that may be unknown to those accustomed to the former spelling.

It has always seemed strange to me that texts in English should unquestioningly adopt French or Castilian variants for place names. To be sure, the vast majority of source material encountered (be it in English, French, or Castilian) will use French or Castilian variants; this, I feel, only adds to the subsumed or *hidden* quality of Basque history. As this is a study focusing on Basque history, I have decided to use the Euskara version of place names (with their French or Castilian equivalents in parentheses on their first appearance in each chapter) as an appropriate means of introducing readers to a specifically Basque perspective.

One further point of usage needs clarification. Throughout the work, the words "Castile" and "Spain" are used. The process by which Spain came into being at the expense of Castile is more thorny than, for example, that of Great Britain in relation to England. According to

Simon Barton, "just precisely when Spain as a nation is born is a moot point," with interpretations ranging from the unification of several kingdoms in the period between 1479 and 1512 to the introduction, by King Felipe V, of the 1716 *Nueva Planta* constitution.[276]

The single term "Spain" (*España*) developed out of an abbreviation of a long list of royal titles bestowed on monarchs after 1512. At that time, the official title of the "Spanish" monarch was "King of Castile and León, King of Aragón, King of Nafarroa, Count of Gipuzkoa," and so on. As such, a term developed to encompass all of these titles: "the Spains" (*las Españas*). The country was therefore known, at the dawn of the modern period, as "the Kingdom of the Spains," a term carrying with it many implications about the nature of the kingdom. I have tried to emphasize the Castilian political influence on the emergence of Spain at the beginning of the work and therefore consciously use the term Castile. Thereafter, and especially in regard to the early nineteenth century and beyond, I use the word "Spain" to refer to the country.

ONE OTHER related point is worth mentioning: The language of Castile, and indeed the dominant language of modern Spain, is Castilian (*castellano*). To use the term "Spanish" for this language is incorrect, as this word comes from "Spain," which was originally a geographic (and later a political) term. Culturally, the language of Castile came to dominate "Spain," but to regard this as the sole language of "the Spains" is inaccurate when Català (Catalan), Euskara (Basque), and Galego (Galician) have also been languages of Spain.

Endnotes

1. Eric Hobsbawm, *On History* (New York: The New Press, 1997), p. 10.
2. See David Lowenthal, *The Past is a Foreign Country* (Cambridge: Cambridge University Press, 1985).
3. Ibn Khaldûn, *The Muqaddimah: An Introduction to History*, trans. Franz Rosenthal, abridged and edited by N. J. Dawood (Princeton: Princeton University Press, 1967), p. 5.
4. Adapted from Carl E. Shorske, *Thinking with History* (Princeton: Princeton University Press, 1998), p. 220.
5. Anthony Smith, "The Origins of Nations," in Geoff Eley and Ronald Grigor Suny, eds., *Becoming National: A Reader* (New York and Oxford: Oxford University Press, 1996), p. 107.
6. Ibid., p. 108.
7. Walker Connor, *Ethnonationalism: The Quest For Understanding* (Princeton: Princeton University Press, 1994), p. 196.
8. Ibid., p. 197.
9. Ian Gibson, *Fire in the Blood: The New Spain* (London and Boston: Faber and Faber, 1992), p. 131.
10. Ibid., pp. 132–34.
11. Ibid., pp. 136–37.
12. Ibid., p. 137.
13. Ibid., p. 146.
14. Mark Kurlansky, *The Basque History of the World* (New York: Walker & Company, 1999), p. 326.
15. Ibid. p. 350.
16. Ibid., p. 351.
17. See Eric Hobsbawm's *The Age of Revolution 1789–1848* (London: Weidenfeld & Nicolson, 1962),

The Age of Capital 1848–1975 (London: Weidenfeld & Nicolson, 1975), and *The Age of Empire 1876–1914* (London: Weidenfeld & Nicolson, 1987).

18. See William A. Douglass and Jon Bilbao, *Amerikanuak: Basques in the New World* (Reno: University of Nevada Press, 1975), pp. 16–20.

19. Rachel Bard, "The Decline of a Basque State in France: Basse Navarre, 1512–1789," in William A. Douglass, Richard W. Etulain, and William H. Jacobs, eds., *Anglo-American Contributions to Basque Studies: Essays in Honor of Jon Bilbao* (Reno: Desert Research Institute, 1977), p. 83.

20. Benedict Anderson, *Imagined Communities: Reflections on the Origin and Spread of Nationalism*, rev. ed. (London and New York: Verso, 1991), p. 4.

21. Eric Hobsbawm, *The Age of Revolution 1789–1848*, p. 22.

22. Douglass and Bilbao, *Amerikanuak*, pp. 16–17.

23. James E. Jacob, *Hills of Conflict: Basque Nationalism in France* (Reno, Las Vegas, and London: University of Nevada Press, 1994), p. 2.

24. See Walter Ong, *Orality and Literacy: The Technologizing of the Word* (London and New York: Methuen, 1982).

25. Clare Mar-Molinero, "The Role of Language in Spanish Nation-Building," in Clare Mar-Molinero and Angel Smith, eds., *Nationalism and the Nation in the Iberian Peninsula* (Oxford: Berg, 1996), p. 74.

26. See Douglass and Bilbao, *Amerikanuak*, pp. 57–58.

27. Robert P. Clark, *The Basques: The Franco Years and Beyond* (Reno: University of Nevada Press, 1979), p. 22.

28. See Francisco Letamendia Belzunce, *Historia del nacionalismo vasco y de E.T.A.*, vol. 1: *Introducción*

histórica. ETA en el franquismo (1951–1976)
(Donostia: R & B Ediciones, 1994), pp. 54–55.

29. Renato Barahona, *Vizcaya on the Eve of Carlism: Politics and Society, 1800–1833* (Reno and Las Vegas: University of Nevada Press, 1989), p. 11.

30. Peter Sahlins, *Boundaries: The Making of France and Spain in the Pyrenees* (Berkeley: University of California Press, 1989), pp. 110–11.

31. Renato Barahona, *Vizcaya on the Eve of Carlism: Politics and Society, 1800–1833* (Reno and Las Vegas: University of Nevada Press, 1989), p. 14.

32. Ibid., p. 19.

33. See Francisco Letamendia Belzunce, *Historia del nacionalismo vasco y de E.T.A.*, vol. 1: *Introducción histórica. ETA en el franquismo (1951–1976)* (Donostia: R & B Ediciones, 1994), pp. 69–80.

34. Robert P. Clark, *The Basques: The Franco Years and Beyond* (Reno: University of Nevada Press, 1979), pp. 20–21.

35. Barahona, *Vizcaya on the Eve of Carlism*, p. 19.

36. James E. Jacob, *Hills of Conflict: Basque Nationalism in France* (Reno, Las Vegas, and London: University of Nevada Press, 1994), p. 15.

37. Rachel Bard, "The Decline of a Basque State in France: Basse Navarre, 1512–1789," in William A. Douglass, Richard W. Etulain, and William H. Jacobs, eds., *Anglo-American Contributions to Basque Studies: Essays in Honor of Jon Bilbao* (Reno: Desert Research Institute, 1977), p. 89.

38. Jacob, *Hills of Conflict*, pp. 5–6.

39. Stanley Payne, *Basque Nationalism* (Reno: University of Nevada Press, 1975), p. 17.

40. Joxe Azurmendi, *Espainolak eta Euskaldunak* (Donostia: Elkar, 1992), p. 488.

41. Robert Darnton, *The Great Cat Massacre and Other Episodes in French Cultural History* (New York: Vintage Books, 1985), p. 191.
42. Ibid., p. 192.
43. Ibid., p. 193.
44. James E. Jacob, *Hills of Conflict: Basque Nationalism in France* (Reno, Las Vegas, and London: University of Nevada Press, 1994), p. 6.
45. Darnton, *The Great Cat Massacre*, pp. 191–93.
46. See Benedict Anderson, *Imagined Communities: Reflections on the Origin and Spread of Nationalism*, rev. ed. (London and New York: Verso, 1991).
47. Eric Hobsbawm, "Introduction: Inventing Traditions," in Eric Hobsbawm and Terence Ranger, eds., *The Invention of Traditions* (Cambridge: Cambridge University Press, 1983), p. 1.
48. Darnton, *The Great Cat Massacre*, p. 193.
49. Jacob, *Hills of Conflict*, p. 35.
50. Ibid., p. 37.
51. Cited in Stacy Burton and Dennis Dworkin, eds., *Trial of Modernity: Europe since 1500*, 2nd ed. (Needham Heights, Mass.: Simon & Schuster, 1998), pp. 106–07.
52. Cited in Joan Mari Torrealdai, *El libro negro de Euskera* (Donostia: Ttarttalo, 1998), pp. 27–28.
53. William A. Douglass and Jon Bilbao, *Amerikanuak: Basques in the New World* (Reno: University of Nevada Press, 1975), p. 105.
54. Stanley G. Payne, *Basque Nationalism* (Reno: University of Nevada Press, 1975), p. 35.
55. Ibid., p. 36.
56. Howard G. Brown, "From Organic Society to Security State: The War on Brigandage in France, 1797–1802," *The Journal of Modern History* 69, no. 4 (December 1997), pp. 662, 669.

57. Renato Barahona, *Vizcaya on the Eve of Carlism: Politics and Society, 1800–1833* (Reno and Las Vegas: University of Nevada Press, 1989), p. 26.

58. Robert P. Clark, *The Basques: The Franco Years and Beyond* (Reno: University of Nevada Press, 1979), p. 26.

59. David Held, "The Development of the Modern State," in Stuart Hall, David Held, Don Hubert, and Kenneth Thompson, *Modernity: An Introduction to Modern Societies* (Oxford and Malden, Mass.: Blackwell, 1996), p. 86.

60. Ernest Gellner, "Nationalism and High Cultures," in John Hutchinson and Anthony Smith, eds., *Nationalism* (Oxford: Oxford University Press, 1994), p. 63.

61. Ibid., p. 64.

62. See Benedict Anderson, *Imagined Communities: Reflections on the Origin and Spread of Nationalism*, rev. ed. (London and New York: Verso, 1991).

63. Geoff Eley and Ronald Grigor Suny, "Introduction: From the Moment of Social History to the Work of Cultural Representation," in Geoff Eley and Ronald Grigor Suny, eds., *Becoming National: A Reader* (Oxford: Oxford University Press, 1996), p. 8.

64. The map provided by Eugen Weber representing knowledge of the French language at this time suggests that the state had made little inroads into the Basque culture of Iparralde. See Eugen Weber, *Peasants Into Frenchmen: The Modernization of Rural France, 1870–1914* (Palo Alto: Stanford University Press, 1976), p. 68.

65. Manex Goyhenetche, *Pays Basque Nord: Un Peuple Colonisé* (Baiona: Elkar, 1979), p. 71.

66. James E. Jacob, *Hills of Conflict: Basque Nationalism in France* (Reno, Las Vegas, and London: University of Nevada Press, 1994), p. 42.

67. Pierre Birnbaum, "Nationalism: A Comparison between France and Germany," *Historical Sociology* 44, no. 3 (August 1992), p. 382.

68. See Marie-Pierre Arrizabalaga, "The Stem Family in the French Basque Country: Sare in the Nineteenth Century," *Journal of Family History* 22, no. 1 (January 1997), pp. 50–69.

69. Xosé Estévez, *Historia de Euskal Herria, Tomo II: Del hierro al roble* (Tafalla: Txalaparta, 1996), pp. 257–70.

70. Stuart Hall, "The Question of Cultural Identity," in Stuart Hall, David Held, Don Hubert, and Kenneth Thompson, *Modernity: An Introduction to Modern Societies* (Oxford: Blackwell, 1996), pp. 611–12.

71. Ibid., p. 612.

72. Robert P. Clark, *The Basques: The Franco Years and Beyond* (Reno: University of Nevada Press, 1979), p. 31.

73. Raymond Carr, *Spain 1808–1975*, 2nd ed. (Oxford: Clarendon Press, 1982), p. 339.

74. Clark, *The Basques: The Franco Years and Beyond*, pp. 31–32.

75. Adrian Shubert, *A Social History of Spain* (London: Unwin Hyman, 1990), p. 173.

76. *William Wordsworth: The Poems*, ed. John O. Hayden, vol. 1 (New Haven and London: Yale University Press, 1981), p. 839.

77. George Borrow, *The Bible in Spain* (London: J. M. Dent, 1906), pp. 341–42.

78. Joseph Harrison, "Heavy Industry, the State, and Economic Development in the Basque Region,

1876–1936," *The Economic History Review*, second series, 36, no. 4 (November 1993), p. 535.

79. Eduardo Jorge Glas, *Bilbao's Modern Business Elite* (Reno and Las Vegas: University of Nevada Press, 1997), pp. 53–54.

80. Eric Hobsbawm, *The Age of Capital 1848–1975* (London: Weidenfeld & Nicolson, 1975), p. 15.

81. Eric Hobsbawm, *The Age of Capital 1848–1975* (London: Weidenfeld & Nicolson, 1975), p. 241.

82. Chris Rojek and John Urry, *Touring Cultures: Transformations of Travel and Theory* (London and New York: Routledge, 1997), p. 3.

83. See Edward Said, *Orientalism* (New York: Vintage Books, 1979).

84. Linda Colley, *Britons: Forging the Nation 1707–1837* (New Haven and London: Yale University Press, 1992), p. 173.

85. *The Picture Guides: Biarritz, Pau and the Basque Country* (London and Boston: The Medici Society, 1926, pp. 69–70.

86. John K. Walton and Jenny Smith, "The Rhetoric of Community and the Business of Pleasure: The San Sebastián Waiters' Strike of 1920," *International Review of Social History* 39, part I (April 1994), p. 6.

87. Rudy Koshar, "'What ought to be seen': Tourists' Guidebooks and National Identities in Modern Germany and Europe," *Journal of Contemporary History* 33, no. 3 (July 1998), p. 326.

88. See William A. Douglass, "Factors in the Formation of the New-World Basque Emigrant Diaspora," in William A. Douglass, ed., *Essays in Basque Social Anthropology and History* (Reno: Basque Studies Program, 1989), pp. 251–67.

89. See Angel García-Sanz Marcotegui and Alejandro Arizcun Cela, "An Estimate of Navarrese Migration

in the Second Half of the Nineteenth Century (1879–1883)," in Douglass, ed., *Essays in Basque Social Anthropology and History*, pp. 235–49.

90. William A. Douglass and Jon Bilbao, *Amerikanuak: Basques in the New World* (Reno: University of Nevada Press, 1975), p. 137.

91. Helen Graham and Jo Labanyi, "Culture and Modernity: The Case of Spain," in Helen Graham and Jo Labanyi, eds., *Spanish Cultural Studies: An Introduction* (Oxford: Oxford University Press, 1995), p. 9.

92. Carolyn P. Boyd, *Historia Patria: Politics, History, and National Identity in Spain, 1875–1975* (Princeton: Princeton University Press, 1997), p. 102.

93. Sebastian Balfour, "The Lion and the Pig: Nationalism and National Identity in *Fin-de-Siècle* Spain," in Clare Mar-Molinero and Angel Smith, eds., *Nationalism and the Nation in the Iberian Peninsula: Competing and Conflicting Identities* (Oxford and Washington, D.C.: Berg, 1996), pp. 113–15.

94. Geoffrey Jensen, "Military Nationalism and the State: The Case of *Fin-de-Siècle* Spain," *Nations and Nationalism* 6, no. 2 (April 2000), p. 268.

95. See Manuel González Portilla, *La formación de la sociedad capitalista en el País Vasco*, vol. 1 (Donostia: L. Haranburu, 1981).

96. E. P. Thompson, *The Making of the English Working Class* (London: Victor Gollancz, 1963), pp. 9–10, 11.

97. Cyrus Ernesto Zirakzadeh, *A Rebellious People: Basques, Protests, and Politics* (Reno and Las Vegas: University of Nevada Press, 1991), p. 55.

98. The party survives to this day.

99. See Shlomo Avineri, "Marxism and Nationalism," *Journal of Contemporary History* 26, no. 3–4 (September 1991), pp. 651–53.

100. Corcuera Atienza, *Orígenes, ideología y organización del nacionalismo vasco 1876–1904* (Madrid: Siglo XXI, 1979), p. 275.

101. Jensen, "Military Nationalism and the State," p. 269.

102. See José Luis de la Granja Sainz, *El nacionalismo vasco. Un siglo de historia* (Madrid: Tecnos, 1995), pp. 23–31.

103. Jeremy Paxman, *The English: Portrait of a People* (London: Michael Joseph, 1998), pp. 30–31.

104. For an overview of how nationalist ideologies changed through the nineteenth century, see Michael Biddiss, "Nationalism and the Moulding of Modern Europe," *History* 7, no. 257 (October 1994), pp. 412–32.

105. Sebastian Balfour, "The Lion and the Pig: Nationalism and National Identity in *Fin-de-Siècle* Spain," in Clare Mar-Molinero and Angel Smith, eds., *Nationalism and the Nation in the Iberian Peninsula: Competing and Conflicting Identities* (Oxford and Washington, D.C.: Berg, 1996), p. 110.

106. Granja Sainz, *El nacionalismo vasco*, p. 34.

107. See Adam Smith, *An Inquiry into the Nature and Causes of the Wealth of Nations* (Oxford: Oxford University Press, 1976), Karl Marx and Friedrich Engels, *The Communist Manifesto* (New York: Monthly Review Press, 1964), and Karl Marx, *Capital* (Harmondsworth: Penguin, 1976).

108. Cited in Santiago de Pablo, José Luis de la Granja, and Ludger Mees, eds., *Documentos para la historia del nacionalismo vasco. De los fueros a nuestros días* (Barcelona: Ariel, 1998), pp. 34–35.

109. Cited in Joan Mari Torrealdai, *El libro negro de Euskera* (Donostia: Ttarttalo, 1998), pp. 40–41.
110. Rogers Brubaker, *Citizenship and Nationhood in France and Germany* (Cambridge and London: Harvard University Press, 1992), p. 8.
111. Ibid.
112. Alfred Cobban, *A History of Modern France* (London: Pelican, 1965), p. 20.
113. James E. Jacob, *Hills of Conflict: Basque Nationalism in France* (Reno, Las Vegas, and London: University of Nevada Press, 1994), p. 40.
114. Herman Lebovics, "Creating the Authentic France: Struggles over French Identity in the First Half of the Twentieth Century," in John R. Gillis, ed., *Commemorations: The Politics of National Identity* (Princeton: Princeton University Press, 1994), p. 240.
115. For an account of how the republic was consciously *ruralized*, see Sudhir Hazareesingh, "The Société d'Instruction Républicaine and the Propagation of Civic Republicanism in Provincial and Rural France, 1870–1877," *The Journal of Modern History* 71, no. 2 (June 1999), pp. 271–307.
116. Eugen Weber, *Peasants into Frenchmen: The Modernization of Rural France, 1870–1914* (Palo Alto: Stanford University Press, 1976), p. 303.
117. Ibid., p. 310.
118. Ibid., p. 313.
119. Ibid., p. 332.
120. Ibid., p. 334.
121. Ernest Renan, "What is a Nation?" in Homi K. Bhabha, ed., *Nation and Narration* (London and New York: Routledge, 1990), p. 20.
122. Homi K. Bhabha, "DissemiNation: Time, narrative, and the margins of the modern nation," in

Bhabha, ed., *Nation and Narration* (London and New York: Routledge, 1990), p. 310.

123. Lebovics, "Creating the Authentic France: Struggles Over French Identity in the First Half of the Twentieth Century," p. 241.

124. See Sudhir Hazareesingh, "The Société d'Instruction Républicaine and the Propagation of Civic Republicanism in Provincial and Rural France, 1870–1877."

125. Jacob, *Hills of Conflict*, p. 54.

126. Ibid., pp. 60–61.

127. Ibid., p. 54.

128. Cited in Eric Hosbawm, *Age of Extremes: The Short Twentieth Century, 1914–1931* (London: Michael Joseph, 1994), p. 1.

129. Eugen Weber, *Peasants into Frenchmen: The Modernization of Rural France, 1870–1914* (Palo Alto: Stanford University Press, 1976), p. 475.

130. Ibid., p. 477.

131. Herman Lebovics, "Creating the Authentic France: Struggles Over French Identity in the First Half of the Twentieth Century," in John R. Gillis, ed., *Commemorations: The Politics of National Identity* (Princeton: Princeton University Press, 1994), pp. 244–45.

132. James E. Jacob, *Hills of Conflict: Basque Nationalism in France* (Reno, Las Vegas, and London: University of Nevada Press, 1994), p. 55.

133. Weber, *Peasants into Frenchmen*, p. 477.

134. Jean Louis Davant, *Histoire du Peuple Basque: Le Peuple Basque dans l'Histoire* (Baiona: Elkar, 1996), p. 109.

135. Jacob, *Hills of Conflict*, p. 55.

136. Pierre Laborde, *Pays Basque: Économie et Société en Mutation* (Baiona: Elkar, 1994), pp. 181–84.

137. Weber, *Peasants Into Frenchmen*, p. 481.
138. Jacob, *Hills of Conflict*, p. 65.
139. Ibid., p. 82.
140. Lebovics, "Creating the Authentic France," p. 247.
141. Sandra Ott, *The Circle of Mountains: A Basque Shepherding Community* (Reno: University of Nevada Press, 1993), p. 10.
142. Jacob, *Hills of Conflict*, p. 128.
143. Weber, *Peasants into Frenchmen*, p. 474.
144. Ott, *The Circle of Mountains*, p. 7.
145. Shlomo Ben-Ami, "Basque Nationalism between Archaism and Modernity," *Journal of Contemporary History* 26, no. 3–4 (September 1991), p. 497.
146. Telesforo de Aranzadi, "Mestizo, za," *Enciclopedia Universal Ilustrada Europeo-Americana*, vol. 34 (Bilbo: Espasa-Calpe, n.d.), p. 1091; cited in Joseba Zulaika, *Del Cromañon al Carnaval. Los vascos como museo antropológico* (Donostia: Erein, 1996), p. 62.
147. Jacqueline Urla, "Reinventing Basque Society: Cultural Difference and the Quest for Modernity, 1918–1936," in William A. Douglass, ed., *Essays in Basque Social Anthropology and History* (Reno: Basque Studies Program, 1989), p. 150.
148. Juan Pablo Fusi, *El País Vasco. Pluralismo y nacionalidad* (Madrid: Alianza, 1984), p. 18.
149. Francisco Letamendia Belzunce, *Historia del nacionalismo vasco y de E.T.A.*, vol. 1, *ETA en el franquismo (1951–1976)* (Donostia: R & B Ediciones, 1994), p. 158, n. 129.
150. Raymond Carr, *Spain 1808–1975*, 2nd ed. (Oxford: Clarendon Press, 1982), p. 529.
151. Cited in ibid., p. 377.
152. Michael Richards, "Constructing the Nationalist State," in Clare Mar-Molinero and Angel Smith,

eds., *Nationalism and the Nation in the Iberian Peninsula* (Oxford and Washington, D.C.: Berg, 1996), p. 154.

153. Miguel de Unamuno, *En torno al casticismo* (Madrid: n.p., 1895); cited in Richards, "Constructing the Nationalist State," p. 154.

154. Letamendia, *Historia del nacionalismo vasco y de ETA*, p. 158, n. 129.

155. Carr, *Spain 1808–1975*, p. 530.

156. See Inman Fox, *La invención de España* (Madrid: Cátedra, 1998), pp. 112–23.

157. Urla, "Reinventing Basque Society," p. 155.

158. Cited in Zulaika, *Del Cromañon al Carnaval*, p. 68.

159. H. H. Stuckenschmidt, *Maurice Ravel: Variations on His Life and Work* (Philadelphia: Chilton, 1968), p. 6.

160. Juan Pablo Fusi, *El País Vasco. Pluralismo y nacionalidad* (Madrid: Alianza, 1984), p. 17.

161. John K. Walton, "Reconstructing Crowds: The Rise of Association Football as a Spectator Sport in San Sebastián, 1915–32," *The International Journal of the History of Sport* 15, no. 1 (April 1998), p. 29.

162. Fusi, *El País Vasco*, p. 20.

163. Helen Graham and Jo Labanyi, "Introduction: Culture and Modernity: The Case of Spain," in Helen Graham and Jo Labanyi, eds., *Spanish Cultural Studies: An Introduction* (Oxford: Oxford University Press, 1995), p. 6.

164. See Sandra Ott, "*Indarra*: Some Reflections on a Basque Concept," in J. G. Peristiany and Julian Pitt-Rivers, eds., *Honor and Grace in Anthropology* (Cambridge: Cambridge University Press, 1992), pp. 193–94.

165. Gorka Aulestia, *Improvisational Poetry from the Basque Country* (Reno: University of Nevada Press, 1995), p. 85.
166. Ott, *"Indarra,"* pp. 209–10.
167. Walton, "Reconstructing Crowds," p. 35.
168. Ibid., p. 29.
169. See Angel Capellán, *Hemingway and the Hispanic World* (Ann Arbor, Mich.: UMI Research Press, 1985), pp. 28–32.
170. Ibid., p. 32.
171. Rodney Gallop, *A Book of the Basques* (1930; reprint, Reno: University of Nevada Press, 1970), p. xi.
172. C. Day Lewis, "The Nabara," in C. Day Lewis, *The Complete Works of C. Day Lewis* (Stanford: Stanford University Press, 1992), pp. 290–91.
173. Fusi, *El País Vasco*, pp. 17–18.
174. Shlomo Ben-Ami, "Basque Nationalism between Archaism and Modernity," *Journal of Contemporary History* 26, no. 3–4 (September 1991), p. 497.
175. Zulaika, *Del Cromañon al Carnaval*, pp. 67–76.
176. Ibid., p. 75.
177. Juan Pablo Fusi, "The Basque Question 1931–7," in Paul Preston, ed., *Revolution and War in Spain* (London and New York: Methuen, 1984), p. 184.
178. Ibid., p. 195.
179. Ibid., p. 191.
180. See Martin Blinkhorn, "'The Basque Ulster': Navarre and the Basque Autonomy Question Under the Spanish Second Republic," *Historical Journal* 17, no. 3 (September 1974), pp. 595–613.
181. Cited in Robert P. Clark, "Language and Politics in Spain's Basque Provinces," *West Eurpean Politics* 4, no. 1 (January 1981), p. 93.

182. Cited in Ronald Fraser, *Blood of Spain: An Oral History of the Spanish Civil War* (London: Allen Lane, 1979; reprint, London: Pimlico, 1994), p. 395.

183. Paul Preston, *Franco: A Biography* (London: Harper Collins, 1993), pp. 243–47.

184. Hugh Thomas, *The Spanish Civil War* (London: Penguin, 1965), p. 689.

185. Robert P. Clark, *The Basques: The Franco Years and Beyond*, p. 76.

186. Cited in Fraser, *Blood of Spain*, pp. 398–99.

187. *Weekend Edition Saturday*, National Public Radio, United States, April 26, 1997.

188. Cited in Fraser, *Blood of Spain*, p. 399.

189. Cited in ibid., pp. 399–400.

190. Cited in ibid., p. 401.

191. Ibid.

192. Claude Bowers, United States Ambassador to Spain, to the United States Secretary of State, Donibane-Lohizune (St. Jean-de-Luz), April 30, 1937, 852.00 / 5276, no. 253, in *Foreign Relations of the United States*, vol. 1 (1937), p. 290.

193. George L. Steer, *The Tree of Gernika: A Field Study of Modern War* (London: Hodder & Stoughton, 1938), pp. 234–45.

194. William Foss and Cecil Gerahty, *The Spanish Arena* (London: The Right Book Club, 1938), pp. 439–40.

195. Mike Richards, "'Terror and Progress': Industrialization, Modernity, and the Making of Francoism," in Helen Graham and Labanyi, eds., *Spanish Cultural Studies: An Introduction* (Oxford: Oxford University Press, 1995), p. 176.

196. Ibid., p. 181.

197. Clare Mar-Molinero, "The Role of Language in Spanish Nation Building," in in Clare Mar-

Molinero and Angel Smith, eds., *Nationalism and the Nation in the Iberian Peninsula: Competing and Conflicting Identities* (Oxford and Washington, D.C.: Berg, 1996), p. 81.

198. Jo Labanyi, "Censorship or the Fear of Mass Culture," in Helen Graham and Jo Labanyi, eds., *Spanish Cultural Studies: An Introduction* (Oxford: Oxford University Press, 1995), p. 208.

199. Mar-Molinero, "The Role of Language in Spanish Nation Building," p. 81.

200. Carolyn P. Boyd, *Historia Patria: Politics, History, and National Identity in Spain, 1875–1975* (Princeton: Princeton University Press, 1997), p. 235.

201. Angel García Sanz-Marcotegui, "La población vasco-navarra entre 1930 y 1960. Los efectos de Guerra y los cambios demográficos," *Boletín del Instituto Gerónimo de Ustaritz* 4 (1990), pp. 98, 102.

202. Robert P. Clark, "Language and Politics in Spain's Basque Provinces," *West Eurpean Politics* 4, no. 1 (January 1981), p. 93.

203. Ibid., p. 91.

204. For the full extraordinary story, see his *Escape via Berlin: Eluding Franco in Hitler's Europe* (Reno and Las Vegas: University of Nevada Press, 1991).

205. Robert P. Clark, *The Basques: The Franco Years and Beyond* (Reno: University of Nevada Press, 1979), p. 232.

206. Mar-Molinero, "The Role of Language in Spanish Nation Building," pp. 81–82.

207. Francisco J. Llera, José M. Mata, and Cynthia L. Irvin, "ETA: From Secret Army to Social Movement–The Post-Franco Schism of The Basque

Nationalist Movement," *Terrorism and Political Violence* 5, no. 3 (autumn 1995), p. 106.

208. Robert P. Clark, *The Basque Insurgents: ETA, 1952–1980* (Madison: University of Wisconsin Press, 1984), pp. 25–26.

209. See ibid., pp. 32–35.

210. Llera, Mata, and Irvin, "ETA: From Secret Army to Social Movement–The Post-Franco Schism of The Basque Nationalist Movement," p. 108.

211. William A. Douglass and Joseba Zulaika, "On the Interpretation of Terrorist Violence: ETA and the Basque Political Process," *Comparative Studies in Society and History* 32, no. 2 (April 1990), p. 241.

212. Llera, Mata and Irvin, "ETA: From Secret Army to Social Movement–The Post-Franco Schism of The Basque Nationalist Movement," p. 128.

213. See Douglass and Zulaika, "On the Interpretation of Terrorist Violence," pp. 241–42.

214. See Cameron J. Watson, "Imagining ETA," in William A. Douglass, Carmelo Urza, Linda White, and Joseba Zulaika, eds., *Basque Politics and Nationalism on the Eve of the Millennium* (Reno: Basque Studies Program, 1999), p. 106.

215. Begoña Aretxaga, "A Hall of Mirrors: On the Spectral Character of Basque Political Violence," in Douglass, Urza, White, and Zulaika, eds., *Basque Politics and Nationalism on the Eve of the Millennium*, p. 117.

216. Robert P. Clark, *The Basques: The Franco Years and Beyond* (Reno: University of Nevada Press, 1979), pp. 272–73.

217. Clare Mar-Molinero, "The Role of Language in Spanish Nation-Building," in Clare Mar-Molinero and Angel Smith, eds., *Nationalism and the*

Nation in the Iberian Peninsula (Oxford: Berg, 1996), p. 82.

218. Ibid., pp. 82–83.

219. Cited in Joxe Azurmendi, *Espainolak eta Euskaldunak* (Donostia: Elkar, 1992), p. 5.

220. See the chapter dedicated to Spain's first "dirty war" in Paddy Woodworth, *Dirty War, Clean Hands: ETA, the GAL and Spanish Democracy* (Cork: Cork University Press, 2001), pp. 44–59.

221. Cyrus Ernesto Zirakzadeh, *A Rebellious People: Basques, Protests, and Politics* (Reno and Las Vegas: University of Nevada Press, 1991), pp. 318–19.

222. For a detailed account of this scandal, see Paddy Woodworth, *Dirty War, Clean Hands: ETA, the GAL and Spanish Democracy* (Cork: Cork University Press, 2001).

223. See, for example, Pedro Ibarra and Antonio Rivas, "Environmental Public Discourse in the Basque Country: The Conflict of the Leizaran Motorway," in David Sciulli, ed., *Comparative Social Research*, Supplement 2: *Normative Social Action* (Greenwich, Conn., and London: JAI Press, 1996), pp. 139–51; and Jacqueline Urla, "Outlaw Language: Creating Alternative Public Spheres in Basque Free Radio," in Lisa Lowe and David Lloyd, eds., *The Politics of Culture in the Shadow of Capital* (Durham and London: Duke University Press, 1997), pp. 280–300.

224. Robert P. Clark, *Negotiating with ETA: Obstacles to Peace in the Basque County, 1975–1988* (Reno and Las Vegas: University of Nevada Press, 1990), pp. 223–24.

225. Jeremy McClancy, "Navarra: Historical Realities, Present Myths, Future Possibilities," in William A.

Douglass, Carmelo Urza, Linda White, and Joseba Zulaika, eds., *Basque Politics and Nationalism on the Eve of the Millennium* (Reno: Basque Studies Program, 1999), pp. 146–47.

226. Two excellent accounts of the Madrid-based campaign against Basque nationalism are Antoni Battitsta, *Euskadi sin prejuicios* (Barcelona: Plaza & Janes, 2001), and Ramón Zallo, *El país de los vascos. Desde los sucesos de Ermua al segundo Gobierno Ibarretxe* (Madrid: Fundamentos, 2001).

227. In August 1999, the PSOE and IU presented a motion in the Spanish parliament to condemn the uprising, which the PP did not support. Woodworth, *Dirty War, Clean Hands*, p. 355, n. 61.

228. *El Mundo (País Vasco)*, October 17, 2002, p. 3.

229. Raymond Carr, "Introducción," in Raymond Carr, ed., *Historia de España* (Barcelona: Península, 2001), p. 16.

230. Woodworth, *Dirty War, Clean Hands*, p. 415.

231. William A. Douglass, "Contesting Control of the Discourse: Basque Nationalism and the Spanish State," Welcome Address, First International Symposium on Basque Cultural Studies, Institute of Basque Studies, London Guildhall University, June 29, 2000.

232. John Loughlin, "A New Deal for France's Regions and Linguistic Minorities," *West European Politics* 8, no. 3 (July 1985), p. 102.

233. Ibid., p. 108.

234. Ibid., p. 102.

235. James E. Jacob, *Hills of Conflict: Basque Nationalism in France* (Reno, Las Vegas, and London: University of Nevada Press, 1994), p. 148.

236. James E. Jacob, "The Future of Basque Nationalism in France," in William A. Douglass, Carmelo Urza,

Linda White, and Joseba Zulaika, eds., *Basque Politics and Nationalism on the Eve of the Millennium* (Reno: Basque Studies Program, 1999), p. 163.

237. John Loughlin, "A New Deal for France's Regions and Linguistic Minorities," *West European Politics* 8, no. 3 (July 1985), p. 108.

238. Herve Michel, "Government or Governance? The Case of the French Local Political System," *West European Politics* 21, no. 3 (July 1998), p. 155.

239. James E. Jacob, "The Future of Basque Nationalism in France," in William A. Douglass, Carmelo Urza, Linda White, and Joseba Zulaika, eds., *Basque Politics and Nationalism on the Eve of the Millennium* (Reno: Basque Studies Program, 1999), p. 159.

240. Ibid., p. 161.

241. See Sarah Waters, "New Social Movement Politics in France: The Rise of Civic Forms of Mobilisation," *West European Politics* 21, no. 3 (July 1998), p. 172.

242. Ibid., p. 175.

243. James E. Jacob, *Hills of Conflict: Basque Nationalism in France* (Reno, Las Vegas, and London: University of Nevada Press, 1994), p. 335.

244. Ibid., p. 337.

245. Hemen Elkartea, *Ipar Euskal Herria: Haren biztanleria eta Ekonomia 1980–2000 / Le Pays Basque Nord: Sa population et son économie 1980–2000* (n.p., 2002), pp. 49–50.

246. Ibid., pp. 3–4.

247. Jean-Jacques Cheval, "Local Radio and Regional Languages in France," in Stephen Harold Riggs, ed., *Ethnic Minority Media: An International Perspective* (Newbury Park, London, New Delhi: Sage Publications, 1992), p. 169.

248. Jacob, *Hills of Conflict*, p. 326.

249. See Eneko Bidegain, "Iparralde: Un cadre institutionnel tant revendiqué," *Les Temps Modernes*, no. 614 (June–August 2001), p. 215.

250. Waters, "New Social Movement Politics in France," p. 170.

251. Cheval, "Local Radio and Regional Languages in France," pp. 169–70.

252. Jacob, "The Future of Basque Nationalism in France," p. 166.

253. Jacob, *Hills of Conflict*, pp. 390–91.

254. Jesús María Lasagabaster, "The Promotion of Cultural Production in Basque," in Helen Graham and Jo Labanyi, eds., *Spanish Cultural Studies: An Introduction* (Oxford: Oxford University Press, 1995), p. 354.

255. Cited in Raymond Carr, *Spain 1808–1975*, 2nd ed. (Oxford: Clarendon Press, 1982), p. 767.

256. Cited in Ignacio Elizalde, *El País Vasco en los modernos escritores españoles* (Baroja, n.d.), p. 255.

257. Cited in ibid., pp. 231–32.

258. Jesús María Lasagabaster, "Introduction," in Jesús María Lasagabaster, *Contemporary Basque Fiction: An Anthology* (Reno: University of Nevada Press, 1990), p. 6.

259. Javier Cillero Goiriastuena, "*Contemporary Basque Fiction* Revisited," in William A. Douglass, Carmelo Urza, Linda White, and Joseba Zulaika, eds., *Basque Cultural Studies* (Reno: Basque Studies Program, 1998), pp. 87–92.

260. Lasagabaster, "The Promotion of Cultural Production in Basque," p. 353.

261. Jaume Martí-Olivella, "Invisible Otherness: From Migrant Subjects to the Subject of Immigration in Basque Cinema," in Douglass, Urza, White, and Zulaika, eds., *Basque Cultural Studies*, p. 207.

262. Interview in *El País*, May 19, 1996; cited in Martí-Olivella, "Invisible Otherness," p. 206.

263. For an overview of the contemporary state of *bert-solaritza*, see Joxerra Garzia, Jon Sarasua, and Andoni Egaña, *The Art of Bertsolaritza: Improvised Basque Verse Singing* (Donostia: Bertsozale Elkartea, 2001).

264. See Sharryn Kasmir, "From the Margins: Punk Rock and the Repositioning of Ethnicity and Gender in Basque Identity," in Douglass, Urza, White, and Zulaika, eds., *Basque Cultural Studies*, pp. 178–204.

265. For an overview of the development of modern Basque music, see Colette Larraburu and Peio Etcheverry-Ainchart, *Euskal Rock 'n' Roll: Histoire du Rock Basque* (Biarritz: Atlantica, 2001).

266. Cited in Mark Kurlansky, *The Basque History of the World* (New York: Walker & Company, 1999), p. 9.

267. Bernardo Atxaga, *Obabakoak: A Novel*, trans. Margaret Jull Costa (London: Vintage International, 1992), pp. ix–x.

268. From Negu Gorriak, *Ideia Zabaldu* (Spread the Word, 1995), Esan Ozenki Records, LG SS 129–95 EO.057 CD.

269. William A. Douglass, Carmelo Urza, Linda White, and Joseba Zulaika, "Introduction," in William A. Douglass, Carmelo Urza, Linda White, and Joseba Zulaika, eds., *Basque Cultural Studies* (Reno: Basque Studies Program, 1998), p. 2.

270. Cited in Tom Nairn, "Nations: Breaking Up Is Hard to Do," *Marxism Today*, November / December 1998, p. 41.

271. From a sociolinguistic survey published by the Euskal Kultur Erakundea (EKE; Basque Culture

Institute) with the cooperation of the Institut National de la Statistique et des Études Economiques (INSEE; National Institute of Statistics and Economic Studies), Aquitaine, the Eusko Jaurlaritza (Autonomous Basque Government), and the Nafarroako Gobernua (Government of Nafarroa) (1996). See http: // www.euskadi.net / euskara_inkestak / 2ENCUES / EHEUS.pdf and *Gara Urtekaria* (Iruñea: Gara, 1999), pp. 278–79.

272. *Euskaldunon Egumkaria*, March 26, 2002, p. 13.

273. *Gara*, December 15, 1999, p. 16.

274. Jesús Azcona, "To Be Basque and to Live in Basque Country: The Inequalities of Difference," in Carol J. Greenhouse, ed., *Democracy and Ethnography: Constructing Identities in Multicultural States* (Albany, N.Y.: State University of New York Press, 1998), p. 172.

275. See Andoni Alonso and Iñaki Arzoz, "Basque Identity on the Internet," in Douglass, Urza, White, and Zulaika, eds., *Basque Cultural Studies* (Reno: Basque Studies Program, 1998), pp. 295–312.

276. Simon Barton, "The Roots of the National Question in Spain," in Mikuláš Teich and Roy Porter, eds., *The National Question in Europe in Historical Context* (Cambridge: Cambridge University Press, 1993), p. 107.

Pictures

Abertzaletasunaren Agiritegia. Sabino Arana Kultur Elkargoa archives. 30, 181, 206, 276, 288, 296, 317, 327
————. Taken from Santoago de Pablo (ed.): *Los Nacionalistas. Historia del nacionalismo vasco, 1876-1960*. Vitoria-Gasteiz: Fundación Sancho el Sabio, 1995. 31, 293, 309, 338
"Les Amis de la Vieille Navarre" Association archives. 16, 147, 150, 211, 228, 236, 241, 244, 261, 268, 391
Hugo Thomas: *Bewick's Woodcuts*. London, L. Reeve & Co, 1870. 88
J.G. Bell: *Scrapbook of Thomas Bewick, Book II*. London circa 1870. 73
Robert Bloomfield: *The Farmer's Boy; a Rural Poem*. With engravings by Thomas Bewick. Edwards and Knibb, London 1820. 184
Gatuzain archives. 404
David Carlson: *Ready-to-use Sports Illustrations*. Dover, New York 1982. 427
Carol Belanger Grafton: *Humorous Victorian Spot Illustrations*. Dover, New York 1985. 224
Editorial Iparaguirre, S.A. archives. 8, 23, 95, 98, 111, 118, 135, 157, 173, 194
Euskaldunon Egunkaria archives. 343, 361, 364, 369, 372, 401
————, Martintxo 364, 372
Grandville (Jean-Ignace-Isidore Gérard): *Scènes de la vie privée et publique des animaux*, Paris 1842. 26, 160
Jim Harter (ed): *Animals*. Dover, New York 1979. 130, 219
Koldo Mitxelena Kulturunea archives. 56, 122, 142, 190, 312, 330, 356, 396

Koldo Mitxelena Kulturunea archives. Flyers; artists unknown 53, 114, 346, 387

————, from *La Voz de España*, November 11, 1975. 304

Charles Philipon, court sketches. 85

PhotoSpin. Artville, Madison, 1997. 41

PhotoDisc, Inc., Seattle, 1995. 48

Pilotell (Georges Raoul Eugène Labadie): *Croquis Révolutionnaires*. Paris, circa 1871. 80

Richard Sutphen: *Old Engravings and Illustrations I, People*. Dick Sutphen studio, Minneapolis 1965. 68

Richard Sutphen: *Old Engravings and Illustrations II, Things.* Dick Sutphen studio, Minneapolis 1965. 256

Iñaki Uriarte. 165

Juan de Vingles: *Arte Subtilissima*, Saragossa 1550. 36

Cameron Watson photographs. 214, 233, 273, 379, 419

Index

A

aberri eguna (basque national day), 313

Abertzaleen Batasuna party, formed by agreement between EMA and EB, 406–407

accession of the French Bourbons, resulted in Basque imports falling under the common tariff system of the country as a whole, 43

Acción Nacionalista Vasca, declared a liberal republican platform rejecting all forms of traditionalist ideology, 270

Action Française (French Action) based on authoritarian and racist values, 215

AEK, organization for teaching Basque to adults, 439

Agriculture, subject to state control through price fixing and marketing, 305

Aguirre y Lecube (President of Basque Republic)
death in 1960 of exiled lehendakari, 386
met with State department officials to discuss policy, 314
settled in Washington, D.C., in 1945, 313

aizkolari (woodchopping), 257

aintzina
bilingual newspaper created to spread ideas of proto-basque nationalists, 231
reestablished in 1942, 233

Ajanguiz, Father Dionisio, 297

Ajuria Enea Pact, all Basque parties signed definitive official statement against ETA, 358

Alaitz eta Maider musical form blending traditional accordian with pop music, 428

Alembert, Jean le Rond d', 49

Alfonso XII completely defeated supporters of Old Regime, 110–111

Alfonso XIII [*sic*], 134

Alfonso XIII, 201

Algeria, French wage warfare in (1954–1961), 383

Alianza Anticommunista Apostolica, 347

E

French nation

cultural pluralism as illegitimate in name of positivist and universalist state norms, 89

imagined or articulated through discursive practices such as state education and even military service, 82

Frente Popular, Azaña and Basque socialist leader Prieto, formed a new liberal-left coalition called, 275

French Second Empire 1851–1871, 81

French state, as a prison that held its ethno nationalities by force, 384–385

Front National,

rise in the 1980s of, 395

serious challenge for ultimate office of France, 397

fueros, 40

Fusi, Juan Pablo

culture of the Basque Country abandoned provincial, elementary and coarse levels characterized Basque culture in previous centuries, 264

"modern" culture was general phenomenon without national identity, 263

G

GAL

affair where entire Spanish democratic establishment had involvement in state terrorism, 373

attacks on French and Spanish citizens by, 401–402

Gallicization of the French state (1870–1914), 204

Gallop noted folklorist who wrote "A Book of the Basques" on folklore, 261–262

Garaikoetxea

becoming first, since Aguirre y Lecube, *lehendakari* to take office, 345

picture of, 356

Garat (Dominique-Joseph) plans to create separate Basque federation, 72

García Sanz-Marcotegui, Angel, 308

Garzon, Judge Baltazar

leading figure in judicial assault on Batasuna, 368

M

N

W

X

Y

Z

Colophon

Cameron Watson's text was edited by Jennifer Knox White. The book was indexed by Lawrence Feldman. It was laid out and produced by Gunnlaugur SE Briem, who also designed the typeface, BriemAnvil.
It was printed and bound by Fidler Doubleday.

The Basque Studies textbook series